THE PIONEERS

THE PIONEERS

By the Editors of

TIME-LIFE BOOKS

with text by

Huston Horn

TIME-LIFE BOOKS / ALEXANDRIA, VIRGINIA

Time-Life Books Inc.
is a wholly owned subsidiary of

TIME INCORPORATED

Founder: Henry R. Luce 1898-1967

Editor-in-Chief: Henry Anatole Grunwald
President: J. Richard Munro
Chairman of the Board: Ralph P. Davidson
Executive Vice President: Clifford J. Grum
Chairman, Executive Committee: James R. Shepley
Editorial Director: Ralph Graves
Group Vice President, Books: Joan D. Manley
Vice Chairman: Arthur Temple

TIME-LIFE BOOKS INC.

Managing Editor: Jerry Korn
Executive Editor: David Maness
Assistant Managing Editors: Dale M. Brown (planning),
Martin Mann, John Paul Porter, Gerry Schremp (acting)
Art Director: Tom Suzuki
Chief of Research: David L. Harrison
Director of Photography: Robert G. Mason
Assistant Art Director: Arnold C. Holeywell
Assistant Chief of Research: Carolyn L. Sackett
Assistant Director of Photography: Dolores A. Littles

Chairman: John D. McSweeney
President: Carl G. Jaeger
Executive Vice Presidents: John Steven Maxwell,
David J. Walsh
Vice Presidents: George Artandi (comptroller);
Stephen L. Bair (legal counsel); Peter G. Barnes;
Nicholas Benton (public relations); John L. Canova;
Beatrice T. Dobie (personnel); Carol Flaumenhaft
(consumer affairs); James L. Mercer (Europe/South
Pacific); Herbert Sorkin (production); Paul R. Stewart
(marketing)

THE OLD WEST

EDITORIAL STAFF FOR "THE PIONEERS"
Editor: George Constable
Assistant Editor: Joan Mebane
Picture Editor: Myra Mangan
Text Editor: Bryce Walker
Designer: Herbert Quarmby
Staff Writers: Lee Greene, David Lawton, Philip Payne,
Suzanne Seixas, Jill Spiller, Peter Wood
Researchers: Loretta Britten, Marilyn Daley,
Catherine Ireys, Mary Leverty, Nancy Miller,
Mary Kay Moran, Gail Nussbaum, Jane Sugden,
Madeleine Walker, Janet Zich

EDITORIAL PRODUCTION
Production Editor: Douglas B. Graham
Operations Manager: Gennaro C. Esposito,
Gordon E. Buck (assistant)
Assistant Production Editor: Feliciano Madrid
Quality Control: Robert L. Young (director),
James J. Cox (assistant), Daniel J. McSweeney,
Michael G. Wight (associates)
Art Coordinator: Anne B. Landry
Copy Staff: Susan B. Galloway (chief),
Barbara H. Fuller, Celia Beattie
Picture Department: Barbara S. Simon
Traffic: Kimberly K. Lewis

THE COVER: Pioneers listen to a guide describe the trail ahead in William Ranney's 1853 painting, *Advice on the Prairie.* The air of resolute purpose characterized most of those who journeyed west across the plains, deserts and mountains—though some faces also reflected the hardships endured en route, as seen in the frontispiece photograph of Mormon pioneer Lucy Smith and her child, emigrants to Utah in 1851.

THE AUTHOR: Huston Horn began his writing career in 1951 as a reporter for his hometown newspaper, the Nashville *Tennessean,* then moved to New York and in 1957 joined the staff of SPORTS ILLUSTRATED. After nine years, he left to study for the Episcopal priesthood, meanwhile continuing to produce magazine articles as a freelancer. He wrote *The Pioneers* during a leave of absence from his parish in Pasadena, California, in the course of which he traveled more than 7,000 miles retracing the major westward routes of 19th Century wagon trains.

CORRESPONDENTS: Elisabeth Kraemer (Bonn); Margot Hapgood, Dorothy Bacon, Lesley Coleman (London); Susan Jonas, Lucy T. Voulgaris (New York); Maria Vincenza Aloisi, Josephine du Brusle (Paris); Ann Natanson (Rome). Valuable assistance was also provided by: Sue Wymelenberg (Boston); Judy Aspinall, Karin B. Pearce (London); Carolyn T. Chubet, Miriam Hsia, Christina Lieberman (New York); Mimi Murphy (Rome); Martha Green (San Francisco); Jane Estes (Seattle).

Other Publications:

LIBRARY OF HEALTH
CLASSICS OF THE OLD WEST
THE EPIC OF FLIGHT
THE GOOD COOK
THE SEAFARERS
THE ENCYCLOPEDIA OF COLLECTIBLES
THE GREAT CITIES
WORLD WAR II
HOME REPAIR AND IMPROVEMENT
THE WORLD'S WILD PLACES
THE TIME-LIFE LIBRARY OF BOATING
HUMAN BEHAVIOR
THE ART OF SEWING
THE EMERGENCE OF MAN
THE AMERICAN WILDERNESS
THE TIME-LIFE ENCYCLOPEDIA OF GARDENING
LIFE LIBRARY OF PHOTOGRAPHY
THIS FABULOUS CENTURY
FOODS OF THE WORLD
TIME-LIFE LIBRARY OF AMERICA
TIME-LIFE LIBRARY OF ART
GREAT AGES OF MAN
LIFE SCIENCE LIBRARY
THE LIFE HISTORY OF THE UNITED STATES
TIME READING PROGRAM
LIFE NATURE LIBRARY
LIFE WORLD LIBRARY
FAMILY LIBRARY:
   HOW THINGS WORK IN YOUR HOME
   THE TIME-LIFE BOOK OF THE FAMILY CAR
   THE TIME-LIFE FAMILY LEGAL GUIDE
   THE TIME-LIFE BOOK OF FAMILY FINANCE

For information about any Time-Life book, please write:
Reader Information
Time-Life Books
541 North Fairbanks Court
Chicago, Illinois 60611

Time-Life Books.
  The pioneers/by the editors of Time-Life Books, with text by
  Huston Horn. — New York: Time-Life Books, [1974]
  240 p.: ill.; 29 cm. — (The Old West)
  Bibliography: p. 236-237.
  Includes index.
  1. Overland journeys to the Pacific.   2. Frontier and pioneer
  life—The West.   3. The West—History—To 1848.
  4. The West—History—1848-1950.
I. Horn, Huston.   II. Title.   III. Series: The Old West
(Alexandria, Va.)
F593.T55   1974   978   73-94242
ISBN 0-8094-1477-5
ISBN 0-8094-1476-7 lib. bdg.
ISBN 0-8094-1475-9 retail ed.

CONTENTS

1|In search of a second Eden

The exodus began in 1841, a stream of men, women and children pouring out of Independence, Missouri. They were headed west, walking beside the covered wagons that held their possessions, going across 2,000 miles to the Pacific Coast. Mostly American-born, they were home-seekers, determined to find the fertile earthly paradise missionaries and mountain men had sworn existed on the other side of the continent.

They were not rich: many were trying to escape economic hardship. But neither were they without funds: it cost from $700 to $1,500 to outfit a family for the trip. They were innocent, and braved the wilderness because they did not know its hazards—its forbidding mountains and pitiless deserts, ruinous fires, sometimes-predatory Indi-

ans. But they met the perils with courage, and most of them won through to become the West's new settlers.

The pictures of their trek shown on these and the following pages, painted by men who had been West but had rarely traveled with a wagon train, are more idealized than accurate. But they convey the spirit of heroic endeavor that characterized this great migration.

6

A wagon train fords Wyoming's Medicine Bow River in Samuel Colman's peaceful painting.

The best time of the pioneers' day is commemorated in Benjamin Reinhart's 1867 scene of a wagon train halted for the night, the men tending the animals as the women cook supper. But Reinhart erred by incorporating huge Conestogas: much lighter wagons were used on the long trip west.

8

9

Menaced by billowing flames, an emigrant brandishes a torch
to scare off panicked horses that threaten to trample his family. Fires such as the one William Ranney painted in 1848
were sometimes started by bands of Indians, in the hope
of stampeding and later capturing the pioneers' livestock.

10

Ranney

Emigrants blast away at their attackers in this 1856 canvas by Charles Wimar. Though Wimar, who traveled with a wagon train and studied Indians as a boy in St. Louis, got the details right, the episode itself is improbable: at that time tribes rarely made a frontal assault on wagon trains this size.

The serene majesty of the plains is captured in William Ranney's 1850 study, *The Pioneers*. In real life, however, at least four oxen would have been pulling the wagon and the people shown in it probably would have been walking: wagon loads were kept light to spare valuable draft animals.

14

15

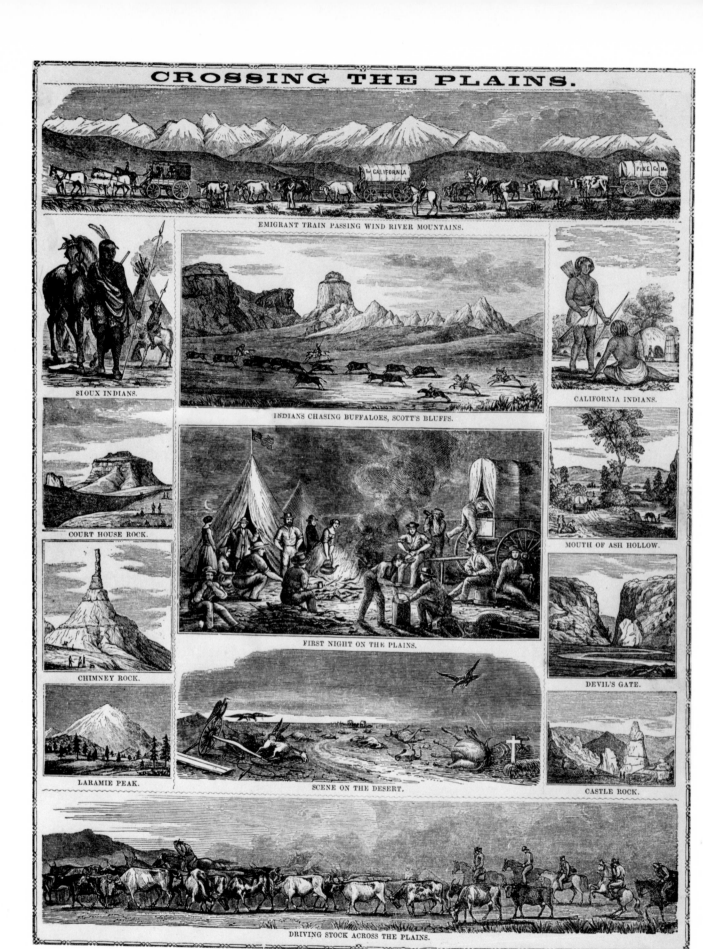

CROSSING THE PLAINS.

EMIGRANT TRAIN PASSING WIND RIVER MOUNTAINS.

SIOUX INDIANS.

CALIFORNIA INDIANS.

INDIANS CHASING BUFFALOES, SCOTT'S BLUFFS.

COURT HOUSE ROCK.

MOUTH OF ASH HOLLOW.

FIRST NIGHT ON THE PLAINS.

CHIMNEY ROCK.

DEVIL'S GATE.

LARAMIE PEAK.

SCENE ON THE DESERT.

CASTLE ROCK.

DRIVING STOCK ACROSS THE PLAINS.

A restless people with a hunger for land

It was the latter part of June, a Tuesday afternoon, in the year 1845. Up since 4 and moving since 7, a wagon train of American pioneer families, some bound for the Oregon country and some for California, had been traveling west all day beside the lukewarm North Platte River in Indian country west of Nebraska. A few of these emigrants — the 19th Century name for pioneers crossing the continent — rode saddle horses, but most of them trudged along the riverbank on foot. Both the riders and the walkers coaxed the loose herd of milk cows and the extra oxen and mules that plodded behind the 41 canvas-covered wagons.

Only the sick, some of the women and the littlest children rode inside the wagons. There was simply no room for anyone else. The wagons were already piled high with flour, pilot bread and beans; bacon, dried fruit and coffee; sugar, salt and vinegar; plows, axes and bucksaws; rocking chairs and chamber pots; tinware, cast-iron skillets and Dutch ovens; linsey-woolsey shifts and buckskin shirts; feather beds and patchwork quilts; water kegs and butter churns; violins and books.

The emigrants had been moving slowly westward from Independence, Missouri, across the Great Plains for nearly two months, and were now approaching the first low foothills of the Rocky Mountains. Here the afternoon temperature soared high into the 80s. The train of wagons, animals and people, perhaps a mile in length, panted across a blackened upland of burned-over prairie grass. With each footfall a puff of ashes and dust rose and clung in the oxen's nostrils.

As the animals strained heads-down against the rattling chains and hickory yokes, a deep coughing shook

---

By 1853 the landmarks, the challenges and the hardships catalogued on this page from a California weekly were indelibly etched on the memories of 180,000 pioneers.

their trail-worn bodies. The teamsters trudging beside them, half-hidden in the clouds of dust, cursed and goaded and lashed at them with whips. Above the din an unattended axle shrieked for want of grease. Inside a wagon something swayed, lurched and tipped over with a splintering crash, and a napping infant woke up with a wail. Down the line a 10-year-old boy, mindless with boredom, jammed a thick stick into a slowly revolving wheel to see what would happen. A wooden spoke fractured.

A day like that, with all its weary frustrations, did not differ very much from any other day on the pioneer trail. But for the pioneers in this particular wagon train, some 150 men, women and children who had set out seven weeks and approximately 600 miles earlier from Independence in the first week of May, the day would end differently from the others. Toward sundown, just above the gently rolling prairie, rose a landmark that the pioneers had been anticipating for almost two months: the turreted and picketed ramparts of Fort Laramie. This was the first habitation of white men the travelers had seen since leaving Missouri. All of them — children and adults alike — were streaked with grime and sweat, and the adults voted unanimously to pass the next day cleaning up and resting on the green meadows just east of the fort.

Despite its name, Fort Laramie, near the eastern edge of what would one day be the state of Wyoming, was not a military installation. The United States Army would eventually buy it and garrison soldiers there, but in 1845 it was simply a fur trappers' trading post surrounded by an adobe wall 15 feet high and by a North American wilderness 600 miles wide. Fort Laramie's only tie to civilization was the wagon track that had brought the 41 covered wagons and the 150 pioneers over the horizon that afternoon.

This track was the Oregon Trail — the route which had already carried fur trappers and other adventurers

Asiatic cholera first reached Eastern cities in the early 1830s, inspiring broadsheets like the one below. Emigrants carried the scourge with them, and cholera killed more pioneers than all other diseases combined.

REMEDIES FOR
CHOLERA

As prescribed by the Edinburgh Board of Health, and approved of by the Faculty of New-York.

CAREFULLY PREPARED BY JEFFERSON B. NONES,
APOTHECARY AND CHEMIST,

NO. 644½ BROADWAY, NEW-YORK.

NO. 1.—CHOLERA MIXTURE.
A table-spoonful with 60 drops of Laudanum, in half a wine-glassful of cold water. If this fail to relieve, repeat two spoonsful, with 30 drops of Laudanum every half hour. Half these doses of mixture and laudanum, for children of 14. One-fourth for children of 7. Do not exceed the doses prescribed; and stop when the vomiting and cramps cease, unless you have medical advice.

NO. 2.—BOTTLE OF LAUDANUM.

NO. 3.—CHOLERA PILLS.
To be used if the mixture No. 1 be vomited. Two pills at first, and then one every half hour, if the first fail to relieve. Half these doses for children of 14; one-fourth for children of 7. Do not exceed the doses prescribed, and stop when the vomiting and cramp cease, unless you have medical advice.

NO. 4.—CHOLERA CLYSTERS.
Inject three tea-spoonsful in a wine-glassful of thin warm gruel, and retain as long as possible by pressure below with a warm cloth; if not retained, repeat immediately, but otherwise not. Half the dose for children of 14—one fourth for children of 7.

NO. 5.—MUSTARD POULTICES.
A fourth part is enough for one person. Dust it thickly over porridge poultices, of which apply a large one on the belly, and others on the soles and calves. Remove when the patient complains much of the smarting.

Greenwich Printing Office, 118 Barrow-street.

into the Rocky Mountains and a smattering of missionaries to the unredeemed Indians of the Oregon country. Now, along with the dreams and possessions of these pioneers and thousands like them, the Oregon Trail was bringing America itself to the unsettled Pacific Coast. Still, it was no great highway across the continent, but simply a pair of parallel wheel ruts traced by the wagons across the sod of the prairies, the rock and the rubble of mountain passes and the sands of the Western deserts. They were intermittent ruts at that; when they arrived at the bank of a river they stopped —and resumed on the other side, leaving the traveler to devise his own connection. Even so, when Oregon itself became an official section of the United States in 1846, the 2,000 rough-and-ready miles of the Oregon Trail combined to make it the longest thoroughfare in the republic—and unquestionably the hardest. "Once started on the journey," one pioneer remembered, "the

problem was to finish. We didn't think much about the unborn generations who would profit by our venturesomeness. It was simply a desperate undertaking."

In 1845, when those 41 wagons had started from Independence, the westernmost edge of the formally constituted United States ended at the Missouri River. California appeared on the map as a northern province of Mexico, and already there was a small but prosperous community of Spanish-speaking cattle ranchers. The Oregon country was a huge tract of wilderness that extended north from California all the way up the Pacific Coast to Alaska, and from the Pacific Ocean in the west to an eastern boundary running along the Continental Divide in the Rocky Mountains—thus encompassing today's states of Oregon, Washington and parts of Canada, Montana, Idaho and Wyoming. No one knew for certain to whom this land really belonged; it was claimed by both the United States and Great Britain, who had signed an unusual treaty allowing for "joint occupation" in 1818.

Thus the overland pioneers were, in a very real sense, emigrants. They went out from their own country into what was basically a foreign land, and an uncivilized one at that, to commence their farming and homemaking. Later, after these Western territories had been duly incorporated as part of the U.S., another term for American pioneers came into use: the sodbusters. This was the name applied to the people who began to homestead the prairies and plains of Kansas, Nebraska, Colorado, Wyoming, Montana and the Dakotas—the determined farmers who sometimes broke the soil with an ax to plant their corn.

Among the emigrants arriving at Fort Laramie, on Tuesday, the 24th of June, 1845, was a high-browed, raw-boned man named Joel Palmer, "an intelligent farmer," as he styled himself, from Laurel, Indiana. A public-spirited man, Palmer had been sent by his neighbors to the Indiana legislature in Indianapolis the year before. But Palmer itched for wider horizons, and so here he was, headed for Oregon where there were no big cities and no state legislature of any kind. He was going for personal observation, he said, "with a view of satisfying myself whether Oregon's advantages were sufficient to make it my future home."

Sixty-nine days previously he had taken leave of his wife and children "with a truly melancholy heart," and

thus became one of a total of 5,000 other west-bound emigrants on the Oregon Trail that summer. Emigration to the Pacific West was still such a new idea at this time — the first pioneer wagons had creaked along the trail only four years earlier — that not many in the 1845 migration knew exactly where they were headed or precisely what they hoped to find. But most of them probably felt the same optimism Joel Palmer did: "I believed that I was right," he said. "I hoped for the best, and pressed onward."

Because of his flair for leadership, Palmer had been appointed captain of his wagon train by the democratic vote of the adults. As captain he had the power to make certain decisions affecting the common life of the train, and he had given his approval to a brief layover at Fort Laramie. While camped there, Palmer and the others spent their time writing letters home, washing out their dirty socks and underwear, mending their wagons

and harness, shoeing their horses and oxen and trading at the fort where flour was selling that week at $15 a hundredweight and a dollar would buy only two cups of sugar or two cups of coffee beans.

Having spruced themselves up and improved their dispositions since Tuesday, Palmer and his companions decided upon a sagacious bit of frontier diplomacy. The next leg of their journey would pass through Indian country, so the pioneers arranged a banquet for Wednesday afternoon in honor of a hundred or so Oglala Sioux Indians who frequented this region and were then camped near the fort on the banks of the Laramie River. Each pioneer family agreed to furnish two dishes of food for the feast.

When the Indians arrived, they seated themselves in two concentric semicircles on the ground. The pioneers formed a single semicircle opposite the Indians. The Sioux chief — nobody caught his name — opened the ceremony with a blunt but careful speech, his words being translated to the pioneers by a white trader. "This country belongs to the red man," said the chief, "but his white brethren travels through, shooting the game and scaring it away. Thus the Indian loses all that he depends upon to support his wives and children. The children of the red man cry out for food, but there is no food." The chief concluded by asking for guns, lead and powder. Only with these arms, he said, could the Indian kill the wild animals that were now too skittish to be taken by bow and arrow.

Joel Palmer replied in kind. "As it devolved upon me to play the part of the white chief," he later recalled in his diary, "I told my red brethren, that we were journeying to the great waters of the west. Our great father owned a large country there and we were going to settle upon it. For this purpose we brought with us our wives and little ones. We were compelled to pass through the red man's country, but we traveled as friends, and not as enemies."

Unfortunately for the Indians, Palmer continued, the suspendered men and bonneted women seated beside him were not traders. They were farmers on their way "to plough and plant the land." Such powder and ball as they possessed were barely sufficent for their own needs and they had none to trade or give away.

Palmer then urged the assembled Indians to help themselves to the food spread out before them, picnic-style, on buffalo robes: meat, cakes, rice mush, bread and coffee. Dipping their fingers in, the Indians ate, understanding all too clearly that nothing would be gained by further talk. The unstoppable American white man was on the move once again and the resistant American Indian was again being told that he would have to settle for apologies and a few handouts of food. The Oglala Sioux, when they got up to leave, glumly collected the leftovers and took them home.

As Joel Palmer watched the Sioux people depart, unrequited, for their tipis that night at Fort Laramie, he was indeed standing witness to one more small but deeply significant scene in the drama of American expansion that had been running for more than 200 years — ever since the first white settlers came ashore at Plymouth. Since then the frontier, which the white settler took west with him like the mud on his boots, had expanded from the Atlantic seaboard with a kind of

pulsing, move-and-hesitate rhythm. Each time it moved deeper inland, the resident aborigines had been given the option of stepping aside or getting pushed. The Indians, and the wilderness itself, were giving way to a new kind of people, who would settle, and eventually dominate, the great empty spaces of America.

The original frontier of colonial times lay east of the Appalachians. Then, following the example of Daniel Boone in 1767 *(page 27),* a few venturesome families began to leave the settled colonies to cross the wilderness mountains. These were the first emigrants — and they filled in the Ohio River valley, the lower Mississippi and the old northwest of Illinois, Indiana and Michigan. At length, by the 1820s, the frontier butted against the wide and coffee-colored Missouri River.

Here the pioneers were stymied for the time. Beyond the river and all the way to the Rocky Mountains some 600 miles distant, lay the generally arid and desolate Great Plains, and beyond them the formidable bastion of the Rockies. This was the land of the Louisiana Purchase, the land Thomas Jefferson had paid Napoleon only $15 million for, sight unseen, in 1803. To the frontiersman, Napoleon had got the best of the trade. There were almost no trees for houses or fences and scarcely any water for farm crops. The forbidding countryside broiled in the summer, froze rock hard in the winter and the buffalo grass which grew on it bent before a wind that never seemed to blow itself out. No one from the forested East had ever seen such a peculiarly inhospitable landscape.

Children's geography books labeled the area as the Great American Desert. In addition, the United States had designated the region as Indian land (what else was it suited for?), officially off limits to everything except the aboriginal savages chasing their wild game herds, and a few fur traders and foolhardy missionaries. Many straight-thinking Americans felt that it should stay that way. For example Zebulon Pike, a U.S. Army explorer most famous for discovering Pikes Peak, had traveled through the region in 1806, surveying it with greatest care. And he concluded that the Great Plains, with all their drawbacks, had been purposely put there by a merciful "Providence to keep the American people from a thin diffusion and ruin." American expansion, it would seem, was all over at a line slightly more than one third of the way across the continent.◉

Le bouvier des grandes plaines et son attelage. — Dessin de Janet Lange d'après des croquis originaux.

LE FAR-WEST AMÉRICAIN,

PAR M. L. SIMONIN.

1867. — TEXTE ET DESSINS INÉDITS.

GO AHEAD!

I

DE PARIS AU MISSOURI.

Arrivée à Brest. — Utilité des années bissextiles. — Petit et grand bateau. — Les officiers du *Saint-Laurent*. — Beau temps en mer. — La *Ville Impériale*. — Un hôtel de marbre. — La discipline des caravansérails américains. — Mes compagnons de voyage. — Craintes au départ. — Un homme scalpé vivant. — En avant! — L'Hudson et le Niagara. — Un coin du Canada. — Détroit, le Michigan, Chicago. — Les *railroads* américains. — Voitures-dortoirs, wagons-palais et salons d'état. — Les merveilles de la *Reine des Prairies*. — De Chicago à Council-Bluff et Omaha.

Le 13 septembre 1867, un vendredi, à huit heures du soir, mauvaise date, mauvais jour et vilaine heure, je quittai Paris pour me rendre à Brest. Le chemin de fer de l'Ouest, qui unit la prosaïque gare de Montparnasse à la poétique Cornouaille bretonne, me porta à Brest sain et sauf, le lendemain. Je ne prétends pas que le train fût rapide, car on le transforma, suivant l'usage, en train omnibus à partir de Rennes, au grand désespoir des voyageurs transatlantiques; mais nous arrivâmes, après un sommeil modéré, sans encombre, et c'était là le principal.

On dit qu'il pleut toujours à Brest, en d'autres termes qu'il y tombe de l'eau trois cent soixante-cinq jours par an. Cela fait désirer, dans cette partie de la Bretagne, les années bissextiles, celles de trois cent soixante-six jours, qui malheureusement n'arrivent que tous les quatre ans. Il pleuvait donc le jour de notre arrivée, et nous n'avions pas lieu d'en être satisfaits, car nous devions, sur un petit steamer, nous rendre à bord du navire français le *Saint-Laurent*, trop grand, sinon trop fier pour venir nous prendre à quai.

Le *Saint-Laurent*, un des meilleurs marcheurs de la flotte française transatlantique, est commandé par le capitaine de Bocandé, un loup de mer, qui aime son

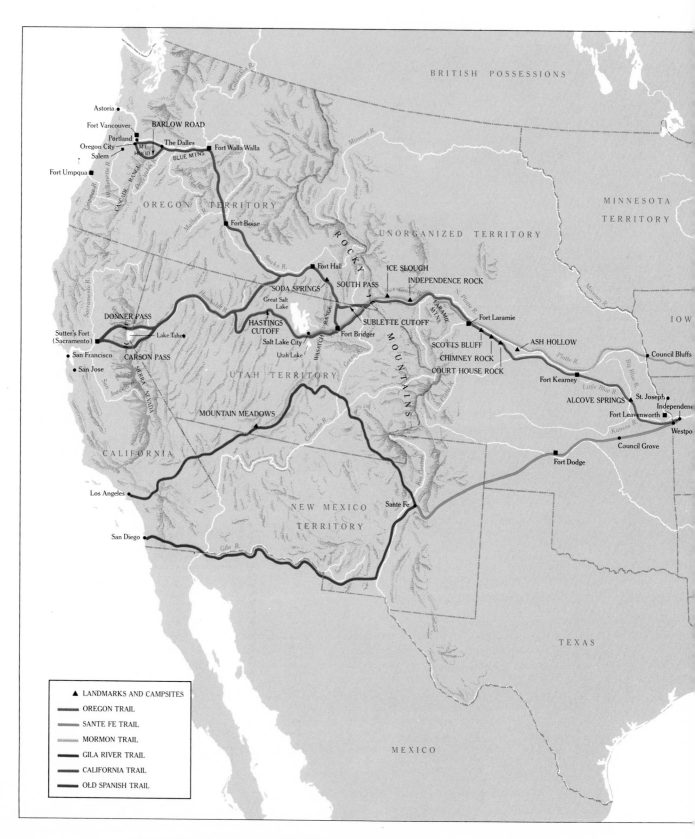

BRITISH POSSESSIONS

MINNESOTA TERRITORY

Astoria
Fort Vancouver
Portland   BARLOW ROAD
Oregon City   The Dalles   Fort Walla Walla
Salem   MT. HOOD   BLUE MTNS
Fort Umpqua

OREGON   TERRITORY

Fort Boise

ROCKY

Fort Hall   ICE SLOUGH
SODA SPRINGS   SOUTH PASS   INDEPENDENCE ROCK
Great Salt
Lake
DONNER PASS   HASTINGS   SUBLETTE CUTOFF
CUTOFF   Fort Laramie
Salt Lake City   Fort Bridger   SCOTTS BLUFF   ASH HOLLOW
Sutter's Fort   Lake Tahoe   CHIMNEY ROCK
(Sacramento)   Utah Lake   WASATCH   COURT HOUSE ROCK
San Francisco   CARSON PASS   Council Bluffs
San Jose   Fort Kearney
                UTAH   TERRITORY   MOUNTAINS   ALCOVE SPRINGS   St. Joseph
                MOUNTAIN MEADOWS   Independenc
CALIFORNIA   Fort Leavenworth
                                                                        Westpo
                                                        Kansas R.   Council Grove
Los Angeles   NEW MEXICO   Fort Dodge
                                        Sante Fe
                                TERRITORY
San Diego   Gila R.

                                                        TEXAS

MEXICO

▲ LANDMARKS AND CAMPSITES
─── OREGON TRAIL
─── SANTE FE TRAIL
─── MORMON TRAIL
─── GILA RIVER TRAIL
─── CALIFORNIA TRAIL
─── OLD SPANISH TRAIL

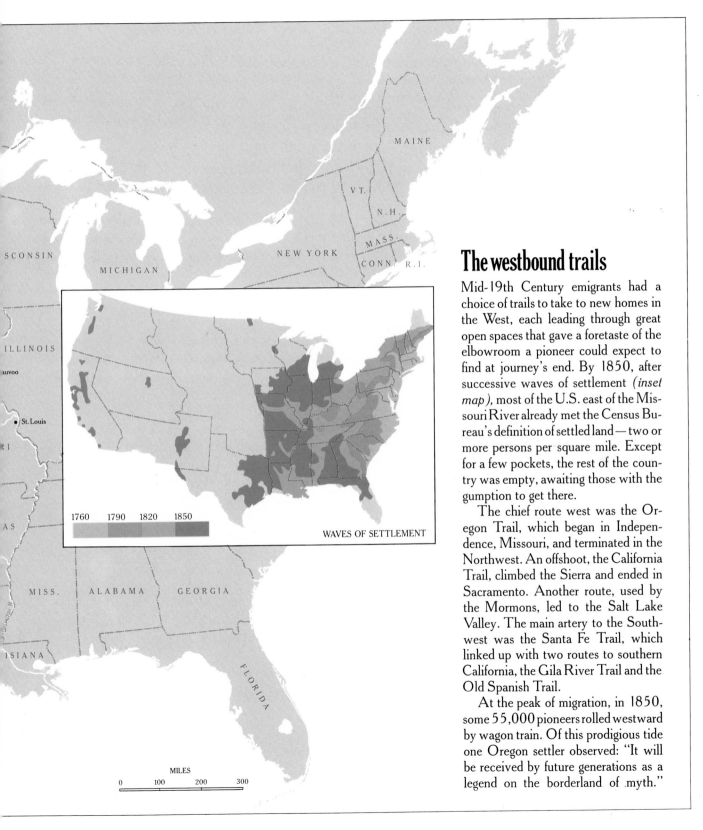

1760   1790   1820   1850

WAVES OF SETTLEMENT

MILES

0   100   200   300

The westbound trails

Mid-19th Century emigrants had a choice of trails to take to new homes in the West, each leading through great open spaces that gave a foretaste of the elbowroom a pioneer could expect to find at journey's end. By 1850, after successive waves of settlement *(inset map)*, most of the U.S. east of the Missouri River already met the Census Bureau's definition of settled land—two or more persons per square mile. Except for a few pockets, the rest of the country was empty, awaiting those with the gumption to get there.

The chief route west was the Oregon Trail, which began in Independence, Missouri, and terminated in the Northwest. An offshoot, the California Trail, climbed the Sierra and ended in Sacramento. Another route, used by the Mormons, led to the Salt Lake Valley. The main artery to the Southwest was the Santa Fe Trail, which linked up with two routes to southern California, the Gila River Trail and the Old Spanish Trail.

At the peak of migration, in 1850, some 55,000 pioneers rolled westward by wagon train. Of this prodigious tide one Oregon settler observed: "It will be received by future generations as a legend on the borderland of myth."

But no mere tract of prairie, however bleak, could check the 19th Century American's westering urge, his quest for a better chance and for more room. Somehow the West always seemed to promise something extra: blacker soil, bluer skies, a rosier future. In large part it was an emotional urge, this inclination to move west, an itch in the brain, a restlessness in the feet, a rising to the challenge of new land no one else had settled. Henry David Thoreau sensed it in the New England woods, where walking in circles, he felt his perplexity change to insight.

"Eastward," he said, "I go only by force, but westward I go free . . . the prevailing tendency of my countrymen." A pioneer woman doodled the same idea in her diary one wintry day in Dakota's Red River valley.

When God made man,
He seemed to think it best
To make him in the East,
And let him travel west.

A popular saying had arisen about it: "If hell lay to the west, Americans would cross heaven to get there."

No one could say for sure why this was so, but one pioneer made a good try in 1846. His name was James Clyman and he had been a mountain man and fur trapper before he turned to guiding the wagon trains of emigrants. "All ages and sects are found to undertake this long tedious and even dangerous Journy," he wrote in his journal, "for some unknown object never to be realized even by the most fortunate. And why? Because the human mind can never be satisfied, never at rest, always on the strech for something new."

And so, having studied the mid-continent barrier which the plains and mountains presented, and seeing little to tempt him in this windy, water-scarce region, the frontier American on the stretch, as James Clyman had put it, began to scan the far horizons of the Pacific West. The refraction of this land of tall trees and deep valleys brimming with rich soil and bathed by dependable rain and sunshine became an image fixed in his eye, inviting him to cross the wide Missouri.

In time the urge to transport oneself to that smiling region seemed almost irresistible. From Maine to Missouri, men and women kept hearing amazing claims that were being made about the beneficent land along the southern Pacific Coast. As early as 1782, an English author named William Frederick Martyn had painted California as a place where "a vast quantity of dew falls every morning; which, settling on rose leaves, candies, becomes hard like manna, and possesses all that sweetness peculiar to refined sugar." More recent reports seemed scarcely less miraculous. Fur trappers, adventurers, merchant seamen who traded with the local Spanish colony brought back fabulous tales of California's perpetually sunny climate. No one, it seems, ever got sick. One old trapper, when asked if the ague was troublesome in the Sacramento valley, replied that "but one man in California ever got a chill there, and that was a matter of so much wonderment that folks went 18 miles into the country to see him shake."

No less marvelous were the stories that circulated about Oregon, where by 1836 a handful of trappers, traders and missionaries had begun settling into the lush, richly timbered Willamette valley. Oregon was a "pioneer's paradise," one of the region's advocates told a party of emigrants as they were about to start out in 1843, where "the pigs are running about under the great acorn trees, round and fat, and already cooked, with knives and forks sticking in them so that you can cut off a slice whenever you are hungry."

A bit more circumspect, but just as enthusiastic, was a Boston man named Hall Jackson Kelley, whose dream was to create a New England town beneath the towering evergreens of western Oregon. "When improved and embellished" by the white man, he wrote, Oregon would become the "loveliest and most envied country on earth." A popular tract summed up the boosterish mood: "As far as its producing qualities are concerned, Oregon cannot be outdone whether in wheat, oats, rye, barley, buckwheat, peas, beans, potatoes, turnips, cabbages, onions, parsnips, carrots, beets, currants, gooseberries, strawberries, apples, peaches, pears or *fat and healthy babies.*"

No wonder, then, that the caravans of wagons began heading west. It mattered not at all that these lands remained wholly or in part under foreign dominion. Both California and Oregon seemed expressly designed for American occupation and settlement. And Americans felt a kind of confidence—indeed arrogance—that America would get them. Surely both Mexico and Great Britain would shortly concede that all this land belonged by God-given right to the United States—by Manifest

made a careful tally of all passing wagons, people and livestock, and the count for 1850 included 7,472 mules, 30,616 oxen, 22,742 horses, 8,998 wagons and 5,270 cows. But still the caravans continued, until by 1869, the year the first transcontinental railroad was completed, no fewer than 350,000 emigrants had rolled and plodded along the trail. In passing, the wheels of their wagons cut gashes in the continent that would still be evident a century and a quarter later.

Beyond any mystic westering urge, or the call of Manifest Destiny, some hard realities prompted Americans to pull up stakes and leave the Eastern United States during the middle decades of the 19th Century. Black slavery, for one thing. Some abolitionists found slavery so repugnant, for humanitarian reasons, that they migrated to fresh territories where they would find no vestiges of the foul practice. Many other people objected to slavery on the simple economic grounds that it put the typical small farmer at an earning disadvantage. A man who owned no slaves just could not raise crops as cheaply and easily as a man who did. Thus he had the choice of going broke or moving on.

Moreover, in 1837, the nation suffered its first major financial collapse, the result of cavalier money and banking policies and feverish speculation in public lands during the administration of Andrew Jackson. On May 10, 1837, just 67 days after Jackson had retired from office, the major New York banks shut their doors, and in the panic that ensued banks all over the country followed suit. Depression enveloped the nation like the smoke of a prairie fire: agricultural prices skidded downward, farm surpluses clogged the produce markets and farmers could not meet the mortgage payments on their land. So they packed everything portable into wagons and headed for the free land on the Pacific.

Epidemics of sickness also drove people west, where both legend and logic suggested the airs were purer. In the East, more people died of such diseases as typhoid, dysentery, tuberculosis, scarlet fever and malaria than from any other cause. Yellow fever so decimated the population of New Orleans and the settlements along the Mississippi River to the north that the regional death rate exceeded its birth rate for nearly a century. And in the 1830s an epidemic of cholera, which had started in Asia, rampaged through Europe, and came across the Atlantic on passenger ships, struck the East

Destiny as President James Polk might have phrased it.

And that, by and large, is how things turned out, due in considerable measure to the visionary persistence of the emigrants. Their thrust to the Pacific began in the spring of 1841, when a party of 69 hardy souls left Missouri for the Pacific Coast, led by a Missouri farmer named John Bartleson and an Ohio schoolteacher named John Bidwell. It continued the following year when 200 pioneers headed west. Another 1,000 crossed the trail in 1843, followed by 4,000 in 1844 and the 5,000 of Joel Palmer's year. By then the magnetism of the West had reached across the Atlantic to Europe, and sturdy English crofters, German farm folk, Irish potato growers and Scandinavian dairy farmers were joining the wagon trains.

The discovery of gold in California in 1848 sent the number of emigrants on the Oregon Trail—foreign and domestic—spurting up to 30,000 in 1849, and to 55,000 by 1850. The latter was the peak year of travel along the trail. Soldiers at Fort Laramie, which had become an official U.S. Army post the year before,

Coast and spread inland. The disease raged for almost two decades, killing some 30,000 in 1850 alone.

Some emigrants headed for the Oregon Trail because of religious persecution. The Mormons—members of the Church of Jesus Christ of Latter-day Saints—were driven from their homes in Nauvoo, Illinois, by unsympathetic neighbors in 1846, and set out on a migration to the Salt Lake valley of Utah.

Eventually, a far greater conflict—the American Civil War—would send another great wave of pioneers westward. In the war's aftermath, thousands looked for an escape from their devastated homes. To all these people the word West sounded, as it had to the first American settlers, like another way of saying health, wealth and happiness. And notwithstanding the fact that most pioneers would reach the end of the trail destitute of property and money, a successful recovery was usually just a matter of time. "The majority," said one man who made the crossing himself in 1846, "were plain, honest, substantial, intelligent, enterprising and virtuous." "They were," he said, "indeed much superior to those who usually settle in a new country."

As a possessor of all those winning attributes, John Minto seemed to embody the pioneer prototype. Good-looking, without guile or vice, John had come from Newcastle, England, and in 1844 was working in a Pennsylvania coal mine. He had been a coal miner in both England and America for 14 of his 22 years, and now he was sick of grubbing black fuel from the earth. By a stroke of paradoxical luck for him, his Pittsburgh mine shut down during a strike that winter. Coal glutted the market and wages were too low to keep any miner in room and board. John Minto, romanced by James Fenimore Cooper's tales of frontier life (he had read *The Pioneers* while sailing to America from Liverpool in 1840), took deck passage on a paddle-wheel steamer down the Ohio River and made his way to St. Louis. There he bought a rifle, some fishhooks and "a hatchet to answer for a tomahawk."

Thus provisioned, he proceeded to Weston, Missouri, one of the bustling towns on the Missouri River where emigrants about to depart for Oregon laid in supplies before striking out on the trail together. John Minto heard encouraging gossip in Weston. A fellow of his strength and willingness, he was told, ought to have no trouble getting a job as a teamster with a family bound for the West. Minto remembered, "I whirled my cap up and said, 'Boys, here is the fellow that goes to Oregon, or dies in a sand bank.'"

At that time the Mississippi valley, no less than Pennsylvania, was having its own economic troubles; prices in farm goods had dropped so low that Mississippi steamboats sometimes burned bacon for fuel. One Missouri farmer who had resolved to walk away from the depressed situation was Wilson Morrison, and he happened to be on the lookout for a hired hand to take West. John Minto got the job; sometime later in Oregon, he also got Farmer Morrison's daughter as his bride. John noticed her on his first day at work—"a girl of twelve or thirteen going from the house to a near by spring for water." Instantly, said Minto, the lines of an English ballad moved through his mind:

The farmer's boy grew up a man,
And the good old farmer died,
And left the lad the farm he had
With the daughter for his bride.

"If my thought had been given voice," Minto decided, "it would have been, 'There, Johnny Minto; there goes your wife that is to be.'"

One evening before they were all to leave Missouri, a friend of Farmer Morrison's dropped by the Morrison's frontier log cabin. He said that a journey to Oregon seemed like plain foolishness, an "unnecessary search for toil and danger." He asked Morrison to explain what prompted him to go. John Minto said his new boss then and there made quite a moving little speech that summed up everyone's best reasons for hitting the trail.

"Well," Morrison began, "I allow the United States has the best right to that country, and I'm going to help make that right good. Then I suppose it is true, there are a great many Indians there that will have to be civilized; and though I am no missionary, I have no objection to helping in that. Then, I am not satisfied here. There is little we raise that pays shipment to market; a little hemp and a little tobacco." Finally he spoke directly to the slavery issue. "Unless a man keeps niggers, (and I won't)," Morrison went on, "he has no even chance. There is Dick Owens, my neighbor; he has a few field hands and a few house niggers. They raise and make all that the family and themselves eat

Daniel Boone: The quiet man behind a flamboyant myth

When Daniel Boone, toward the end of his 86th year, died peacefully in bed in his son Nathan's elegant stone Missouri farmhouse on September 26, 1820, the surge of emigrants along the Oregon Trail was still a generation away. But Boone already exemplified the pioneer at his best. He was neither the physical giant (five feet nine) nor the innocent child of nature that legend has made of him. He was an intelligent, soft-spoken family man who cherished the same wife for 57 years. Though he never learned to spell — he had left school early after putting an emetic in a hated teacher's hidden whiskey bottle — he could read *Gulliver's Travels* aloud to hunting partners by the light of campfires. He befriended Indians, preferred company to solitude and when he told his wife it was time to move because a newcomer had settled some 70 miles away, he was joking. He loved the forest but it was also his place of business: in it, he was out for a buck — literally — because of a buckskin's worth.

Pennsylvania-born, Boone was one of 11 children in a family of Quakers who migrated to North Carolina. There Boone was recruited at age 40 to undertake a scheme designed to open up Kentucky to settlers and establish it as a 14th colony. He arranged a deal by which the Cherokees sold 20 million acres for £10,000 worth of goods to Boone's employers, the Transylvania Company. It was all fair and square — the Indians had an attorney, an interpreter and the sound advice of their squaws. The deal completed, Boone led a party from Tennessee through the Cumberland Gap, hacked out the Wilderness Road and set up a town — Boonesboro — and a government. Elected a legislator, he introduced on the first session's first day a bill to protect game against wanton slaughter and a second bill to "im-

In a characteristic portrait, Boone carries a coonskin cap. In fact, he never wore one.

prove the breed of horses." He got 2,000 acres for his work, but after the Revolution — in which Boone won considerable fame as a militia commander — the scheme of the Transylvania Company was declared illegal and Boone lost his land.

Undaunted, he staked out more claims — and lost them because he impatiently neglected to register his deeds. Ever hopeful, he accepted an invitation from Spanish-held Missouri to come and settle there and bring others with him. The Spanish gave him 8,500 acres and made him a judge. But the Louisiana Purchase, which embraced Missouri, again left him — but not his children — landless. Old and broke, Boone cheerfully continued hunting and trapping long after his hands shook. Shortly before he died, he was talking knowledgeably with young men about the joys to be experienced in settling California.

In choosing an obviously well-to-do family for his painting *Leaving the Old Homestead,* artist James Wilkins, who traveled the Oregon Trail in 1849, made the point that pioneers came from all walks of life.

and wear, and some hemp and tobacco besides. If markets are good, Dick will sell; if not, he can hold over, while I am compelled to sell all I can make every year in order to make ends meet. I'm going to Oregon where there'll be no slaves, and we'll all start even."

Later that evening, Johnny Minto sang the household to sleep:

> *Will you go lassie,*
> *go to the braes of Balquihidder,*
> *Where the blaeberries grow,*
> *mang the bonny highland heather....*

Then, with their songs sung and their farewells done, John Minto, his staunch employer and his future bride made ready in early May to join the battalions of other emigrants who, in the three decades following, rolled westward in their wagons toward the green and bountiful farmlands of the Pacific Far West. Like the great majority of those pioneers, Morrison and Minto headed off along the best known and most traveled overland route. It was called the Oregon Trail *(map, pages 22-23)*—though it also led to California. At a point slightly beyond halfway, in the eastern section of the huge Oregon country, the trail forked, one branch knifing south toward California, the other beckoning on to Oregon. Either way, throughout most of its length the trail was already well marked, having been traveled by a full generation of mountain men who trapped the beaver streams on the slopes of the Rockies and beyond.

From the main jump-off point at Independence, Missouri, the Oregon Trail angled west across the Kansas grasslands, and north into Nebraska. From there it continued west by a bit north along the broad, silt-clogged Platte River, rising imperceptibly through the Nebraska prairies and onto the dry, desolate High Plains.

Past Fort Laramie, in what would one day become the state of Wyoming, the trail climbed gradually through an undulating landscape covered with sagebrush and bunch grass toward the snow-capped ranges of the Rocky Mountains. It crossed the Continental Divide at an unprepossessing place called South Pass, a wind-swept upland between the mountains. This broad, flat corridor through the Rockies had been discovered in 1812 by a beaver trapper named Robert Stuart who had worked for the fur magnate, John Jacob Astor. During the roistering decades of the 1820s and 1830s,

bearded mountain men had used the pass to freight pro-visions to a rendezvous point, where the trappers would gather to trade pelts, swap stories and drink raw whis-key in one of the valleys west of the Continental Di-vide. Now in the middle decades, South Pass's gradual slope provided emigrants with the only feasible wagon route across the divide north of New Mexico, and so made the Oregon Trail possible.

After crossing South Pass the trail entered the arid eastern regions of the Oregon country, an area too harsh and intemperate to invite settlement. It then moved downslope through an increasingly tumbled landscape toward the more benign Pacific Coast. Near the border of present-day Idaho the route split into its two main branches (plus a maze of shortcuts and bypasses). Northwest, of course, lay the fertile valleys of western Oregon, the trail descending the slope of the continent along the tortuous curve of the Snake River that cut through a succession of difficult mountain ranges before joining the Columbia. This was the route opened ear-lier by fur trappers going to the Oregon forests, and the one taken by John Minto and William Morrison, who were eight dangerous, wearisome months on the trail. They did not arrive at Oregon's Willamette valley un-til December 30, 1844, having floated the last 200 miles down the Columbia River on a raft, through gales and snowstorms, and over rapids that Minto described in his diary as the worst hazard of the whole trip.

The emigrants' other choice at the great fork in the trail was the route blazed in 1833 by the most cel-ebrated of all the mountain men, Joe Walker. Walker's keen pathfinding instinct had led him to the most direct feasible way to California: north of Great Salt Lake and along the brackish Humboldt River through the al-kali wastes of the Nevada desert and then over the 13,000-foot peaks of the Sierra Nevada into the cen-tral valleys beyond. Walker crossed the mountains at Yosemite, through some of the most spectacular but dif-ficult country in the entire West. A decade later, in 1844, another famous mountain man, Kit Carson, dis-covered an easier crossing near Lake Tahoe to the north —and this eventually became a standard route across the mountains for the wagon trains.

A few pioneers with their eyes on the Far West tried other basic routes to the promised land. One was the old Santa Fe Trail, which also jumped off from In-dependence. The Santa Fe Trail had been opened in 1821 as a trading route between the United States and Mexico. An annual caravan of freight wagons, piled high with merchandise from Eastern factories, headed out on the 800-mile trek through present-day Kansas and New Mexico to the old provincial capital of Santa Fe. To protect their cargo, and also provide themselves with a reasonably snug shelter against prairie storms, the Santa Fe wagoners fitted their wagons with canvas covers stretched over wooden frames. From a distance these slow-moving vehicles with their white canvas top-ping looked like ships of the plains. Thus they acquired the nickname of prairie schooner, and the sobriquet—to-gether with the wagon cover itself—became a symbol of the entire pioneer movement.

For almost a decade the trail went no farther than Santa Fe. But in the 1830s the traders began to ex-pand their operations into California, extending the trail with branches that reached to San Diego and Los An-geles. These extensions, known respectively as the Gila River Trail and the Old Spanish Trail, got heavy use after the gold rush as later settlers took up land in south-ern California and Arizona.

If he possessed the money and the stomach for it, an emigrant bound for the coast had yet another, dramatic alternative. He could ignore the overland roads alto-gether and take passage on a sailing ship from New York or Boston for the six-month, 13,000-mile sea voyage around Cape Horn. (Pressed for time, the voy-ager could also save three months—and risk yellow fever —by shortcutting across the Isthmus of Panama.)

As with the overland trails, the sea lanes to Cali-fornia and Oregon had been opened by commerce many years earlier. Even before the first beaver trappers had reached Oregon, and Astor's fur company had estab-lished the initial American settlement of Astoria in Or-egon in 1812, Yankee sea captains had developed a thriving trade for sea-otter pelts with the Northwest In-dian tribes. In fact so many New Englanders reached the Oregon coast that for years afterwards the Indians called all white people Bostons.

Yankee shipowners had also made America aware of the seaports and verdant ranches of California, as they plied an immensely lucrative trade in hides and beef tallow with Mexican cattlemen. Beginning in the 1820s and continuing for the next quarter century,

Yankee enterprise in Spanish California

Journey's end for the pioneer usually meant unsettled wilderness, like the little-explored country beyond the Oregon Trail. But in California the first emigrants from the East found a thriving foreign colony. It included many Americans like Jacob Leese—seen with his family at right—who had been drifting into California since the early 19th Century.

The Mexican laws then governing the region made it difficult for aliens to enter or live there, but Mexican citizens generally winked at these laws. Eager for a touch of the outside world, they welcomed newcomers, even Joseph Chapman, a crewman on a pirate ship that was captured in 1818 during a raid on Monterey. Chapman married his captor's daughter, entered the boatbuilding business, and became a pillar of the community.

Other sailors wrote home describing a cattle-rich, trade-starved land of promise, and alert Boston merchants sent flocks of white-winged brigs to pick up cargoes of cowhide. Some smart seafarers stayed on in the region as local agents, enriching both their firms and themselves as merchants and rulers of vast ranches.

In the late 1820s a second wave of newcomers began arriving from the land side. Gaunt, leathery fur trappers made it through the snowy Sierra passes, and settled down as carpenters, masons, coopers, silversmiths, soapmakers, shipwrights, millers and vintners. Among these foot-loose fellows was Jacob Leese.

An Ohio clerk turned trapper, Leese crossed the Sierra in the winter of 1833; during that harrowing jour-

Proud and still prosperous, the Leeses and their children sit for a family portrait in 1849.

ney he ate his faithful hound to stave off starvation. Within three years he emerged as an up-and-coming merchant in Yerba Buena—later to be renamed San Francisco—and the owner of the hamlet's biggest house, for which he paid $440 in merchandise. ("I think itts a Dam Good Traid," he wrote to a friend.)

In this rambling redwood structure he staged the town's first Fourth of July celebration in 1836 with a congenial mix of some 60 Americans, Britons and Mexicans. The guests included the Mexican General Mariano Guadalupe Vallejo, whose pretty sister, Rosalia, captivated Leese. Such romances were not unusual. A well-connected wife could help in dealings with officialdom; and besides the dark-eyed señoritas were beguilingly exotic. They smoked cigarettes in gold holders, rode like vaqueros,

danced, sang and played the guitar.

Some had whims of iron. Vallejo had bestowed a large ranch and Rosalia's hand on an Irishman named Timothy Murphy, who had been scratching out a living as an otter hunter. But the spirited and tart-tongued Rosalia jilted Murphy (although he kept the ranch) and married Leese instead. Their daughter Rosalia, the eldest of their seven children, was born in 1838.

Leese prospered for a time in enterprises as diverse as a cattle drive to Oregon and a trading trip to China. Then his luck left him. Like many a pioneer, he eventually lost the lands he had acquired to hordes of squatters who poured into California during the gold rush of 1849. He died impoverished at 82, run over by a wagon in San Francisco while he was walking home from an oldtimers' get-together.

A cornucopia of natural treasures, plus the promise of modern industry and communications — all these things would be inherited by the intrepid

American trade ships arrived by the hundreds carrying, as one observer vividly described, a cargo of "spirits of all kinds: teas, coffee, sugars, crockery-ware, tin-ware cuttlery, boots and shoes from Lynn, calicoes and cottons from Lowell, crapes, silks, necklaces, jewelry, and combs for the ladies; furniture; and in fact, everything that can be imagined, from Chinese fireworks to English cartwheels." So wrote Richard Henry Dana Jr., who made the voyage as a deck hand in 1834 and described the experience in a hugely popular book, *Two Years before the Mast*—which helped to whet American curiosity and enthusiasm for seeing California. On the return voyage, the ships would carry great sheaves

of stiffened cowhides for the Lynn shoe factories, and large leather bags filled with beef tallow, used for making candles. Permanent shore posts were needed to handle the trade with the ranchers, and a few ships' agents used their earnings to buy ranches themselves — thus becoming California's first American settlers.

Until the gold rush began, however, only a few emigrants shipped west by sea, and despite a spurt of sea travel immediately following the gold strike at Sutter's Mill, the total number of voyagers never equaled the many thousands who trudged along the Oregon Trail. Besides the high cost of passage (about $300 a head), the food aboard ship was terrible and living quarters

emigrant in California, according to this imaginative 1857 engraving from the unabashedly boosterish *Wide West*, a San Francisco weekly.

abominably crowded. The one advantage of the voyage was that it could be undertaken during the northern winter, giving passengers a head start on overland travelers who were obliged to wait until the spring thaw.

Yet, according to the diaries of voyagers, such advantages were more than offset not only by the discomforts but especially by the crushing boredom of a half-year odyssey around the Horn. One man told how he passed the time. "Today," he wrote in his diary, "I opened my big box and spread all its contents out on my bunk, examining each article carefully and then stowing it away again. One man came below and seeing me thus engaged, proceeded to unpack *his* trunk.

We both agreed that it was a pointless proceeding, yet the time passed pleasantly." Another man who was caught in a storm shortly after sailing told his diary: "Commenced reading today a work entitled *What I Saw in California* by Edwin Bryant. Mr. Bryant traveled the overland route to California, and I regret very much that I did not take the same."

No one knows how many strong-stomached pioneers braved the sea voyage; perhaps 100,000, including the ones who took the Panama shortcut. But three times that many emulated the prudent Edwin Bryant. As these emigrants streamed into the coastal region, whether by wagon or ship, and the Pacific wilds began to give way to vegetable farms and dairies and fruit orchards, a strange thing happened. The frontier took a giant step backwards, over the Rocky Mountains and east to those same plains of Kansas and Nebraska that the first emigrants had found so bleak and monotonous when they crossed them on the trail.

A number of events had occurred meanwhile to make settlement on the plains seem somewhat more appealing. One was a bald-faced political maneuver by a short, feisty Illinois Senator named Stephen A. Douglas. As a natural booster of his home state—and an important landowner there—Douglas hoped to secure a northerly route for the proposed transcontinental railroad, with an eastern terminus in Chicago and track running through the Indian lands west of the Missouri River. Therefore the Senator, in 1854, slipped through Congress a piece of legislation known as the Kansas-Nebraska Act, which turned the Indian country into U.S. territories and officially opened them up to settlers. The act also opened up the prickly issue of whether these territories would be slave or free. Vicious guerrilla warfare broke out in the new territories. But still the pioneers rolled in; the population rose from almost nothing to 136,000 in the six years before the Civil War.

Even more important than the Kansas-Nebraska machinations for most pioneers was the promise of free land, provided by the Homestead Act of 1862. By its terms, for a filing fee of only $10, any U.S. citizen or alien immigrant could claim 160 acres of the public domain. All he had to do was live on the land and farm it for five years. By adding more government land at a guaranteed low price of $1.25 an acre, he could acquire —at modest expense—a farm of considerable size. And on the vast sweep of the plains and prairies, there was room for at least half a million such farms.

Though the economics and some aspects of the politics of settling on the plains had thus improved, the physical fact of living there decidedly had not. There was still no timber for houses nor indeed wood to burn in kitchen stoves. The plains settlers had to build their homes out of earthen chunks cut with a plow or a broadax from the sod beneath their feet, using the prairie itself for a floor, and dried buffalo dung or dead grass for heating and cooking fuel.

No amount of wifely energy could bring much cheer to such a dwelling with its dank, half-lit interior and vermin-infested roof. A visitor, spending her first night in a pioneer family's soddy, as the houses were called, woke with a start: "Something similar to fine hail was falling on my face and hands," she said. Go back to sleep, her hostess reassured her. It was only the wind redistributing the building materials.

If a settler landed upon a spot where the sod would not hold together for house building, he would be forced to scoop a lateral dugout in a hillside, hang a blanket over the front and urge his family to move into their new home. "Floors are a luxury rarely seen here," wrote a pioneer. "I noticed yesterday a member of our family making up his bed with a hoe."

Throughout the 1850s and 1860s, settlers like these all across the plains existed with a constant dread of attack by Indians. "We do not go to bed at night without fear, and my rifle is always loaded," wrote a farmer from Dodge County, Minnesota, in 1862. And though some tribes along the westward trail had been reduced to begging handouts or perhaps stealing an occasional calf, for a lone emigrant man at his plow or woman in her soddy, the sudden appearance of Indians could mean death. So it was for the two older children of Peter Ulbrick, who were hoeing corn in their parents' Nebraska homestead on July 23, 1867, when a party of Indians rode up. The Indians bashed in the head of young Peter, aged 12, with a tomahawk, and carried off Veronica, aged 15, held her captive for eighteen months, during which time they abused her so savagely she never fully recovered. Another family fared only slightly better when George Martin, out haying with his two sons, Nathaniel and Robert, caught an arrow in the jugular vein while standing in the hay

ARMCHAIR WESTERING FOR ONE SLIM DIME

Through the rose-colored imagination of pulp fiction authors like Ann Stephens, whose popular novel *Esther* appeared in 1862, the plodding monotony and the nagging hardship of the pioneer experience became the backdrop for rousing tales of adventure. Esther, Mrs. Stephens' heroine, wanders away from the wagon train with which she and her father are traveling and is captured by Dakota Indians. (In the cover illustration at right she is being warned of her impending fate, albeit too late, by Waupee, a friendly squaw.) Many hair-raising trials and tribulations later, the fair maiden is rescued and, in a truly happy ending, is duly wed to the scion of a rich and socially prominent St. Louis family.

COMPLETE. **BEADLE'S** NUMBER 45.

DIME NOVELS

UNITED STATES OF AMERICA
ONE DIME

THE CHOICEST WORKS OF THE MOST POPULAR AUTHORS.

ESTHER:
A STORY OF THE OREGON TRAIL.

BEADLE AND COMPANY.

NEW YORK: 141 WILLIAM ST. LONDON: 44 PATERNOSTER ROW.

General Dime Book Publishers.

Urging his brothers back East to join him, a 26-year-old Oregon settler named Medorem Crawford wrote a detailed letter of instruction including the promise that "we could in five years all be wealthy farmers."

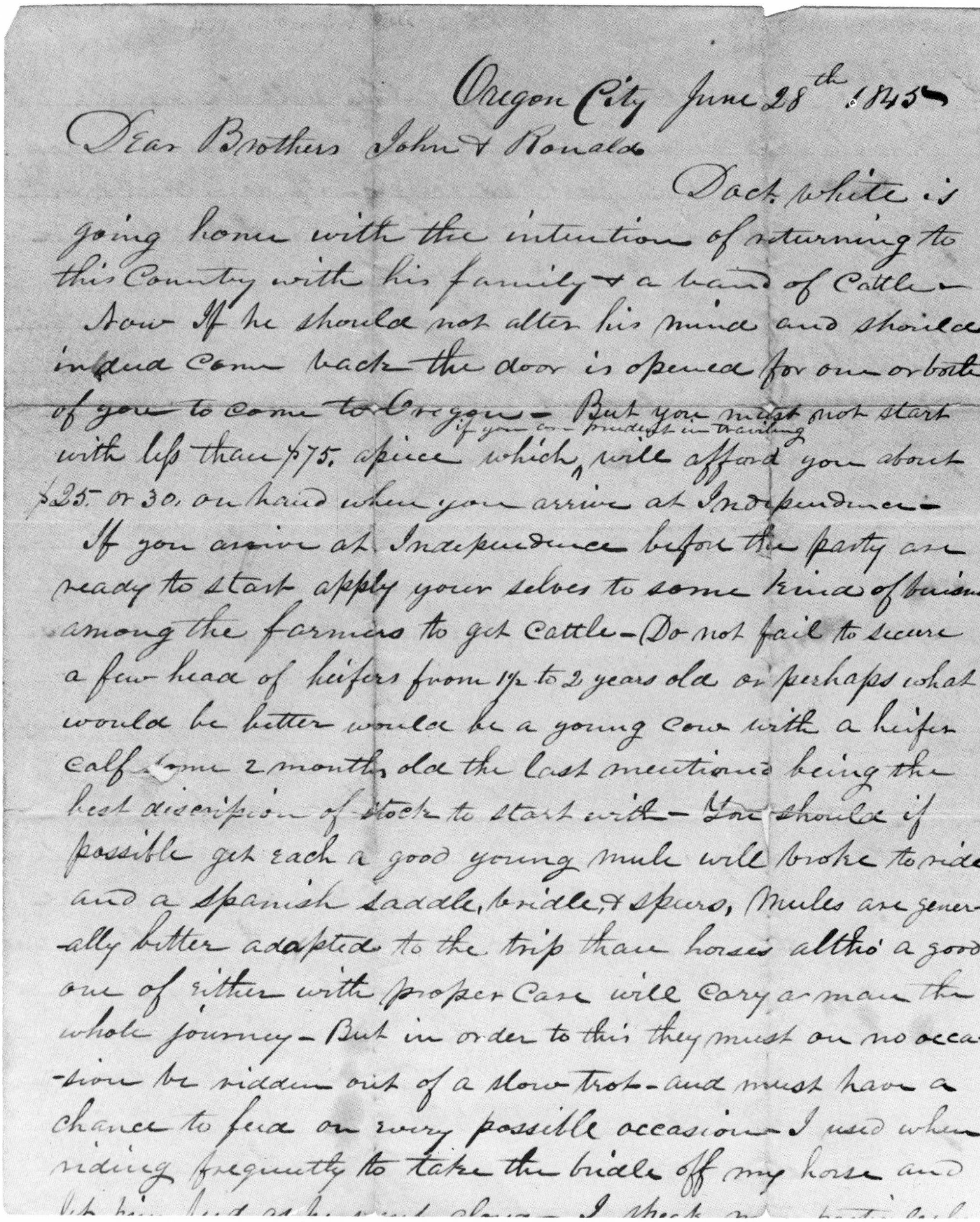

Oregon City June 28th 1845

Dear Brothers John & Ronald

Doct. White is going home with the intention of returning to this Country with his family & a band of Cattle — Now If he should not alter his mind and should indeed Come back the door is opened for one or both of you to come to Oregon — But you must not start with less than $75. apiece *if you are prudent in traveling* which will afford you about $25. or 30. on hand when you arrive at Independence —

If you arrive at Independence before the party are ready to start apply your selves to some kind of business among the farmers to get Cattle — Do not fail to secure a few head of heifers from 1½ to 2 years old or perhaps what would be better would be a young cow with a heifer calf some 2 months old the last mentioned being the best discription of stock to start with — You should if possible get each a good young mule well broke to ride and a Spanish saddle, bridle, & spurs, Mules are gener- ally better adapted to the trip than horses altho' a good one of either with proper Care will Carry a man the whole journey — But in order to this they must on no occa- sion be ridden out of a slow trot — and must have a chance to feed on every possible occasion — I used when riding frequently to take the bridle off my horse and

36

Joel Palmer—farmer, legislator, Indian agent —made two trips to Oregon. Before the second journey he published a guide for pioneers advising them to "lay in a good supply of school books for their children."

wagon. The wagon team bolted for home, where Martin's wife closed up the farmer's severed vein with a pin, thus saving his life. The two boys, riding double on the same horse, also lit out for home, followed by a hail of arrows. Three hit, including one which went completely through the body of one boy and lodged in the backbone of his brother, skewering both together. Somehow the pair survived.

A more constant and only slightly less lethal hazard was the weather on the High Plains. The wind seemed merciless, its incessant buffeting and moaning so oppressive that more than one sod-house wife, left alone for days on end while the men were off plowing or hunting, went mad. Summer temperatures regularly rose above 100 degrees, and winters could be so unspeakably cold that settlers sometimes moved livestock inside the house for body heat. One Dakota woman wrote that "the mercury goes into the ball at forty below and it is now out of sight and Katie is thawing the frost from the front windows with a warm flatiron so as to let in the light." Another diarist reported that he could not keep up his journal because his ink had frozen hard.

Not everyone could take it at first. Said Mollie Sanford, a pretty young schoolteacher moving into a Nebraska cabin with her parents, "Father tried to look cheerful, but I could see tears in mother's eyes." Mollie vowed to become a heroine, "A brave, brave girl, and I said it would be jolly. I did not think so." A pioneer farmer from Council Grove, Kansas, did not even try to say so. "Between the drouth, the cinch bugs, and the grasshoppers," he observed, "we will be forced to go to Egypt or somewhere else for our corn."

Enough was enough for some people, and they went back to where they came from, glad they had the strength to retreat. One plains farmer chalked across the door of his deserted cabin: "250 miles to the nearest post office; 100 miles to wood; 20 miles to water; 6 inches to hell. Gone to live with wife's folks."

Such disillusionment and dashed hopes met pioneers in the Far West, too—the place that had seemed so promising in the beginning. On a 320-acre claim facing Washington's Puget Sound, Phoebe Judson and her husband, Holden, constructed a cabin and began to farm their land. Back in Vermillion, Ohio, Phoebe had pictured her cabin in the West covered with vines and trellised with roses. But the gravelly soil of their claim produced scrubby crops and spindly roses, and what with high prices for store-bought goods in nearby Olympia, cougars stealing pigs, floods threatening the house and Indians massacring neighbors, Phoebe lamented that "the inconveniences of our environment and the constant drudgery effectually took all the romance and poetry out of our farm life." She stuck it out, however, and in a book of memoirs entitled *A Pioneer's Search for an Ideal Home,* she concluded that she had, indeed, found the perfect place to live.

No such letdown awaited Joel Palmer who, 200 days after his melancholy departure from his home in Indiana, arrived in Oregon City in the Oregon territory on November 1, 1845. First he took stock of the place: Oregon City had been established earlier by Methodist missionaries and retired trappers from the Hudson's Bay Company, a British-based fur-trading enterprise of enormous influence in the Northwest. Palmer counted "a neat Methodist church, a splendid Catholic chapel, two grist mills, two sawmills, four stores, two taverns, one hatter, one tannery, three tailor shops, two cabinet makers, two silversmiths, one cooper, two blacksmiths, one physician, three lawyers, one printing office and a good brick yard." Palmer then took a brisk hike through the surrounding countryside, pronounced it delightful, and after the winter had passed returned west-to-east over the Oregon Trail to his family. An absence of one year, three months and one week had passed but, he said, "I had the pleasure of finding my family enjoying good health."

The following spring—it was 1847—all of them were traveling on the Oregon Trail. And riding at the head of the wagon train, elected by the democratic vote of the adults in the company, rode Captain Joel Palmer.

When Emanuel Leutze evoked the pioneer spirit in a canvas commissioned by Congress in 1860, he titled it with a clarion call for Manifest

Destiny: *Westward the Course of Empire Takes Its Way*. The line is from a poem by the 18th Century British philosopher George Berkeley.

2 | Prophets and propagandists

Although most emigrants were content to dream of building their own homes and growing their own crops, the men pictured here sought to influence the shape that the political and social order would finally take in the West. Booster John Marsh encouraged emigration in the hope that it would lead to American annexation of — and be followed by statehood for — California. Among his converts was John Bidwell, a young Ohio schoolteacher. Heeding Marsh's call to come West, Bidwell stayed on to fight for California's independence from Mexico. Later he was elected to the new state's first senate.

Then there were the missionaries, men like Samuel Parker and Jason Lee, who went West to ensure the Indians' survival in the face of the increasing number of white settlers. Parker's search for sites for Indian missions led him to explore unmapped areas of Oregon; and the missions that Lee established attracted settlers to the territory.

There were also colonizers: Nathaniel Wyeth hoped to set up a trading community in the fish and lumber country around Oregon's Columbia River, while the half-mad Hall Jackson Kelley dreamed of founding a huge farm commune on the coast. These men's stories are told in the following chapter. Some achieved their goals, others did not. But each played a seminal role in popularizing, exploring and settling the West.

SAMUEL PARKER

JOHN MARSH

JOHN BIDWELL

HALL JACKSON KELLEY

NATHANIEL WYETH

JASON LEE

41

JAMES K. POLK.

THE PEOPLES CHOICE.

Lith. & Pub. by N. Currier 2 Spruce St N.Y.

Bold forerunners of a great emigration

Hall Jackson Kelley was a wonderfully versatile man. Born at the turn of the 19th Century, he introduced the first blackboard into Boston's public schools and he founded the first Sunday school in a Boston church. And in 1829 he devised and announced a heroic plan to move 3,000 New England farmers, en masse, to the banks of the Columbia River in Oregon. The blackboards and the Sunday school have survived for a century and a half. Kelley's grandiose scheme to carve a proper Yankee farm community out of the Pacific forests, on the other hand, brought him nothing but frustration and grief. Yet this turned out to be his most significant endeavor.

Never before had anyone seriously attempted to transplant American families to the Far West. And though Kelley personally would never escort a single pioneer past Boston's city limits, his zealous propagandizing triggered a score of other determined visionaries to follow their own dreams to the West, and in the process to blaze the pioneer trail to the Pacific. These forerunners of the emigrant movement would take the first covered wagons across the Rocky Mountains, and the first women as well; they would celebrate the first marriages, build the first schools and establish the first towns. They were a determined, gutsy, slightly madcap bunch — Yankee traders out to make a dollar, Protestant missionaries out to convert the Indians, and at least one adventurous rascal a half step ahead of the law. But all had one thing in common: they showed the way for the grand procession of pioneers to come.

Kelley himself did not seem like the sort of man to found a colony in the wilderness. Pious, introspective, bookish (he had ruined his eyes as a child reading Vergil by moonlight), he appeared more suited to the ministry or to teaching school. Indeed, after graduating from Middlebury College in Vermont he became a grammar teacher in Boston and wrote several spelling primers. But an urge for high adventure festered in Kelley's blood, based on his reading of the journals of Lewis and Clark. Thereafter the schoolmaster devoured every piece of Far West literature he could find — tracts, pamphlets, and particularly the transcripts of the Congressional debates over the status of Oregon.

Congress had taken up the Oregon question (*page 50*) at the clamorous behest of a Virginia Representative, John Floyd. Great Britain, said Floyd with splendid 19th Century chauvinism, was stealing the region away from the United States. Actually Britain, whose Hudson's Bay Company trading posts were so far the only settlements in Oregon, probably had a sounder claim to the territory than did the United States. Nonetheless Floyd urged Washington to annex Oregon immediately and fill it with U.S. settlers. "With two oceans washing our shores, commercial wealth is ours and imagination can hardly conceive the greatness, the grandeur, the power that await us," the Virginian boomed. His fellow Congressmen were not impressed. Oregon seemed far too savage and remote for anyone to go and live there, and no less a figure than Secretary of State John Quincy Adams judged Floyd's proposal to be based on a "tissue of errors; there was nothing could purify it but the fire."

But in Boston, Floyd's words took hold of the fervent imagination of schoolmaster Kelley. While Congress talked, Kelley decided to act. He would lead the first American settlers himself. For he had received in a vision direct endorsement to do so from God. "The word came expressly to me," Kelley declared, "to promote the propagation of Christianity in the dark

Presidential candidate James Polk boldly bestrides his horse in this 1844 campaign poster. During his tenure, California and the Oregon country became U.S. land.

43

Independence, Missouri, long the jumping-off point for wagon trains headed west on the Oregon and Santa Fe trails, appears here as seen by an

unknown artist in 1853. The main street, with its steepled brick courthouse, also had stores where emigrants laid in last-minute supplies.

and cruel places about the shores of the Pacific."

Thus inspired, Kelley left his post in the Boston school system in 1823, and devoted all his energies for the next 10 years to drumming up excitement for Oregon—a country which, of course, he had never seen. Such a gap in experience, however, was no inhibition to a visionary like Kelley. He described the region as a place brimming with salmon, beaver, timber, and with farmland so rich that "the production of vegetables, grain, and cattle will require comparatively but little labor." Even the trip from Boston to the Pacific Coast would be no more taxing than a pleasant summer outing. The settlers would move overland in comfortable wagons; cumbersome freight would go safely by ship around Cape Horn. Congress would underwrite most of the expenses, and costs would be negligible—ranging from $50 for adults to $5 for children under two.

Congress paid even less attention to the schoolmaster than it had to the Oregon boosters in its own ranks.

But Kelley managed to stir considerable attention in Boston, and by 1829 he had won enough followers to establish formally the American Society for Encouraging the Settlement of the Oregon Territory—whose membership soon reached 500. Its express purpose was "planting, in the genial soil of those regions, the vine of Christianity, and the germ of Civil Freedom." Under Kelley's stewardship, the society met, debated, drew up bylaws, shuffled its feet and debated some more. But it never seemed able to keep a firm departure date.

To at least one of the society's members, a farsighted 29-year-old Boston entrepreneur named Nathaniel Jarvis Wyeth, such lack of decision seemed unforgivable. Wyeth was already engaged in the ingenious and profitable business of cutting ice each winter at a pond in nearby Cambridge and shipping it to the West Indies. Now, attracted by Kelley's sunny propaganda about the Pacific Coast but fed up with the society's inaction, Wyeth resolved to go there on his own, establish the first American colony and sniff out the prospects for profits in fur, salmon and lumber.

Wyeth quit Kelley's American society, decided to leave on March 1, 1832, and with bustle and dispatch began gathering his own group of colonists. He soon had a group of 20 "industrious and temperate men" that included his 19-year-old cousin, John Wyeth; his brother, Dr. Jacob Wyeth, who would act as physician; a gunsmith; a blacksmith; two carpenters; two fishermen; and an assortment of farmers and laborers.

Wyeth loved efficiency and organization. He outfitted his recruits in uniforms: pantaloons, striped shirts and cowhide boots. He armed them with muskets, bayonets, axes and clasp knives "for eating and common purposes" until, said one observer, "they were Yankee all over." A bugle was provided for signaling, and three wagons were built with gondola-shaped bodies so that they could double as boats at river crossings. The energetic leader next took his men to an island in Boston harbor for 10 days of pretrail toughening. Thus hardened and equipped, the company sailed to Baltimore, where it picked up four more recruits.

From this time, all the Cambridge ice merchant's careful planning began to come unstuck. At St. Louis, trail-wise fur traders told Wyeth that his boat wagons were too flimsy to get across the Rockies; he would have to get rid of them (which he did, at less than half

WESTERN CHARACTERS

Redfield

price). His men began to have doubts about traveling into "a dark region of savages," and by the time the party reached Independence, Missouri, six had defected.

Independence itself must have seemed like the edge of nowhere to the Bostonians. The town's first cabins had been thrown together only five years earlier, in 1827. A traveler, Charles Joseph Latrobe, who passed through Independence in the same year as Wyeth, described it as "a ragged congeries of five or six rough-hewn log-huts, two or three clap-board houses, two or three so-called hotels, alias grog-shops, a few stores." But for all its air of makeshift, Independence was a town with special advantages and a unique importance: it would serve as the main gateway to the trails west.

Here was the staging point for the trading caravans that had been rattling down the Santa Fe Trail to Mexico for more than a decade. Each year the heavy Conestoga wagons would start west, laden with trade goods —bolts of calico and denim; cutlery and rugs; bracelets, beads and hairpins; brushes, razors, mirrors; sugar, flour and whiskey. The wagons would return with Mexican silver and gold, furs and raw wool. Fur traders, too, completed provisioning in Independence before setting off for the summer rendezvous in the Rockies.

Nat Wyeth hitched his company to the 1832 fur brigade. The famous trail veteran William Sublette guided the expedition; and the seasoned fur trader gave the greenhorn Bostonians every help. "We must have perished for want of sustenance in the deserts of the Missouri had we been by ourselves," wrote cousin John.

By July, when the company finally straggled into the rendezvous at Pierre's Hole, seven more colonizers decided to drop out, including both John Wyeth and the ice merchant's brother, Jacob. The return party started back with Sublette, but not in time to escape a week of intermittent skirmishing with 150 Blackfoot warriors —an incident that became celebrated in Rocky Mountain lore as the Battle of Pierre's Hole. Seven trappers and one colonist perished. Perhaps a dozen men were wounded, including Sublette, who caught a Blackfoot arrow in his left shoulder.

Gathering up the remnants of his band, Wyeth struggled west once more. He eventually reached Fort Vancouver, the main Hudson's Bay Company trading post in Oregon, on October 29, 1832, eight months after his departure from New England. There, another shock

awaited him. A ship he had sent out from Boston, carrying beaver traps, trade goods, barrels for packing dried salmon—all the paraphernalia for his various business schemes—had been lost in a Pacific storm.

Even this disaster could not stop Nat Wyeth. Although his first expedition had flopped badly, Wyeth made up his mind to try again. He had already performed an extraordinary feat, having brought the first emigrants over the Oregon Trail to the Pacific Coast. Some of Wyeth's men went to work for the Hudson's Bay Company. One of them, a former lawyer named John Ball, started teaching the half-breed children of the fur men—thus founding Oregon's first school. And Solomon Smith and Calvin Tibbetts stayed on to build farms in the Willamette valley, becoming the first U.S. citizens to take up permanent residence in Oregon.

Shortly after Wyeth's arrival in Oregon, Hall Jackson Kelley finally started west from Boston. In 1833 he went by ship to Mexico, crossed overland and then wandered north through California. At Monterey he joined traders who were driving horses and mules to sell at Fort Vancouver. En route, a small band of strangers had attached themselves to the party. The strangers turned out to be horse thieves fleeing the California authorities, and when the expedition reached Fort Vancouver everyone attached to it was assumed to be a horse thief as well. The visionary schoolteacher eventually cleared himself and shipped back to Boston. But the experience left him a broken man, and he finished his days in poverty and obscurity.

Nat Wyeth's misfortunes were less devastating, and in any event he was not the kind of man to give up. After spending the winter exploring the Oregon wilds, the Yankee merchant headed east to prepare for a second expedition, stopping en route at the 1833 trappers' rendezvous and picking up a contract to deliver supplies to them the following year. Soon he was back in Boston stocking provisions and signing up recruits for a journey to start in the spring of 1834.

Among the first to sign up was a 30-year-old Methodist clergyman named Jason Lee, who, in his own way, would bring the mass of future pioneers a step closer to the Far West. Tall and brawny, with clear blue eyes and a massive jaw, Lee came well equipped for the hardships of the trail. An ex-farmer, he could, according to a contemporary, chop a cord of wood in two hours, and he "possessed a stomach like that of an ostrich, which could digest anything." His credentials as a messenger of God were just as sound. Lee's devotional zeal, said the Methodist bishop in Boston, ran "deep and uniform." What better man to save the heathen natives from Satan? None, thought the bishop, and Jason Lee was charged forthwith by his church to convert the Indians of Oregon to Christianity.

This same evangelical instinct bloomed strong among all the Protestant churches of the mid-19th Century. As early as 1820, the American Board of Commissioners for Foreign Missions, with a sense of dreadful urgency, had sent representatives to plant the church's banner in the Hawaiian Islands. With similar enthusiasm, evangelists would now descend upon and bring salvation to the lost souls of the Oregon tribesmen. In setting up their wilderness missions they would also establish the first American towns in the Pacific Northwest, and provide the oases of American civilization toward which future pioneers would head. Nathaniel Wyeth, whose own zeal was purely commercial—a "perfect infidel," as one divine called him—was going to help by taking the first Oregon missionary, Jason Lee, along the Oregon Trail.

The immediate inspiration for Lee's trip was an impassioned letter that ran in an 1833 issue of the *Christian Advocate and Journal,* a Protestant religious publication. It described a visit by four Indians "from west of the Rocky Mountains" to St. Louis. According to this letter, written by a Methodist convert who was part Indian himself, the visitors had acquired a driving hunger for the white man's religion. Someone had told them, the letter said, "that the white people away toward the rising of the sun had been put in possession of the true mode of worshipping the Great Spirit; they had a book containing directions." So the Indians, three Nez Percés and one Flathead, had traveled 3,000 miles to St. Louis to learn the contents of the Great Spirit's book. No sooner did they arrive at the doorstep of the Superintendent of Indian Affairs—who was none other than the great trailblazer General William Clark himself—than two of them dropped dead from sickness and exhaustion. Martyrdom in pursuit of the True God! The missionary societies stood agog.

The *Christian Advocate* offered a sketch on one dead Indian. His head, from the tip of his nose to the top of his crown, sloped backward like the hypotenuse of a triangle. These Indians, the letter explained, mutilated their foreheads by binding a board against them in childhood. Thus the name Flathead. In fact, none of the Indians at St. Louis had flattened heads, and indeed very few Flatheads anywhere ever followed the bizarre custom of head-binding. But readers believed the drawing, and were horrified. All over the Eastern U.S., volunteer evangelists began applying to their churches for assignment to Oregon.

Jason Lee, as the first to go, started along the Oregon Trail from Independence in late April, 1834, with Nat Wyeth's second expedition. Wyeth was carrying a heavy load of provisions to the fur trappers' rendezvous, and this time had gathered a formidable group of trail companions—70 men in all. Lee himself headed a small delegation consisting of four fellow missionaries—his nephew, the Reverend Daniel Lee; a lay schoolteacher; and two lay assistants. This tiny band had been given an exceedingly weighty charge by the Methodist church: to find the nation of Flathead Indians and "live with them, learn their language, preach Christ to them and, as the way opens, introduce schools, agriculture, and the arts of civilized life."

The expedition went smoothly until it reached the rendezvous at Pierre's Hole, where Wyeth discovered that his old friend William Sublette had arrived before him and provided all the supplies the trappers needed. Left with a caravan of unwanted goods, Wyeth pushed on toward Oregon. Along the trail he built a trading post, Fort Hall, on the Snake River in what is now southern Idaho, from which he hoped to unload his rejected supplies. Here Jason Lee met his first Flathead Indians, and with a grieved spirit glimpsed the magnitude of the evangelizing job that lay ahead. "The Indians play foot-ball on Sunday," he wrote, "and (tell it not in Christendom) it has been taught them by people, calling themselves Christian, as a religious exercise."

When Lee finally arrived at Fort Vancouver on the Pacific Coast, he was genially welcomed by Dr. John McLoughlin, the Quebec-born director of the Hudson's Bay Company enterprises there. As the effective reigning magistrate in the vast Oregon territory, McLoughlin felt a certain sense of responsibility toward all newcomers, even Americans. He gently informed the missionaries that the Flatheads lived in dangerously un-

thereof, may be observed and fulfilled with good faith by the United States and the citizens thereof.

In witness whereof, I have hereunto set my hand and have caused the seal of the United States to be affixed.

Done at the city of Washington, this fifth day of August in the year of our Lord one thousand eight hundred and forty-six, and of the Independence of the United States the seventy-first.

James K. Polk

By the President:

James Buchanan

Secretary of State.

Signed on June 15, 1846, by President Polk and Secretary of State James Buchanan, the Oregon Treaty ended talk of war.

A negotiable ultimatum:"54° 40′ or fight!"

The influx of Americans into Oregon in the 1840s ignited a dispute between Britain and the United States that, in its more intemperate phases, was punctuated by shrill demands in both countries for war. The wrangle originated in the fact that the boundaries of Oregon had never been clearly fixed. The name vaguely embraced the territory west of the Rockies between the northern boundary of Mexican-held California and the southern edge of Russian-held Alaska, which at the time extended south to parallel 54° 40′. In 1818 when America proposed a boundary at the 49th parallel—an extension of the border with Canada that already existed east of the Rockies—and the British suggested a line farther south, statesmen of both nations detoured the resulting impasse by agreeing to accept temporary "joint occupancy."

But by the early 1840s, the issue could no longer be avoided: Oregon fever and Manifest Destiny had become potent political forces. Though many eastern Americans considered the Oregon country too remote to become excited about, demands for its occupation were shouted with almost religious fervor. Senator Thomas Hart Benton, for one, urged Congress to muster "thirty or forty thousand American rifles beyond the Rocky Mountains that will be our effective negotiators." The Democratic Party made "54° 40′ or fight" an issue of the 1844 Presidential election and just managed to install James K. Polk, an ardent expansionist, in the White House. But despite their seeming intransigence, neither Polk nor the British government wanted to fight. And just about the time that Polk learned that the land lying north of the 49th parallel was useless for agriculture, the British decided the American market for goods was worth far more than Oregon's fast-dying fur trade. So they quietly settled for the 49th parallel, the boundary that the United States had proposed in the first place.

In a popular 1846 lithograph, President Polk—backed by the American eagle—defies the British lion as all Europe relishes the row.

protected country hundreds of miles east of Fort Vancouver. He advised them to forget the Flatheads and settle instead in the nearby Willamette valley, where he could keep an avuncular eye on them. Here the missionaries could proselytize the local Callapoewahs. Lee agreed, presumably reasoning that one heathen Indian soul was as worth saving as another.

Lee selected a homestead beside the Willamette River and built a cabin near the east bank beneath a grove of oak and fir trees. There, he and his four fellow evangelists lived in a tent for four weeks while work went on —felling trees, hewing boards for floors, doors and tables, splitting shingles and hurrying against the approaching winter rains. Once he was comfortably settled and had staked out 20 acres of land for spring planting, Lee wrote to his mission board in February 1835, asking for reinforcements—men with families, and especially female teachers.

"White females," Lee cautioned, "would be of the greatest importance to the mission, and would have far more influence among Indians than males." Women would be helpful in still another way. Lee's men complained that they spent far too much time in household chores that were, they thought, women's work.

Two years passed while Lee's letter traveled East and the mission board responded. Meanwhile the crops grew, were harvested, the seeds replanted and a trickle of Indian and half-breed children started to attend a school that the mission had established. Then in May 1837, a ship arrived around the Horn with the requested reinforcements: 13 staunch Methodist men, women and children, including three unattached females. On July 16, Jason Lee married one of the latter, Anna Maria Pittman from New York, in Oregon's first Christian marriage ceremony.

Meanwhile, the same year that Lee traveled to Oregon with Wyeth, other devout Protestants from the East had read the Flathead letter in the *Christian Advocate* and volunteered to evangelize the Western Indians. One of these was a small-town physician from upstate New York, age 34, named Marcus Whitman, who would accomplish more for Oregon settlement than anyone else. The doctor had always felt a strong missionary urge and had dreamed of becoming a minister, but family finances could not support the seven years of training required by Whitman's Congregational church.

So he decided to become a doctor instead, medical schools demanding considerably less time and, hence, far less money. In 1832, Whitman began practicing; in his spare time he gave evening temperance lectures and taught Sunday school.

Two years later he applied to the American Board of Foreign Missions at Boston, asking to be sent to Oregon as "physician, teacher or agriculturalist." The board had already begun looking into the practicability of an Oregon mission, and had commissioned the prim and dignified Reverend Samuel Parker, age 55, to go West and look the country over. The board told Whitman he could go along with Parker.

Besides exploring the feasibility of an Oregon mission, Whitman had a personal quest. He wanted to know if a woman could endure the hazardous overland journey. Shortly before leaving, he had met a girl in nearby Prattsburg, the buoyant, blond Narcissa Prentiss. Whitman found Narcissa pretty, engaging and full of delightful good humor—though in ecclesiastical circles humor was considered next to ungodliness.

But Narcissa was also deeply devout. She, too, informed the American board of her hope "to be employed in their service among the heathen, if counted worthy." If Whitman and Parker's reconnaissance should show that women could travel the Oregon Trail, why, said Miss Prentiss to Dr. Whitman, they would certainly travel it together as man and wife.

Sam Parker and Marcus Whitman arrived in St. Louis on their fact-finding tour in April of 1835. They made an odd couple: the purse-lipped minister with a plug hat and white stock around his throat, and the rough-and-ready country doctor in frontier garb, robust and amiable, with a compact, muscular build. Like all unattached travelers on the Oregon Trail, the pair hitched up with a westbound caravan of rowdy fur traders—who found the missionaries strange fish indeed.

"Very evident tokens," said Whitman, "gave us to understand that our company was not agreeable, such as the throwing of rotten eggs at me." Worse for Whitman was Parker himself. As a pastor in Danby, New York, and also a teacher at a girls' academy in nearby Ithaca, Sam Parker enjoyed a sense of his own importance. He considered himself in charge of the entire trip, and had worked out a careful division of labor between himself and the uncomplaining Whitman. For ex-

A Cowlitz Indian mother and child by frontier artist Paul Kane reveals a curious tribal belief—that a sloping forehead marked a man as free. A board tightly tied to the infant's head produced the desired effect.

ample, while the physician struggled to tie up loose ends of the pack rope on their overburdened pack mule (Parker had thriftily purchased only one mule to carry the baggage of both men), the minister found fault with Whitman's "unskillful management." While Whitman pitched in to lift wagons out of mudholes, helped the fur men build rafts, and treated them all for Asiatic cholera when an epidemic broke out, the Reverend Mr. Parker kept to himself, contemplating the day when the "church-going bell will sound far and wide" across the prairies. And when Whitman, who also doubled as cook, was stricken by dysentery and temporarily left behind by the caravan, Parker rode ahead and took his meals with the fur brigade's captain.

Parker did give an occasional bow to Whitman's competence in his account of the journey. He mentioned that the physician extracted from Jim Bridger's back a Blackfoot arrowhead that the mountain man had carried for several years. (When Whitman expressed astonishment that the arrow had caused no infection, Bridger said, "Meat don't spoil in the Rockies.") However, Parker did not hesitate to claim glory for himself. He vividly recalled the day at Fort Laramie, Wyoming, when a band of Oglala Sioux Indians had stood in solemn reverence while Sam Parker rendered, hat over heart, a verse or so of "Watchmen, Tell Us of the Night." They liked it so much, Parker said, that they brought back friends for an encore.

While Parker was thus busily sizing up the Indians' conversion potential, Whitman had been gauging the success the fur men were having at moving their wagons full of trade goods. For wagons, the doctor felt, were the key to founding a mission, and to all other settlement in Oregon. If wagons could be taken to Oregon, so could women and children, together with all the domestic hardware and provisions needed for setting up a household in the wilderness. Without wagons, the land of Oregon was beyond the practical reach of most Eastern Americans.

By the time the missionaries had reached the fur traders' rendezvous at the Green River, they had managed to conclude, albeit on the scantest of evidence, that the experimental phase of their journey was over. Parker decided the Indians of the West were eager to receive the word of God. Whitman had become convinced that other wagons could travel the Oregon Trail. While Par-

ker continued ahead to check out mission sites in Oregon, Whitman rushed back East for reinforcements (and to pick up his bride-to-be).

As treasurer of the expedition, Parker magnanimously gave Whitman $5 to buy a new pack horse. Since good horses cost anywhere from $75 to $100, the doctor had to make do with the scrawniest animal imaginable, one that was "a disgrace for any man to pack on account of his extreme sore back." For himself Parker engaged two servants, one to act as interpreter, the other to cook and mind his horses, and gave them $18 in goods for the 56 days they served him. The divine then jogged off on a hymn-singing, Bible-reading odyssey through the precipitous Salmon River Mountains of central Idaho, and on toward the Pacific. He was attended by a swarm of jubilant Indians reciting the Lord's Prayer and the Ten Commandments, which Parker had taught them by rote. Despite his pompous ways, Parker showed remarkable mettle as he careened through the mountains and forests of the Northwest, riding five hours a day along bone-wrenching trails, shaken by fever and dizziness, but nevertheless converting virtually every Indian in sight.

He finally pulled into Fort Vancouver on October 29, 1835, carrying notebooks crammed with information on everything he had seen: the geological formations of the country, its flora, fauna, climate and the customs of its Indians. All through that winter he moved about the coastal areas, completing his studies. Then, exhausted by his travels, he embarked by ship for home, where he eventually published the story of his trip. His book, *Journal of an Exploring Tour beyond the Rocky Mountains,* was immensely popular and sold an estimated 10,000 copies.

Whitman himself arrived home in December, reported to the American board and immediately started laying plans for his second trip the following spring. At the same time he pursued his courtship of Narcissa, who was about to turn 28. "Have you carefully ascertained and weighed the difficulties in the way of conducting females to those remote and desolate regions and comfortably sustaining families there?" the secretary of the board wrote to Whitman that December. Yes, he had done that, and the marriage took place in February as planned. Narcissa wore a bombazine dress of Puritan black which she had sewed together herself, to be worn

Narcissa Whitman's journal expresses her eagerness not to spend the winter and bear her expected baby in the comparative comfort of Fort Vancouver but to press onward to Walla Walla with her husband.

Doct McLaughlin promises to loan us enough to make a begining and all the return he asks is that we supply other settlers in the same way. He appears desireous to afford us every facility for living in his power. No person could have received a more hearty welcome, or be treated with greater kindness than we have since our arrival.

14th A subject is now before the minds of a certain number of individuals, in which I feel a great interest, especially in its termination. It is that we ladies spend the winter at Vancouver. While our husbands go seek their locations & build. Doct McLaughlin our host is certain that it will be best for us, and I believe is determined to have us stay. The thoughts of it is not very pleasing to either of us, for several reasons. I had rather go to Walla Walla where if we failed of making a location or of building this fall. we could stay very comfortably and have enough to eat. but not as comfortably nor have as great variety to eat as here. and besides the difficulty of ascending the river in high water. not to say any thing of a six month separation when it seems the least desirable. but all will be ordered for the best. 18th Sab Mr Beaver held two services in a room in Doct McLaughlin house to day. This form of worship or that of the Church of England differs in no we expect from the form of the Episcopals in States. Enjoyed the priveledge much.

not only at the wedding ceremony but to serve her well in her new life in Oregon. Along with that she made some gayer print dresses and purchased a pair of smallish gentlemen's boots to wear while riding sidesaddle. For crossing streams along the trail, she completed her trousseau with an inflatable life preserver. Later, she stitched up a conical tent of striped bed ticking, oiled to make it water-resistant.

The tent appeared to be uncommonly roomy for a couple on their honeymoon; and indeed it was. Narcissa had designed it not only as a bridal bower but as shelter for a number of people who signed up for Whitman's second expedition: a carpenter and mechanic named William Gray, and Eliza and Henry Spalding, another missionary couple. This collection of oddly assorted personalities did not add up to an ideal trail crew for a 2,000-mile hike through the wilderness. Eliza Spalding, though full of a grim and resolute courage, was too physically weak to travel anywhere; she had given birth to a stillborn baby girl. When her husband expressed concern, she pluckily declared: "I like the command just as it stands—'go ye into all the world,' and no exceptions for poor health." Gray, well suited for carpentry, wanted to be a doctor, and that irritated Whitman's pride. Whitman himself still wished that he were a minister; and the Reverend Mr. Spalding har-

Western headquarters of the British-owned Hudson's Bay Company, Fort Vancouver provided a friendly stopover for Americans in transit.

Narcissa Whitman, impressed by its array of trading stores, warehouses, workshops and docks, labeled it "the New York of the Pacific."

bored a smoldering resentment at not having been put in charge of the overland expedition.

Spalding disliked Whitman for still another reason: both men had been rivals for the hand of Narcissa. Spalding had met Narcissa several years earlier while a student at Prattsburg and had mistaken her natural friendliness for personal affection. Enchanted, he had proposed marriage. When Narcissa refused as gently as she could, Spalding's love turned to bitterness. "I do not want to go into the same mission with Narcissa, as I question her judgement," he declared after the American board proposed that he join the Whitman expedition. But Spalding was persuaded to reconsider. Now here he was, married to ailing, humorless Eliza, tagging along on Narcissa's wedding trip. Arguments erupted between the ex-suitor and the bridegroom. Narcissa, in a letter to her father, wrote that "the man who came with us is one who never ought to have come. My dear husband has suffered more from him in consequence of his wicked jealousy, and his great pique towards me, than can be known in this world."

Fractious and combustible as the Whitman party was, it nonetheless embodied certain far-reaching goals. Never before had women attempted the overland journey to Oregon. Even more significant, perhaps, was the fact that the missionaries were traveling with wagons. They had brought two: a heavy farm wagon and a light Dearborn belonging to the Spaldings. And Marcus Whitman was determined to prove that these utilitarian vehicles could be wrenched and cajoled along the full length of the Oregon Trail.

In addition to the multiple sense of mission, Whitman's humble party, like so many of those to follow, was propelled westward by a sense of adventure and discovery. At the outset, Narcissa found the frontier people she met in St. Louis a sketch. "I should like to tell you how the western people talk," she wrote to her parents. "Their language is so singular that I could scarcely understand them. They say, 'How does your wife do today?' 'O she is smartly better, I reckon, but she is powerful weak.'"

Later, when the wagon party had started west from Independence, at the tail end of the fur caravan, Narcissa found a bizarre domesticity in trail life. She described it at length in her letters. "Just take a peep at us while we are sitting at meals," she wrote. "Our table is the ground, our table cloth is an India rubber cloth, used when it rains as a cloak; our dishes are made of tin —basins for tea cups, iron spoons and plates for each of us, and several pans for milk and to put our meat in when we wish to set it on the table—each one carries his own knife in his scabbard. Husband," as Narcissa was wont to refer to Marcus, "always provides my seat, and in a way that you would laugh to see us. It is the fashion of all this country to imitate the Turks. We take a blanket and lay down by the table."

At Fort Laramie, to Marcus' intense disappointment, the captain of the fur caravan, a rough and rangy trail veteran named Broken Hand Fitzpatrick, insisted the missionaries abandon their heavy freight wagon. Fitzpatrick was certain it would never negotiate the mountains ahead. However, the party was able to keep the smaller Dearborn, which—if it could get through —would still provide some proof of Marcus' theory. And when the caravan rattled into the rendezvous point, again located beside the Green River in Wyoming, the missionaries were vastly cheered and diverted by the scene. Here were assembled the savage Indians of half a dozen tribes along with 400 semi-savage white men, all of whom were there for the express purpose of getting drunk, raising Cain and trading off their accumulated pelts for enough coin and supplies to see them through another winter.

Upon this plain of Babel arrived the charming Narcissa and the demure Eliza—to become instant celebrities. "As soon as I alighted from my horse," bubbled Narcissa, "I was met by a company of native women, one after the other, shaking hands and saluting me with a most harty kiss." The fur trappers had to content themselves with awkward but chivalrous respect. Scores of them suddenly got religion, turning out faithfully for the morning and evening devotions conducted by the missionaries. During the 12 days the party rested at the rendezvous, Narcissa reckoned she and Eliza could have passed out all the Bibles and tracts that could be carried on two stout mules. What a shame, she mused, they had not thought to bring any extras.

Narcissa left the rendezvous flushed and happy. "This is a cause worth living for!" she declared. But as she descended into the rocky sagelands to the west, her spirits sagged—a letdown most later pioneers would

A Presbyterian stairway to heaven and hell

The pictorial chart at right, vigorously executed in the best folk-art tradition, was produced around 1845 by Eliza Spalding, wife of Presbyterian missionary Henry Spalding, as an aid in teaching Christian history to the Indians of Oregon. The history starts at the bottom of the chart with Old Testament stories and moves up chronologically, forming a "learning ladder" that Spalding's heathen charges could readily understand.

Painted on a six-foot-long, two-foot-wide sheet of heavy paper that was attached to a roller at the top, the ladder is marked by two vertical columns, the narrow one at right representing the way to salvation, the broader path at left the way to damnation. Between them, at center, is the Crucifixion, with the 12 disciples dressed in mix-matched variations of Henry Spalding's best suit.

Some of Eliza's other images revealed a decidedly Protestant bias that infuriated rival Catholic missionaries in the field. Slightly above and to the right of the disciples is Saint Paul, in frock coat, pointing to a black-garbed sinner who has left his wife and children to become a Catholic priest. He is moving toward the Pope, who is shown as a giant straddling the road to perdition. The Pontiff holds a sword in one hand and a torch in the other, and above him are illustrations of reprehensible behavior: he battles a rival Pope, he receives the severed head of a Protestant, he burns the Bible. Finally, at the top of the ladder, he comes to a bad end. As Henry Spalding explained it, "He falls back into hell at the approach of the

Lord who is coming in the clouds of heaven with his holy angels."

Beyond such blasphemies, what enraged the Catholics was the fact that the learning-ladder device was a Catholic invention, developed by two priests who worked among Oregon's Cowlitz tribe. To give the Indians a sense of time past, they hit upon the idea of using a rectangle of wood on which they marked a ladder of 40 horizontal bars, representing 40 centuries before Christ. Above the bars they placed a series of 33 dots, for the years in Christ's life. Eighteen more bars and 39 more dots brought the chronology up to the current year, 1839. The tribesmen called these boards *sahale,* meaning wood from heaven, and soon the missionaries embellished them with pictures alongside the ladder illustrating Bible stories.

Some ladders also depicted Martin Luther and his followers heading for hell. A Protestant missionary complained of one ladder that portrayed "Protestants as the withered ends of the several branches of Papacy, falling into infernal flames."

Incensed by the Catholic ladders, the Protestants countered with ladders of their own. Now it was the Catholics' turn to fume. "Protestant ministers stop at nothing in sowing tares in the field," wrote one bishop. "They have fabricated an imitation of our historic ladder and have not hesitated to place a mark at the 16th Century showing the rise of their religion." Caught in the middle of this propaganda war, the Indians grew understandably disillusioned, and in the end few joined any Christian church.

feel. Food became scarcer. "I thought of Mother's bread and butter many times as any hungry child would," she wrote while in the arid mountains. "I fancy pork and potatoes would relish extremely well."

Besides, during one of the moonlit nights along the trail, Narcissa had become pregnant. Furthermore, Husband Marcus, despite the responsibilities of impending fatherhood, had begun to expend a disproportionate amount of his time and energy coaxing their one remaining wagon across the jagged terrain.

Narcissa did not share her husband's obsession with bringing wagons to Oregon, and she devoutly hoped he would give up the whole idea. "Husband had a tedious time with the waggon today," she wrote in her diary. "Waggon was upset twice. Did not wonder at all this. It was a greater wonder that it was not turning a somerset continually."

She confessed to being "a little rejoiced" the day an axle broke at Soda Springs in Idaho; surely he would leave it now. No. He simply rigged up a cart with the two rear wheels and kept going.

Narcissa gloomily pondered the trail ahead: "Have six weeks steady journeying before us. Will the Lord give me patience to endure it. Long for rest but must not murmur." Narcissa's mood reached its nadir at Salmon Falls on the Snake River, where Husband lightened the load on his precious vehicle by dropping her clothes trunk, which contained among other things her black bombazine wedding dress. "Poor little trunk," she lamented, "I am sorry to leave thee, thou must abide here alone."

But when the missionaries reached Fort Boise, a Hudson's Bay trading post at the junction of the Snake and Boise rivers, Narcissa recovered her customary good cheer. With Eliza, she was able to do the laundry for only the third time since they had left their homes six months before. The men spruced up. Better yet Marcus, after 1,500 miles of tribulation, reluctantly gave up on the confounded cart. "Perhaps you will wonder why," Narcissa told her parents. "Our animals were failing & the route in crossing the Blue Mountains is said to be impassable for it."

And at long last, it seemed the end of the trail was at hand. Past Fort Boise the route carried through woodland slopes of the Blue Mountains, which reminded Narcissa joyfully of her New York Catskills. The tempo of the journey increased with the party's spirits. Husband's Indian horse, noted Narcissa, was a "hard rider upon every gate, except a gallop," so they all pounded on at that rate.

When on August 29 they camped at an altitude of 5,000 feet, she wrote, "just as we gained the highest elevation the sun was dipping his disk behind the western horizon," back-lighting with a burst of rays the snowy cone of Mount Hood 200 miles to the west. Beyond it, she knew, lay the Pacific Ocean. Three days later they sighted their final landmark—the wooden palisade of Fort Walla Walla, an 18-year-old Hudson's Bay post in the southeast corner of what would become, 53 years later, the state of Washington.

"You can better imagine our feelings this morning than we can describe them," said Narcissa. After snatching at a breakfast, she wrote, "we started while it was quite early, for all were in haste to reach the desired haven. If you could have seen us you would have been surprised for both man & beast appeared alike propelled by the same force. The whole company galloped almost all the way to the Fort."

They had arrived, the first emigrant families to conquer the overland trail to the Far West.

The missionaries pulled up at the fort's gate on the morning of September 1, 1836. After nearly 4,000 miles and six and a half months of travel the Whitmans had reached the place where they would build their own home, plant their own garden—and by springtime celebrate the birth of their daughter Alice Clarissa. A resident cock at Fort Walla Walla crowed, heralding the start of a new era of American growth.

Only one significant unhappiness niggled at the corner of Marcus Whitman's mind on that exuberant September morning: his failure with the wagon. He knew, with the same kind of stubborn conviction that had brought him West in the first place, that someday wagon trains of American pioneers would inevitably start rolling along the Oregon Trail.

And in a few short years Whitman was proved right. On May 19, 1841, the first cavalcade of wagon-borne emigrants left the Missouri frontier for the Pacific Coast. The party consisted of some 70 people, including five women and at least seven children, with all their movable goods piled into a dozen covered wagons. At the head of the caravan rode, again, Broken Hand Fitz-

A gathering of emigrants and Indians — not always an amiable experience for the westbound pioneer — is memorialized by primitive painter E. L.

Spybuck. Fittingly, this sociable encounter took place at Council Grove, Kansas, site of the federal government's 1825 treaty with the Osages.

patrick, on his way to the Flathead country with a delegation of Catholic missionary priests, all Jesuits. The emigrants themselves were bound mostly for California, and had elected a Missouri settler named John Bartleson as their nominal captain. Bartleson had a certain degree of experience in pioneering; 14 years earlier he had been commissioned by the Missouri legislature to help lay out the town of Independence.

From its first ragged beginnings in 1827, Independence had burgeoned by 1841 into a rich, roistering frontier metropolis of some 5,000 souls, most of whom were transients journeying to and from various parts of the West. The original log huts had given way to a collection of rather more refined structures holding dry-goods stores, barbershops, grog houses and emporiums that housed wheelwrights, blacksmiths, harness makers and every other sort of craftsman needed to outfit an expedition across country.

Most of the emigrants in that 1841 caravan had been drawn together by letters from California written by a former Independence resident named John Marsh. One of the region's most persistent boosters, Marsh had wandered down the Santa Fe Trail in 1836, bought some land in California's San Joaquin Valley, and through sharp business dealings had acquired a large herd of cattle. But John Marsh had a dream that went far beyond this personal success. He wanted to bring California, then still a province of Mexico, under the jurisdiction of the United States. The best way to do this, Marsh reasoned, was to persuade other Americans to settle there.

Marsh never tired of writing to friends in the States extolling California's beauties. Unknowingly paralleling the words of Oregon-booster Kelley so many years before, Marsh spoke of "the vast superiority of California in both soil and climate," where free land was available for the asking. Nearby San Francisco, he wrote, "is considered one of the finest harbors in the world." The surrounding land, he declared, "is the finest country for wheat I have ever seen." Labor, furthermore, was plentiful and willing. Local Indians "when caught young, are most easily domesticated, and manifest a great aptitude to learn. They submit to flagallation with more humility than negroes."

The remark was typical of John Marsh, who never hesitated to push people around to get what he wanted.

Tall, domineering, he seemed in some ways a sinister variation on the selfless missionaries who were concurrently settling Oregon. Born in Danvers, Massachusetts, in 1799, he attended Andover Academy and then Harvard to study for the ministry. He gave up the idea when, in his sophomore year, he was tossed out for breaking windows during a student riot. He then decided to become a doctor, and talked his way back into Harvard to earn the requisite bachelor of arts degree.

After graduating, the apostate theology student got a job tutoring children at an Army post in the Minnesota wilderness where he pursued his medical studies with the post surgeon. But soon, a far more fascinating subject caught his attention: the Sioux Indians who lived near the fort. Marsh set to work compiling a Sioux dictionary and grammar, and shortly he acquired a part-Indian mistress, who bore him a son. A little later he managed to get himself appointed subagent for Indian affairs at Prairie du Chien, a garrison post situated at the edge of the Iowa frontier.

He began to dabble in clandestine merchandising of arms — and thereby got into trouble with the law. In the course of going half native, Marsh had become involved in a long-standing feud between his friends, the Sioux, and their sworn enemies, the Fox and the Sauks. The three tribes' old hatreds had erupted in 1832 into a series of battles that collectively became known as the Black Hawk War. During the fighting, Marsh organized and led a band of Sioux warriors into battle, meanwhile turning a tidy profit on the side by illegally selling them guns and ammunition. The U.S. government did a sharp double take, and issued a warrant for Marsh's arrest. He piled into a canoe and paddled down the Mississippi River at top speed.

Marsh spent the following summer hiding out in the company of Rocky Mountain fur trappers along the Oregon Trail. Then in November 1833, he turned up in Independence, where he briefly operated a general store. With its brawling teamsters and its opportunities for sharp traders, Independence seemed to be exactly the kind of place where a man like John Marsh would fit in: no questions were asked, and no answers volunteered. But, while the fugitive did manage to escape detection, his general store went under. So Marsh once again packed his saddlebags — tucking in his old prep-school hymnal, two Bibles (one of them in French) and his

MONTERRY, U. CAL
July 3, 1840.

DEAR SIR:—Since my residence in this country I have frequently received letters from various parts of the United States, but have never received one letter, and seldom any intelligence, from Jackson county. Pray what has become of all the zeal for emigration to this country? I can hear nothing from my old friends and acquaintances. Captain Sutter came last year, who, as he says, formerly resided in Jackson county., and obtained an immense tract of country, and has collected a few people from the Sandwich Islands and elsewhere; and has begun a new settlement in the worst place he could find; but, notwithstanding goes on well. A ship from the United States went to the Oregon last month with fifty families of emigrants. I see by the papers that great preparations are making in the United States for settling the Oregon, and that population must eventually extend to this place, as this is beyond all comparison the finest country and the finest climate. The only thing we lack here is a good Government; but for my part I have but little cause to complain, I have got as much land as I want, and have no apprehension of being molested. What we want most here is more people. If we had fifty families here from Missouri, we could do exactly as we please without any fear of being troubled. I live near the mouth of the rivers Sacramt and St. Joaquin, and the whole country south and east is unoccupied. The nearest farm to mine belongs to R. Livermore, an Englishman. He has a large stock of cattle, and will soon have some thousands. My own affairs go on well. Here is certainly a fine field for enterprise. If you had come here at the time that I did, you might by this time have governed the country. I myself have very little or no ambition if you have I hesitate not to say you had better come here, though I doubt not you are doing very well where you are.

Public attention from without is being attracted to this country, and probably in a few years the most desirable places will be occupied. The difficulty of coming here is imaginary. The route I would recommend, is from Independence to the hunter's rendezvouz on Green River, which is well known to many of your neighbors, thence to the Soda Spring on Bear River, above the Big Salt Lake, thence to Portneuf, thence to Mary's River, down Mary's river till you come in sight of the gap in the great mountain, through that gap by a good road of less than one day and you arrive in the plain of the Tulares & Joaquin, and down that river on a level plain through thousands of Elk and horses, three or four days journey and you come to my house. An old man by the name of Yunt, whom you probably know, came from the rendezvous to Monterry in 30 days, with pack horses; any body else could not do it in much less time. In this route there is no danger to be apprehended, and plenty of water and grass. You will perceive that the difficulty by this route not great. Ten men or even five could pass with perfect safety, with a moderate degree of prudence and woodcraft. You will have heard by the newspapers of a disturbance here between the foreigners and the Government That you may not attach an undue importance to the affair, I will give you a brief account of it.

When the former Mexican Governor and other officers were expelled by the present Governor, it was principally done by means of foreigners, under the command of Isaac Graham, of Kentucky. In process of time an animosity arose between the Governor and the military commandant, and the former apprehending that the foreigners were more in favor of the commandant than himself, pretended that the Americans intended to rise against him and forcibly sent them in a ship to St. Blas. An American and a French ship of war immediatly came here to look into the business, and the Government is now more afraid of us than we are of them. One or more ships of war are to be constantly stationed here. The harbors of this place and St. Francisco, are full of Merchant ships, principally from Boston, all kinds of produce bears a good price.

This I send you by the U. S. ship of war, St. Louis, which is on the eve of sailing or I would write you more fully.

Please let Mr. A. Overton and others of your neighbors know the contents of this, and tell them not to be asleep if they ever intend to come to this country.

Very sincerely,
Your friend and servant,
JOHN MARSH.

P. S. Nathan Daily, of Jackson co., was sent to St. Blas with the others, but he will probably return before long.

Harvard diploma. He headed southwest on the Santa Fe Trail with two companions.

Traveling at night to avoid the heat, Marsh became separated from his friends, and was captured by a Comanche war party. The Indians' chief had been wounded in battle; they demanded Marsh's life as a sacrifice to appease the evil spirits in possession of their chief.

The ailing chief dispatched his granddaughter to fetch Marsh for an interview, whereupon the girl became so infatuated with the prisoner's good looks that she begged he be spared. Marsh for his part removed an arrowhead lodged in the chief's elbow, and asked to be freed to go on his way. No, said the chief; he would never release so useful a man. Fortunately for Marsh, he had been allowed to keep his horse; some days later, he spotted a passing wagon train, he rode hell-for-leather to its sanctuary, and so escaped his Comanche captors.

Marsh pushed on beyond Santa Fe, traveling along the Gila River Trail to the Pacific Coast. In February 1836, he arrived at the little pueblo of Los Angeles, penniless. Ever resourceful, he resolved to pick up some quick cash by practicing medicine, even though he had never completed his training. The town authorities looked doubtfully at the bedraggled traveler and asked: If you are a doctor, where is your proof? Marsh ceremoniously produced his B.A. diploma from Harvard. The authorities could not read Latin, and the diploma looked official. They placed this entry in the archives on February 25, 1836: "Don Juan Marchet has permission to practice medicine, as his diploma was found to be correct, and also for the reason that he would be very useful to the community."

Marsh remained useful to the Angelenos only as long as they remained useful to him—about one year. Then, with $500 he had managed to save, he moved north, had himself baptized a Catholic (a prerequisite for landowners) and bought a 17,000-acre ranch in the San Joaquin Valley. Soon after he moved in, Indian thieves stole 500 horses and ransacked his papers, destroying his license to practice medicine, his new baptismal certificate and his old Harvard sheepskin. Marsh formed a posse, overtook the Indians in the Sierra foothills and summarily killed 11 of them.

It was about this time that Marsh began sending out his letters about the joys of the area. The letters were passed around in Independence and published in news-

papers along the frontier. In the letters Marsh gave directions for the trail to his San Joaquin ranch. He recommended starting along the Oregon Trail — a route he personally had never taken west of the Rockies. And he suggested that, at some vague location in present-day Idaho, the emigrants cut south for California. Such imprecision was no deterrent to the prospective settlers. "We had learned the latitude of San Francisco Bay," said one mesmerized emigrant, "and we thought the sun sufficient to guide us."

Marsh's letters, obviously, were doing their work. John Bartleson, nominal captain of the 1841 wagon train, had been completely sold by the letters. A member of the party, in fact, carried one such document, with its trail directions, in his pocket. Thus equipped, Bartleson and eight fellow California-bound emigrants turned out with their wagons at Sapling Grove, a few miles west of Independence.

A number of other westbound travelers were gathered at Sapling Grove, some ready to push off for California, others for Oregon. The company agreed to journey together along the Oregon Trail to the California fork on the far side of the Rockies, where it would split. In all, it was a grand scheme — bold, hopeful, naïve and historic. And the people who carried it forward were representative of the great waves of pioneers who would follow in their wagon ruts: farmers, schoolteachers, wives and children, missionaries and a small band of fur trappers. Among them were:

♦ John Bidwell, a good-looking frontier schoolteacher of 21. A year earlier he had left home in Ohio with $75, the clothes on his back and, as he noted ruefully in his diary, "nothing more formidable than a pocket knife." In Missouri he had heard people talking about bountiful California, and in the winter of 1840 he joined a California emigration society. The society's members had signed a pledge with 500 signatures to meet in Sapling Grove in early May. John Bidwell arrived on the appointed day to discover that only one other wagon had shown up. Then John Bartleson and his friends arrived, and Bidwell joined them. Bidwell soon showed himself to be a far more capable leader than Bartleson, and the journey came to be known afterwards as the Bidwell-Bartleson Expedition.

♦ Nancy Kelsey, age 18, traveled with her husband, Benjamin Kelsey, whom she had married in Kentucky

three years earlier. Now they had a year-old daughter. "Where my husband goes, I go," Nancy said. "I can better endure the hardships of the journey than the anxieties for an absent husband." Nancy and daughter Ann became the first American mother and child to reach California via the Oregon Trail.

♦ Joseph Chiles, a Missouri farmer who had fought Indians in Florida in 1838, was now, at 31, restless for new adventure. Chiles would make seven journeys across the continent in the next 14 years, often piloting other emigrants and cutting new trails to California. When at home on his 1,600-acre wheat farm and cattle ranch in California, he would become well known for his fine flour and his "Pure Napa Wheat Whiskey."

♦ Nicholas Dawson was a schoolteacher and the descendant of three generations of pioneers along the Ohio River. He left home at 19, intending to spend "about six years in seeing the world." His gallivant to California was part of that odyssey. Dawson strayed from camp one evening, was captured by Cheyennes who took his mule and his clothes, and left him to find his way, in his underwear, back to the wagon train. "Cheyenne" Dawson was his name forever after.

♦ The Reverend Pierre De Smet, five feet seven inches tall and a jovial 210 pounds, was a Jesuit priest from Belgium on his way to build missions among the Flathead Indians — the same ones Jason Lee had passed by in 1834. It was De Smet who had hired veteran fur trapper Broken Hand Fitzpatrick as a guide.

♦ The Reverend Joseph Williams, 64, left his home near Napoleon, Indiana, with only his horse for company. "I want to preach to the people of Oregon," he said, "and also to the Indians, as well as to see the country." Mr. Williams, who was not easily fazed, could scarcely believe what he saw and heard along the Oregon Trail. Most of the emigrants, he suspected, were "deists," his term for ungodly, and "there were some as wicked people among them as I ever saw in all my life." Of their oaths as they drove the mules and oxen he lamented, "O the wickedness of the wicked!"

♦ Talbot H. Green was the assumed name of Paul Geddes; Paul Geddes was a bank embezzler. The emigrants did not know that, and found Talbot charming, intelligent and a most agreeable trail companion. A brick of "lead" which he carried to California with great difficulty was actually the gold bullion missing from his bank. Eventually, Green Street in San Francisco was to be named for the popular Mr. Geddes.

Some of the travelers in the expedition gave up half-way and went home. Thirty-two decided to go to Oregon. The rest, 34 in all, turned off at Soda Springs for California; they barely made it. Water and grass in the Utah and Nevada deserts were far scantier than Marsh had indicated. "We could see nothing before us but extensive arid plains, glimmering with heat and salt," wrote Bidwell in his diary. "The ground was in many places white as snow with salt & perfectly smooth—the midday sun, beaming with uncommon splendor upon these shining plains, made us fancy we could see timber upon the plains, and wherever timber is found there is water always. We marched forward with unremitted pace till we discovered it was an illusion."

As the draft animals weakened from thirst and hunger, it became necessary to dump the heaviest wagons amid the sand and sagebrush. By the time the emigrants had reached the grim escarpment of the Sierra Nevada, they were forced to eat the oxen in order to survive. Bidwell's diary began to reflect a growing discouragement. It seemed to him that "only a bird could get through" the tangled web of woods and canyons. "Having come about 12 miles," he wrote on October 19, "a horrid precipice bid us stop—we obeyed and encamped. Men went in different directions to see if there was any possibility of extricating ourselves from this place without going back but could see no prospect of a termination of the mts., mts., mountains."

Talbot Green staggered along under the weight of his lead brick. Nancy Kelsey, barefoot to relieve her blisters, carried Ann in her arms while leading her horse down the stony mountainsides—"a sight," said Cheyenne Dawson, "I shall never forget." But the pioneers kept plodding, and by sheer fortitude they made it. When they broke into the San Joaquin Valley, they found an abundance of fowl, deer, antelope and, said Dawson, "the most delicious grapes I had ever eaten." This was the California of Marsh's letters. "My breakfast this morning," wrote Bidwell on November 1, "formed a striking contrast with that of yesterday which was the lights of a wolf"; he had feasted on antelope.

That was Monday, and by Thursday evening the expedition had found John Marsh's little house. Marsh produced a meal of fat pork and flour tortillas, and they all talked late into the night. Bidwell, noting that Marsh charged each man $3 for the Mexican passports he had obtained for them without charge, decided later that Dr. John Marsh was "the meanest man in California."

No one could deny, however, that John Marsh had provided the inspiration that had set in motion the first emigrant wagon train. And thanks to his boosterism and his makeshift travel guide—as well as the kind of determination that had enabled Nancy Kelsey to carry Baby Ann over the wintry Sierra Nevada, shoes or no shoes—the settlement of California by American overland emigrants was established, fragile for the moment, but nonetheless assured.

The following year Joseph Chiles, a member of the Bidwell-Bartleson party, returned to Missouri to lead a second group of emigrants along the Oregon Trail to California in 1843. Each year thereafter new American settlers arrived in the Mexican province, and the inevitable confrontation with Mexico finally exploded into war. Then, with the discovery of gold at Sutter's Mill on the American River in 1848, the Far West suddenly overflowed with newcomers. That same year Mexico acknowledged defeat, and the United States acquired California in the negotiations that followed. John Marsh's dream had been realized.

In the Oregon wilderness the roly-poly Father De Smet had founded a string of Catholic missions among the Flatheads. Meanwhile settlers began to arrive. In 1842 some 200 pioneers plodded along the Oregon Trail, most of them heading for the Willamette valley. Next season so many emigrants took the Oregon Trail that 1843 became known as the year of the Great Emigration. They traveled in an immense caravan of 120 wagons, with Marcus Whitman, who had returned East on mission business, acting as trail guide. This time he made good on his promise to himself; he brought the wagons, along with 875 men, women and children, to Fort Hall, and they proceeded along the Oregon Trail to the Pacific Coast.

In all, more than 1,000 pioneers crossed the continent to various destinations in the Far West during the year of the Great Emigration. Most of them stopped, at least for a short period, at the small nuclear settlements established by John Marsh, Jason Lee and Whitman himself—the early visionaries who had blazed the pioneer trails. But this, too, was just the beginning.

Catholic missionaries among the Indians

In the effort to win converts among the Indians of the Northwest, Protestants found themselves competing with a small but diligent band of Catholic missionary priests led by Pierre Jean De Smet and Nicolas Point. The Catholics labored so successfully in this cause that Protestant Narcissa Whitman was moved to warn: "Romanism stalks abroad on our right and our left, and with daring effrontery boasts that she is to possess the land."

De Smet, a burly Belgian, emigrated to the United States when he was 20 and joined the Jesuit order, which had long been active among the Indians of Canada and the Mississippi valley. In 1840 his superiors in St. Louis dispatched him to the Oregon country to convert and minister to the Flathead and Coeur d'Alene tribes. He was to spend 32 years among these and other Indians of the region, living the life they led, eating the food they ate and making long journeys on horseback — Indian fashion, without a saddle. In seeking out remote tribes, he logged some 100,000 miles through mostly uncharted mountains.

In 1841 he was joined by Father Point, a French Jesuit. Point became the official diarist of the Catholic missionary endeavor, keeping meticulous notes on his own experiences and those of his colleagues. Although he had little schooling as an artist, he enhanced his text with several hundred vivid oil paintings and drawings that comprise a unique pictorial record of a little-known era in the history of American Indians.

Flathead Indians greet Fathers De Smet and Point on their arrival at Fort Hall in Idaho. Point's diary noted that the date inscribed at far right in French — August 15 — also marked the Feast of the Assumption.

Usually jovial, Father De Smet assumes a solemn mien for the camera.

In their missionary travels, Father De Smet *(left)* often suggested that his colleague put his artistic gifts to use: "Here is something beautiful. Sketch it for me." Father Point needed no urging. He was equally adept at oils *(right and overleaf)* and drawings, some of which were later colored and lithographed *(below and lower right)* for a volume of De Smet's letters published in 1847. Point had a humble opinion of his own talent, believing that an art critic would rate him as "neither a painter nor even a doodler." Point's legacy was to prove more valuable than he realized. Though his themes were mainly religious, his settings were authentic, preserving a mine of information about the intertwined lives of the Catholic missionaries and the Indians of the Northwest.

A church built by Father Point with the help of the Coeur d'Alene Indians dominates the tiny Sacred Heart mission settlement in Idaho.

In a rough-hewn church, Father Point sits close to the fireplace while hearing a Coeur d'Alene tribesman's public confession of sins.

Flathead Indians at St. Mary's mission receive Easter communion from Father De Smet in a galleried chapel festooned with greenery.

In an imaginative mood, Father Point depicted an Indian much given to vices experiencing a visitation from messengers sent by heaven. The

Indian, according to the missionary-artist, underwent a complete and sudden conversion to the Christianity that Point had been preaching.

An 1860 wagon train pulls into Manhattan, Kansas, for a last purchase of supplies before crossing the plains.

3 | Hopeful novices on a perilous journey

"In prosecuting this journey," warned an 1849 guidebook to the West, "the emigrant should never forget that it is one in which time is every thing." Thus, while pioneers had a sense of making history, they could rarely afford to halt for the hour or so needed to assemble and sit for portraits in front of the cumbersome cameras of the day.

History had to be content, in the main, with the often blurred visual record made by itinerant photographers who snatched glimpses of wagons in transit.

But there were other observers to help round this record out. In 1846 a veteran mountain man wrote of seeing a train on the Oregon Trail in which 30 wagons were "all busily engaged in crossing a river which was found not to be fordable." To him the pioneers were the greenest of greenhorns—farmers who had no idea how to live off wild country. Many oldtimers shared his belief, but they failed to take into account the pioneers' iron determination to press on. And in the end, most of the greenhorns got through to their goal.

Teams of oxen stand ready to resume the trail. Relatively few of the lumbering beasts were destined to complete their journey. Though warmly regarded by their owners—and given such names as Tom or Dick or Sam—they were summarily slaughtered when other sources of food ran out.

Floating their wagons on improvised ferries and swimming
their horses alongside, emigrants cross a river. Chaos often
attended the maneuver; at a Kansas river in 1850, a traveler
noted, "the fiendish swearing shouted in all languages by furious madmen would becraze Christendom's greatest stoic."

80

Stealing precious moments from their tightly scheduled passage across the continent, members of a wagon train pause triumphantly for a group portrait on an auspicious occasion: they have reached South Pass, the broad, saddle-like valley on the Oregon Trail that marks the Continental Divide.

THE
NATIONAL
Wagon Road Guide.

In the trail of the Buffalo, followed first the Indian, then the White Man.

"Over the Rocky Mountains' height,
Like ocean in its tided might,
  The living sea rolls onward, on!
And onward on. the stream shall pour
And reach the far Pacific's shore,
  And fill the plains of Oregon."

SAN FRANCISCO:
PUBLISHED BY WHITTON, TOWNE & CO
125 Clay St., corner Sansome.
1858.

Caravans laboring toward a promised land

Every year during the middle decades of the 19th Century, pioneers moved west in wagon trains so long they sometimes stretched to the horizon. Nothing had prepared the majority of these travelers for the ordeals of the trail. Back in Illinois — or Tennessee or Pennsylvania or wherever it was — they had pictured themselves building new homes and creating bright futures in the West. But the strain of getting there proved far worse than any guidebook had hinted at. Life on the trail was a story of an ever-more-difficult roadway, of failing supplies of food and water, of bone-wrenching weariness, of accumulating miseries of every sort. As the pioneers pushed overland, perhaps 15 miles a day, many lost sight of the vision that had set them going. In its place, they saw only the tragic signs of families that had preceded them: the wolf-pawed graves of the dead, the putrefying carcasses of mules and oxen, the splintered wrecks of abandoned wagons.

The weight of their own privations was enough, on occasion, to bring tears to the eyes of the women and buckle the knees of the men. Yet they kept going. After a few weeks on the trail, most of them had come too far to return. There was little choice except to trudge on, setting one foot doggedly ahead of the other. "The trail west," said one emigrant, "is a treadmill."

Along the treadmill most pioneers summoned up reserves of indomitable courage. They endured everything from heat prostration to a mule kick to the shins. If they went hungry for a time because so many things could go wrong at a trailside cookfire, they simply waited and made do. One woman, suspending her soup kettle on a makeshift tripod, saw it upset five times as the fragile legs of the tripod kept giving way. Five times she hung the kettle up again. "I intend having that soup," she vowed, and finally sat down to her dinner — or what was left of it.

More than heroics, what got the pioneers through was the kind of unyielding determination shown by that soup maker. Another woman whose patience proved more than a match for the trials of the trail was Amelia Knight. She and her husband, Joel, left Iowa in 1853 bound for Oregon with their children — seven in all: Plutarch, Seneca, Frances, Jefferson, Lucy, Almira and Chatfield. Plutarch, the eldest, was 16; Chatfield was a year old. Their trip turned out to be an odyssey of minor disasters. On one day or another, Amelia added these notes to her diary: "Made our beds down in the tent in the wet and mud. . . . Cold and cloudy this morning and everybody out of humor. Seneca is half sick. Plutarch has broke his saddle girth. Husband is scolding and hurrying all hands (and the cook) and Almira says she wished she was at home, and I say ditto. . . . Have to eat cold supper. . . . We are creeping along slowly, one wagon after another, the same old gait; and the same thing over, out of one mud hole and into another all day. . . . Them that eat the most breakfast eat the most sand. . . . It has been raining all day long. The men and boys are all soaking wet and look sad and comfortless. The little ones and myself are shut up in the wagons from the rain. Take us all together we are a poor looking set, and all this for Oregon."

All this and more, in fact. Amelia's litany of aggravations went on throughout her journey; if anything, her tribulations became more rather than less trying. "It's 'children milk the cows, all hands help yoke these cattle, the devil's in them.' Plutarch answers, 'I can't, I must hold the tent up, it's blowing away.'. . . Chatfield, the rascal, fell under the wagon. Somehow he kept from

A guidebook for pioneers, one of dozens published in the mid-19th Century, carries an inspirational verse on its cover. Some carelessly researched manuals left many a traveler floundering in desert or mountains.

A rare printed agreement between emigrants and a transportation supplier spells out the terms of a package deal to carry the group — first by steamboat and then by wagon train — from Cincinnati to Sacramento.

MEMORANDUM OF AGREEMENT,

Between Joseph Dana & Co., and E. Butler *Witnesseth —*

Said Dana & Co. agree to take E. Butler to Council Bluffs on the Missouri River, in cabin of steamboat, and from thence will provide good strong wagons, and at least three yoke of oxen to each wagon, to go over the Plains to Sacramento City, in the State of California; and will furnish provisions for the journey, to consist of Bacon, Flour, Meal, Sea Biscuit, Hommony, Beans, Sugar, Coffee, Pepper, Salt, &c., so that each man can have at least three pounds of provisions per day. The Company will be required to select a Committee of five men from the Company before leaving Council Bluffs, to examine the quantity and quality of provisions provided, and their decision shall be conclusive as to sufficiency. Said Dana & Co. shall have the privilege to direct the train or teams in regard to stopping or starting. The teams will be required to keep together, and rest as often as one day in each week, unless otherwise directed by said Dana & Co. Any one of the Company may be expelled by a vote of the majority of the company, and in case he is expelled, shall have a proportionate quantity of provisions set off to him, and shall not again be taken into said Company without the concurrence of the whole Company. Each member, in consideration here mentioned, agree to pay said Dana & Co., one hundred and fifty dollars, as follows: One hundred dollars upon signing this contract, and fifty dollars when landed at Council Bluffs, and will furnish for themselves, a gun, ammunition, knife, and two blankets. The Company will form themselves into messes of five, and will cook for themselves, and stand sentry by turns. Each man will procure a sack for his clothes, and will be entitled to take only twenty-five pounds of baggage, exclusive of blankets and gun. Dana & Co, also agree to furnish one tent and cooking utensils to each mess, and such other articles as the proprietors think necessary to facilitate the journey. Any man of this Company taking his family will be provided with a light spring wagon and will be charged two hundred dollars for each one of the family and the man will perform same duties as other members of the Company. All the members of this Company will be in readiness to leave Cincinnati about the 1st of April next.

CINCINNATI, *March 2* 1852.

Joseph Dana } Proprietors.
L. Dana

under the wheels. I never was so frightened in my life. I supposed Frances was taking care of him. . . . Chatfield quite sick with scarlet fever. A calf took sick and died before breakfast. . . . Here we left, unknowingly, our Lucy behind. Not a soul had missed her until we had gone some miles when we stopped a while to rest the cattle; just then another train drove up behind us, with Lucy. It was a lesson to all of us. Lost one of our oxen; he dropped dead in the yoke. I could hardly help shedding tears. . . . Passed a sleepless night as a good many of the Indians camped around us were drunk and noisy. . . . I was sick all night and not able to get out of the wagon in the morning. . . . Yesterday my eighth child was born." Nothing to it, Amelia might well have summed up: merely a matter of outlasting the trail.

And the trail lasted long indeed. From the Missouri River to the West Coast *(map, pages 22-23),* it ran 2,000-odd zigzag miles, with constant detours for pas-

ture or water. But the distance in miles mattered less than the distance in time. It usually took about four and a half months to reach the Far West, and the trip became a race against the seasons, in which sure timing made the difference between success and failure.

Late April or early May was the best time to get rolling, though the departure date had to be calculated with care. If a wagon train started too early in the spring, there would not be enough grass on the prairie to graze the livestock. Then animals would start to sicken, slowing up the train and causing alterations of schedule that might bring trouble later. On the other hand, a train that pushed off after other trains were already on the trail found campsites marked by trampled grass and fouled water holes. Worse still, an emigrant company that dallied too long could get trapped at the far end of the journey by early winter blizzards in the coastal mountains. Obviously it was important to get to the

In 1844, mountain man Elisha Stevens led the first wagon train over the snowy Sierra Nevada to California. Two years later his trail through Truckee Pass took the Donner party *(pages 111-118)* to its doom.

jump-off point on the Missouri at the right moment, and keep pretty close to schedule.

To reach the jump-off point, a family from the East could either buy steamboat passage to Missouri for themselves, their wagons and their livestock or — as happened more often— simply pile everything into a wagon, hitch up a team and begin their overland trek right in their front yard. Lodisa Frizzell's diary tersely recorded her departure in 1852 from her home near Ewington, Illinois: "We (that is George, Westall, Bethel, Elliot, my husband and myself) started for California on the 14th day of April, with five yoke of cattle, one pony and sidesaddle and accompanied by several of our friends and neighbors as far as the first town, where we parted and said our last goodby."

Along the macadamized roads and turnpikes east of the Missouri River, travel was comparatively fast, camping easy and supplies plentiful. Then, in one river town or another, the neophyte emigrants would pause to lay in provisions. For outfitting purposes, the town of Independence had been preeminent ever since 1827, but the rising momentum of pioneer emigration had produced some rival jump-off points. Westport and Fort Leavenworth flourished a few miles upriver. St. Joseph had sprung up 55 miles to the northwest; in fact, emigrants who went to Missouri by riverboat could save four days on the trail by staying on the paddle-wheelers to St. Joe before striking overland.

At whatever jump-off point they chose, the emigrants studied guidebooks and directions, asked questions of others as green as themselves and made their final decisions about outfitting. They had various, sometimes conflicting, options. For example, either pack animals or two-wheel carts or wagons could be used for the overland crossing. A family man usually chose the wagon. It was the costliest and slowest of the three, but it provided space and shelter for children and for a wife who likely as not was pregnant. Everybody knew that a top-heavy covered wagon might blow over in a prairie wind or be overturned by mountain rocks, that it might mire in river mud or sink to its hubs in desert sand — but maybe if those things happened on this trip they would happen to someone else. Anyway, most pioneers, with their farm background, were used to wagons.

A new wagon cost anywhere from $60 to $90, and a prudent man laid in as many spare parts as he could af-

ford. Wheels were high, for clearance, which meant that maneuverability was low, because a wagon could not make sharp turns unless front wheels were small enough to swivel underneath the wagon box. Wagon tongues often snapped in two when the draft animals pulled too far right or left. The wheels themselves, unless they were exceptionally well made, often fell apart. The dry air of the plains and deserts shrank the wooden spokes and rims of the wheels until the iron tires wobbled off. A blacksmith could fix a thrown tire by heating it red-hot and replacing it on the rim; as it cooled it would shrink to a snug fit. More unexpected breakdowns required quick improvisation. When one caravan's cattle stampeded on the trail and wrecked the undercarriage of a wagon (prompting the train captain to report drily: "Three wheels broke all to smash and 50 miles to timber") somebody's dining-room table was promptly sawed up into new wheels.

The cover of a wagon was made of heavy cotton twill or canvas or some other strong cloth, waterproofed with linseed oil; an inventive wife would sew pockets and slings to the inner surface of the fabric for extra storage space. Supported by hickory bows, the cover provided about five feet of headroom. Pucker ropes at either end could be tightened to screen the interior of the wagon from the weather and from neighbors' eyes. The pioneers called their combination parlor-kitchen-bedrooms prairie schooners, as apt a phrase as was ever coined. Not only did they resemble sailing ships, but on occasion they actually did become vessels of a sort. With its seams calked and its wheels removed, a wagon became amphibious and could be floated across rivers too deep to be forded.

Having selected a wagon, the pioneer next had to choose his draft animals. Horses were expensive, so emigrants generally reserved them for saddle riding. The real choice lay between mules and oxen, and any trail-experienced salesman could make a strong case for or against either. A man risked life and limb just becoming acquainted with an unbroken mule, but once trained to harness, it proved sure-footed, smart, quick-moving and durable. Oxen could pull heavier loads, would eat anything, did not run away at night, did not cost as much ($50 apiece, against $90 for a mule) and were less often stolen by Indians. Some emigrants swore by oxen; Peter Burnett, after his trek to Oregon in 1843, pro-

claimed: "The ox is the most noble animal, patient, thrifty, durable, gentle. Those who come to this country will be in love with their oxen by the time they get here." But oxen had their drawbacks, too. Their cloven hoofs splintered to the quick on mountain rocks, and they took about 15 more days on the road than mules. "They don't walk," said one exasperated emigrant. "They *plod.*"

Whichever animals he finally chose, an emigrant needed plenty of them. Generally a minimum of two teams of mules or two yoke of oxen were required to pull a loaded wagon, and the more one had above that minimum, the better. With extra mules or oxen to share the load, the chance of their lasting the entire journey was greatly increased. A few well-to-do emigrants took several wagons and sets of oxen, and they even hired teamsters to drive them. But most pioneers were not well-to-do; a man of ordinary means, with perhaps a wife and four or five children, would try to manage with one wagon and perhaps four yoke of oxen.

Within its average 10-by-4-foot body a wagon would not hold very much, but the trail ahead held even less. Because they knew full well that they had better take with them whatever they would need, emigrants piled their wagons high with every bit of food and clothes and furniture they reckoned essential *(pages 102-103)*. A. J. McCall found his fellow travelers' tendency to leave nothing behind ludicrous. "They laid in," he wrote, "an over-supply of bacon, flour and beans, and in addition thereto every conceivable jim-crack and useless article that the wildest fancy could devise or human ingenuity could invent—pins and needles, brooms and brushes, ox shoes and horse shoes, lasts and leather, glass beads and hawks-bells, jumping jacks and jews-harps, rings and bracelets, pocket mirrors and pocket-books, calico vests and *boiled shirts.*" A passerby who watched one family pack its wagon was reminded of birds building a nest.

Mainly, however, a packing list consisted of foodstuffs, chosen according to what would stay fresh and what would not. Sometimes, of course, an item failed to keep. "We had been imposed upon in St. Louis in the purchase of bacon," Alonzo Delano discovered two days out. "It began to exhibit more signs of life than we had bargained for, having a tendency to walk in insect form." Ordinarily, thick slabs of smoked bacon would

With tomahawk in hand and lance planted athwart the trail, an Indian hunter orders the leader of an advancing wagon train to retreat. Such confrontations were usually resolved peaceably by an exchange of gifts.

keep as long as they were protected from the heat of the plains. Packing bacon in a barrel of bran was one way of insulating the meat. Similarly, eggs often were packed in barrels of corn meal; as the eggs were used up, the meal was used to make bread. Coffee was drunk by man and beast, adult and child; it disguised the taste of bitter, alkali-laden water so effectively that one man whose horse "declined the water with decision" induced it to drink coffee instead.

In the early years of emigration, pioneers could often kill a few buffalo and antelope along the trail, but a more dependable supply of fresh meat was a herd of cattle led behind the wagon. A cow for milking purposes was also recommended. "Milk is relished upon the plains," wrote J. L. Campbell in his 1864 *Emigrant's Guide Overland*. "In case of a storm when cooking can-

not be done, it serves a tolerable purpose." Surplus milk could always be churned into butter simply by hanging it in pails beneath the jolting wagon; at day's end the butter would be ready.

With their wagons loaded and their animals assembled, all that remained for the pioneers to do at the jump-off point was to organize themselves. Here the American town-meeting tradition proved useful. As if by reflex, they would nominate candidates, hold elections and set up temporary governments. Some of these trail governments were so elaborate that they soon collapsed under their own weight. Alonzo Delano heard of one that contained a court of appeals, an executive branch and a legislative body, all set forth in a written constitution. So many privileged officials of this bureaucracy were exempted from taking their turns at night

The shape of a day on the Oregon Trail

In the early morning bustle of eating, loading up the wagons and yoking the teams, a trumpeter on horseback sounds a call to assemble the caravan.

One of the best firsthand accounts of emigrant life en route west was provided by Jesse Applegate, captain of a contingent of several hundred pioneers whose horde of cattle and horses made the trek an especially ponderous undertaking. This extract from Applegate's memoir, "A Day with the Cow Column in 1843," describes an 18-hour period that advanced his party some 20 miles nearer Oregon despite logistical—as well as human—complications.

It is four A.M.; the sentinels on duty have discharged their rifles—the signal that the hours of sleep are over; every wagon and tent is pouring forth its night tenants, and slow-kindling smokes begin to rise. Sixty men start from the corral and by five o'clock they have begun to move the herd of 5,000 cattle and horses toward camp.

From six to seven o'clock is a busy time; breakfast is eaten, tents struck, wagons loaded, and teams yoked. There are 60 wagons in 15 divisions or platoons of four wagons each.

The women and children have taken their places in the wagons. The pilot stands ready to mount and lead the way. Ten or 15 young men set off on a buffalo hunt. As the unfriendly Sioux have driven the buffalo out of the Platte, the hunters must ride 15 or 20 miles to reach them.

It is on the stroke of seven that the clear notes of the trumpet sound in the front; the leading division of wagons moves out of the encampment and the rest fall into their places with the precision of clockwork until the spot so lately full of life sinks back into that solitude that seems to reign over the broad plain and the rushing river.

The hunters are a full six miles from the line of march; though everything is dwarfed by distance, it is seen distinctly. The caravan has been about two hours in motion. First, near the bank of the shining river, is a company of horsemen. A member of the party has raised a flag, no doubt a signal for the wagons to steer their course to where he stands. The wagons form a line three quarters of a mile in length; some of the teamsters ride upon the front of their wagons, some walk beside their teams; scattered along the line companies of women and children are taking exercise on foot; they gather bouquets of rare and beautiful flowers that line the way.

Next comes a band of horses, the docile and sagacious animals scarce need attention, for they have learned to follow the wagons. Not so with the large herd of horned beasts that bring up the rear; lazy, selfish and unsocial. They move only in fear of the whip; there is never a moment of relaxation of the tedious and vexatious labors of their drivers.

At the nooning place, the teams are not unyoked, but simply turned loose from the wagons. Today an extra session of the Council is being held to settle a dispute between a proprietor and a young man who has undertaken to do a man's service on the journey for bed and board. The high court, from which there is no appeal, will define the rights of each party.

The evening is far less animated than the morning march; a drowsiness has fallen apparently on man and beast; teamsters fall asleep on their perches and even when walking by their teams. A little incident breaks the monotony of the march. An emigrant's wife whose state of health has caused Dr. Whitman to travel near the wagon is now taken with violent illness. The doctor has had the wagon driven out of the line, a tent pitched and a fire kindled.

We must leave it behind for the sun is now getting low in the west, and at length the painstaking pilot is standing ready to conduct the train in the circle 100 yards deep which he has marked out. So accurate the measurement and perfect the practice, that the hindmost wagon always precisely closes the gateway. Within ten minutes from the time the leading wagon is halted, the barricade is formed.

Everyone is busy preparing fires of buffalo chips to cook the evening meal, pitching tents and otherwise preparing for the night. There are anxious watchers for the absent wagon. But as the sun goes down it rolls into camp, the bright, speaking face of the doctor declares without words that both mother and child are well.

It is not yet eight o'clock when the first watch is to be set; the evening meal is just over. Near the river a violin makes lively music, and some youths improvise a dance; in another quarter a flute whispers its lament to the deepening night. It has been a prosperous day; more than 20 miles have been accomplished.

All is hushed and repose from the fatigue of the day, save the vigilant guard, and the wakeful leader who still has cares upon his mind that forbid sleep. The night deepens. At length a sentinel hurries to him with the welcome report that a party is approaching. He is at no loss to determine that they are our missing hunters who have met with success. He does not even await their arrival, but the last care of the day being removed, he too seeks the rest that will enable him to go through the same routine tomorrow.

As the first wagons get underway, an outrider gallops off to hunt, a teamster cracks his whip and three women indulge in a last-minute chat.

guard duty that the put-upon plain citizenry eventually threw the lot of them out of office.

A simpler setup might consist of a train captain and a few lesser officials, with the captain making most decisions—ordering the train underway in the morning, choosing a site for the midday noonings, or rest stops, and deciding where the train would camp for the night. His reward, normally, was a great deal of criticism for his poor judgment, especially if the train started later than it should have.

Finally the day arrived when the wagons had been given their last overhaul, the animals were sleek and healthy, the weather promising. It was time to move out, and the train captain gave the signal. Slowly the wagons rolled forward, each taking a previously assigned position in the line. With a whoop and a holler, outriders galloped out far ahead of the line, working off some of their pent-up impatience. The prairie schooners lumbered across the Missouri border and onto the prairie. It was a moment of excitement tinged with nostalgia for old homes and old friends left behind. "Farewell to America!" cried John East of Missouri, as he set out with a wagon caravan in 1843.

By mid-May the grass all across the plains would be luxuriant, and with the grass came the wild flowers; the Kansas prairies, rolling in soft, pillowy mounds, were lovely at that time of year. The spring storms were magnificent, too, and some travelers sought to capture their grandeur in words. "King Lear in the height of his madness would have been troubled to have got his mouth open to vent his spleen on such a night," Alonzo Delano wrote one evening. Francis Parkman, soon to become the great historian of the Oregon Trail, was trapped on it in a memorable downpour during the summer of 1846: "Such sharp and incessant flashes of lightning, such stunning and continuous thunder I had never known before. The woods were completely obscured by the diagonal sheets of rain that fell with a heavy roar and rose in spray from the ground."

Did Parkman mention lightning? "Enough of the article was manufactured for home consumption and to spair to batter down the walls of Sebastopol," said Edwin Bird in 1854. And against a deluge of rain, what chance was there for a cotton cover brushed with linseed oil? Moreover, these epic storms sent the waters of creeks and rivers flooding up and across their banks, obscuring or completely obliterating the trail. One company, arriving at a creek at day's end, wearily decided to postpone crossing it until the morning. They never made a poorer decision. A rainstorm came up during the night and the party remained stalled beside that little stream for two more weeks before it subsided sufficiently for them to cross.

All the same, the emigrants often had it easy in their first weeks on the trail, following it northwest toward Nebraska and the Platte River. The climate was mild, the land bucolic. It was a good place to learn to handle a prairie schooner, to shake down the routine, to adjust to the extraordinary adventure on which they were launched. One traveler noticed that as they passed through this Indian country, "Every man displayed his arms in the most approved desperado style." But in dealing with the Kanza Indians who populated the area, bargaining skill was more important than marksmanship. Some enterprising tribesmen had established ferries across the wider rivers and did a good business, charging whatever the traffic would bear. Other Indians pestered the pioneers for gifts of sugar, coffee and whiskey. Under the supervisory heel of the U.S. government, the Indians of Kansas were a dejected, beaten people; and John Minto, who encountered them in 1844, remarked of his disillusionment that he had to give up "a great lump of Fennimore Cooper's ideal Indian, which I had previously imbibed."

Because the lengthening spring days did not drain and exhaust the travelers, evenings in the campgrounds were given over to children's games and to parties and dancing by their elders. "There was a tall time last night in the shape of a fandango," one man reported, and another told about the night the men formed a "French Four with Cottillion. The way the prairie grass suffered was a sight." Sundays were spent according to the tastes of the travelers; as Joel Palmer put it, the emigrants formed "a miniature of the Great World." In John Minto's train, one Sunday morning, an Oregon-bound missionary "preached to those who would listen, and gave bibles to those who would take them; while at no great distance others were noisily racing horses with Indians of their sort." The worship service was a deep disappointment to one member of the congregation—a teen-age boy who heard the minister pray to God "to remove the wild beasts and savage men from our pathway." The boy, said Minto, was "bound to kill a buffalo and would like to see a grizzly bear."

About two weeks out of Independence the trail crossed the Big Blue, a tributary of the Kansas River. The Blue was a changeable river that could be forded some of the time but had to be ferried when the water was up. Yet for those who were detained at the crossing there was a compensation: the campsite was one of the most idyllic along the entire length of the trail. Edwin Bryant, a one-time Louisville newspaper editor who camped there in 1846, described the spot: "We found a large spring of water, as cold and pure as if it had just been melted from ice. It gushes from a ledge of rocks, which composes the bank of the stream, falling some ten feet into a basin. Altogether it is one of the most romantic spots I ever saw. We named this the 'Alcove Spring'; and future travellers will find the name graven on the rocks."

Beyond the Big Blue crossing, the trail ran up into Nebraska to meet the Platte River, then turned west to follow its south bank. "Nebraska" is an Indian word meaning "flat and shallow"; and "Platte" is a French equivalent. Both descriptions are appropriate to the Platte's broad band of flowing silt, which forms lazy S's from the Rocky Mountains to the Missouri. The river ran "near the top of the ground," observed a lady euphoniously named Martha Missouri Moore. Someone else reckoned the river's measurements at "a mile wide and an inch deep." A third traveler called the Platte "a complete burlesque of all the rivers of the world," and another described it as "bad to ford, destitute of fish, too dirty to bathe in and too thick to drink."

The plains on either side of the Platte were covered with short grass but were bare of trees—"like the wild regions of Africa," said Sarah Cummins. What little timber there was—most of it had been burned off by the Indians in small-game hunts—survived on the river's sandy islands. At a distance of about three miles on both sides of the Platte, the land rose in sandstone cliffs, higher and more broken as the trail moved west. It all seemed most peculiar to people from the forested regions of Eastern America.

They marveled, too, at the prairie wildlife—antelope and coyotes, grizzlies and black bears, buffalo and innumerable prairie dogs. The prairie-dog villages sometimes covered 500 acres, according to one man's estimate, and the rodents' busy urban life intrigued the emigrants. During the 1840s, buffalo also were plentiful through this stretch of country, "some grazing quietly on the prairies," wrote an 1843 traveler, "and others marching, and moving and bellowing, and the great herds making a roaring noise as they trampled along, a half mile or a mile away. Sometimes buffalos were found among our cattle of mornings, quietly grazing with them." But the numbers steadily diminished. In the flush early times, emigrants shot and used buffalo wastefully, bringing the choice cuts back to the wagons and leaving the bulk of the carcass for the wolves. Later pioneers cut all the meat into strips and dried it for future use.

The buffalo could be a nuisance. Sometimes potable stream water turned dark and redolent after they ambled through it; at other times the emigrants' oxen and cows might stray off with a buffalo herd, never to be seen again. But the buffalo were invaluable as a source of fuel as well as meat. To cook their meals and warm their bodies on the timberless plains, the pioneers depended heavily upon the deposits of buffalo chips—dried dung—that littered the ground. These chips could be brought to a blaze only in a well-drafted fire pit; so the emigrants' sheet-iron stoves became useless, and successful cooking called for new, improvised skills. "There was one young lady," wrote James Clyman, "which showed herself worthy of the bravest undaunted poieneer of the west for after having kneaded her dough she watched and nursed the fire and held an umbrella over the fire and her skillit with the greatest composure for near 2 hours and baked bread enough to give us a verry plentifull supper and to her I offer my thanks of gratitude for our last nights repast."

Trouble with Indians was rare, for the Platte valley lay in a kind of no man's land between the warlike Pawnees to the north and the Cheyennes to the south. All along the trail, in fact, meetings between Indians and emigrants were generally peaceable affairs in which the tribesmen traded buffalo meat for tobacco, ironware and the travelers' worn-out clothing. Precautions were taken nevertheless; the wagon trains were drawn up into a corral at every campsite. This also served the practical purpose of enclosing some of the livestock overnight so they could graze. The corral was formed by interlocking wagons, with the tongue of one extending under the

At Independence Rock a pioneer adds his name to those inscribed by earlier emigrants while his companions watch wagon trains approaching

along the Sweetwater River. William Henry Jackson created the panoramic scene from on-the-spot studies that he made in the late 1860s.

Caught in a prairie storm, an emigrant tries to calm his terrified horses while his wife clings to a teetering wagon. Storms struck without warning, blackening the skies with dust whirled by 80-mile-an-hour winds.

rear wheels of the next; heavy chains then laced the circle of wagons together like a necklace. Before the final link was made fast, the animals were brought in; then the last wagon was rolled in place.

Throughout the night, guards were posted around the corral perimeter. As the campfires burned low, the guards sometimes nodded with fatigue and took pot shots at noises off in the darkness. But almost never in all the history of Western migration did an Indian war party descend upon a circle of corralled wagons. Such a strategy would have assured heavy casualties among the Indians; safe within their circular fortress, the defenders could easily have picked off the besiegers.

Indians did occasionally draw emigrant blood. A single wagon traveling alone or straggling at the end of a long train would sometimes be attacked and robbed, and those who resisted might get themselves killed. And in 1865, the Sioux and Cheyennes, in furious reaction to a defeat by the U.S. Cavalry, temporarily shut down the trails west. Nor did the Indians always act alone. After the Civil War, white renegades, army deserters and border ruffians sometimes joined hostile Indians to prey upon prairie travelers.

In the summer of 1867 the U.S. Army forbade travel by single wagons in western Kansas because of Indian danger. Nevertheless, pioneers John Royer and Ed Schammel decided to go on ahead of their caravan and hired as a guide an old Indian-fighter known only as Long Texas. As the men drove their wagon up a small draw, Texas spotted three armed white men on horse-

More menacing than windstorms, a prairie blizzard could devastate a wagon train overnight. As temperatures plummeted to 40° below zero, cattle would inhale particles of sleet and snow and die of suffocation.

back blocking the trail ahead. When the trio closed in, Texas shot the leader. The two others retreated, but they returned a few minutes later accompanied by a score of Indian warriors armed with rifles, bows and arrows. A long running battle began, with the wagon rolling full tilt across the prairie and the Indians galloping alongside on their ponies.

The fighting lasted two full days, with brief respites at nightfall while the attackers caught their breath. By the second evening both Royer and Schammel had been killed, and Texas' left wrist had been shattered by an Indian bullet. After nightfall, with an icy north wind blowing, he resorted to a desperate diversionary tactic: he set fire to the wagon, and in the ensuing hubbub managed to escape. Half-crazed with pain and fatigue, the

old Indian-fighter wandered about the prairie on foot until morning, when a passing wagon train spotted him and took him to safety.

Less dramatic but far more common than attacks by Indians were the everyday trail hazards of accident and disease. Particularly disease. At least 20,000 emigrants, about one of every 17 who started, were buried beside the Oregon Trail, and most of them succumbed to the very illnesses that pioneers went west to escape. Along some stretches of the route graves were so numerous that the trail developed a saw-tooth edge—a border of footpaths worn by the curious going off to the side to read the wooden grave markers.

"Died: Of Cholera." That was the most frequent epitaph. The virulent Asiatic plague had moved up the

97

Mississippi valley from New Orleans. It spread its horror of diarrhea, vomiting, fever, convulsions and death along the roads from Independence and St. Joe and out into the lowlands of the Platte valley. Only the higher elevation of the Rocky Mountains could stop it, and at some of the larger campsites before the mountains were reached—at the crossing of the Big Blue, for example—an entire cemetery was required.

Death was so certain for cholera victims that their companions would sometimes dig graves while the last hours of the dying ran out. Burial rites were stark and pragmatic. Since the emigrants had no lumber for coffins, they usually wrapped the bodies in cloths and buried them under rocks and packed earth. Some graves were dug in the ruts of the wagon trail, in hope that the Indians would not be able to find them, dig up the bodies and mutilate them. Wolves, however, could unearth bodies despite the best precautions. A 20-year-old girl named Agnes Stewart, spying a snarl of woman's hair on the trail with a comb still in it, confided to her diary that night that she "would as soon not be buried at all as to be dug out of my own grave."

Some 460 miles west of the Missouri River—and after at least a month on the road—the emigrants arrived at the confluence of the Platte's north and south forks. To reach the north fork, which the trail followed, wagon trains first had to cross the south fork. But, depending on where they crossed, the south fork might be a half mile to a mile wide, and the crossing almost invariably posed problems. At times of high water, wagon wheels would be removed and the wagon box turned into a flat-bottomed boat that could be floated across the river. One way to waterproof the boxes was to tack buffalo skins over them. But the buffalo had to be caught first, as William Newby noted in this 1843 diary entry: "Hunted buffalo and killed 2. We wonted thare hides for to make bots to craws the river."

Phoebe Judson's party was lucky enough to catch the water of the south fork at a lower level in the summer of 1853, but still had trouble in making the crossing. "We were obliged to double teams," she wrote, "making eight yoke of oxen to each wagon. The beds of the wagons were raised a number of inches by putting blocks under them. We plunged into the river, taking a diagonal course. It required three quarters of an hour to reach the opposite shore. We found the river so deep in places that, although our wagon box was propped nearly to the top of the stakes, the water rushed through it like a mill race, soaking the bottoms of my skirts and deluging our goods." On the other hand, George Donner's wife, Tamsen, took the crossing of the south fork in almost carefree fashion, cheerfully noting in a letter back to Illinois: "If I do not experience something far worse than I have yet done, I shall say the trouble is all in getting started."

Beyond the river crossing, the trail presented a distinct contrast to its route through the flat Platte valley. It now began to provide one adventure after another. First it tilted sharply uphill, then went 22 miles straight across a high, waterless tableland, then, at the far edge of the plateau, dropped suddenly toward the valley of the North Platte. Special care was needed to bring the wagons down the steep drop. At the crest of the hill men would lock the wagon wheels by chaining them to the wagon boxes, then slowly skid the wagons by ropes down to the bottom of the 45° grade. If a wagon broke loose—and many did—it went tumbling down the hill in a shower of splinters.

But getting to the bottom of the valley generally seemed worth the risk because of the woodsy glen located there. Ash Hollow, as it was named, provided the first shade in weeks of travel. William Kelly drew upon a rich lode of 19th Century rhetoric for his description of Ash Hollow in a book entitled *An Excursion to California.* "The modest wild rose," he wrote, "forgetting its coyness in the leafy arbours, opened out its velvet bosom, adding its fragrant bouquet to that of the various scented flowers and shrubs which form the underwood of the majestic ash. Cool streams prattled about until they merged their murmurs in a translucent pond, reposing in the centre of a verdant meadow, whose bespangled carpet looked the congenial area for the toys and gambols of the light-tripping beings of fairyland." Charles Tinker's observations were more concise: "A furstrate spring of cold water here."

After the brief respite of Ash Hollow the trail followed the sandy banks of the North Platte for about 50 miles. The uphill grade through this stretch was slight but constant, and even in late June the nights grew steadily colder with the rising altitude. Far off on the horizon rose the snow-patched Laramie Mountains, forming stepping stones to the Rockies. Closer by, at various points beside the trail, strange formations of earth and rock commanded the emigrants' attention. With days to observe these odd natural structures, diarists whittled fresh points on their pencils and searched their minds for just the right phrase.

A many-tiered, 400-foot-high heap of clay and volcanic ash bore a certain resemblance to a municipal building in St. Louis. It was inevitably dubbed the Court House (off to its side stood a smaller satellite rock—the Jail House). The Court House inspired many a simile—"like a cathedral in ruins," "the Tower of Babel," "the Capitol at Washington"—and many a side trip. "I clim over 200 feet high and rote my name here," said one man, who also recorded a scare on the rock: "I had like to fall down."

More dramatic than the Court House was Chimney Rock, 14 miles to the west. Thrusting up some 500 feet in the air and surrounded at its base by great mounds of debris, the slim stone shaft was likened not only to a chimney but also to a pole in a haystack, a minaret, a church steeple, an inverted funnel and a lightning rod. Some travelers attempted to measure its assorted dimensions (it took 10,040 steps to walk around the base, for example) and most of them realized that the chimney was constantly diminishing through erosion by wind and water. "Every year washes away some of its glory," said Edwin Bird, and he went on to predict that in a few years the spire would collapse completely.

After another 20 miles the emigrants arrived at Scott's Bluff, a weathered contortion of parapets, towers and gulches: a Nebraska Gibraltar, somebody called it. Hiram Scott, a fur trader, had died among its crags in 1828. No one knew exactly how, so a number of legends grew up—that he had sickened and been cruelly abandoned by selfish companions, that he had been murdered by Indians or maybe killed by a grizzly bear, that his skeleton, when found, was twisted in a death agony or that it was propped against a rock, placidly supine.

A wagon train that was traveling more or less on schedule would reach the bluff in late June. Two days more would bring the emigrants to Fort Laramie. This frontier outpost, situated in what is now the southeast corner of the state of Wyoming, stood like a lightship at the far edge of the American sphere of influence. In a passage describing the fort, J. M. Shively's guidebook offered its readers a sobering thought: "You are now 640 miles from Independence, and it is discouraging to tell you that you have not yet travelled one third of the long road to Oregon."

In most cases, more than a third of an emigrant's supplies, and much of the strength of his mules and oxen—to say nothing of his patience—had been used up by this time. What was worse, the road beyond Fort Laramie began the ascent of the Rockies in earnest, trying the tempers of the men and further draining the energies of the animals. Sarah Cummins noted that some men became vexed beyond endurance in the mountains and "would resort to volumes of enathemas and the lashing of their great whips would almost deafen those of refined feelings or considerate natures." To spare Sarah's sensibilities, her "dear mother would almost invariably say, 'You go on ahead,'" and Sarah would ride out of earshot on her saddle horse.

A more effective measure than raving and cursing at the animals was lightening the load. That could mean dumping a burdensome sheet-iron stove, an anvil, a hand-rubbed claw-foot table or even food. The road beyond Fort Laramie acquired a rich deposit of household goods and groceries, stuff that had seemed beyond price in Missouri but now was valuable to no one.

The land was mostly barren. At long range the mountainsides looked like green meadows; up close they turned out to be dry sand and rock, dotted by stunted clumps of sage and greasewood. But after a 50-mile trek along the North Platte the trail reached the Sweetwater River—named, it was said, in blessed relief from the bitter (and sometimes poisonous) springs just passed. And as the Sweetwater led the trail deeper and deeper into the Rockies, the scenery grew steadily more and more spectacular. At least, so most people thought—but William Henry Russell, who had at one time served as secretary to Senator Henry Clay and who crossed the trail in 1846, was not of them. "It may captivate mad poets," Russell said in a grumpy letter to a Missouri newspaper, "but I will swear I see nothing to admire." Perhaps Russell, who was nearsighted, simply could not make out the grandeur that was unfolding about him. Once, it was said, he encountered a flock of owls calling "tu-whooo, tu-whooo." Drawing himself up stiffly, he replied: "Colonel William H. Russell of Kentucky, that's who—a bosom friend of Henry Clay." ◉

This prairie schooner—with a plow and hoe tied to its side—carried three men and a boy from Missouri to Oregon in 1845.

The sturdy wagon that crossed a continent

Nothing affected the outcome of the pioneers' gamble more directly than the wagons that had to carry them across 2,000 jolting miles of wilderness. There was no standard solution to the problem of conveyance. Some emigrants rolled west in farm wagons that had been modified by craftsmen in jumping-off towns; others bought rigs specifically built for the one-way journey. But most wagons incorporated certain features (*shown at right*) that heightened the chances of a successful passage.

A wagon had to be light enough not to place undue strain on the oxen or mules that pulled it, yet strong enough not to break down under loads of as much as 2,500 pounds. To meet these requirements, most wagons were constructed of hardwoods such as maple, hickory and oak. Because of its weight, iron was used only to reinforce parts that took the greatest pounding. These included the tires, axles and hounds—bars that served to connect and provide rigidity to the undercarriage.

The wagon's sole concession to passenger comfort was the cloth cover, which shielded travelers—imperfectly, to be sure—from rain and dust. When the interior became stifling in midsummer heat, the cover could be rolled back and bunched, permitting freer circulation of air. Passengers could also count on plenty of exercise. Since the wagon lacked springs, everybody who could walk had to take to the footpaths when the wagon trail hit a rocky stretch. Yet these evictions could be an enjoyable es-

cape: there was hardly any place to sit inside the wagon; most space was taken up by the diverse cargo needed to sustain emigrants during the trip and to set up homes at its conclusion. An inventory of typical articles that were crammed into a prairie schooner appears on the following pages.

As oxen wearied and weakened, the load had to be lightened, and many a family heirloom suffered the fate of the "massive bureaus of carved oak" that one emigrant sadly reported seeing abandoned along the Oregon Trail in 1846. But apart from such losses and other contingencies, a pioneer who exercised "all due and proper diligence in traveling," as one guidebook said, could "cherish a reasonable hope that he will arrive at his journey's end safely and in season."

The three main parts of a prairie schooner were the wagon bed, the undercarriage and the cover. The wagon bed was a rectangular wooden box, usually about four feet wide and 10 to 12 feet long. At its front end was a jockey box to hold tools.

The undercarriage was composed of the wheels; the axle assemblies; the reach, which connected the two axle assemblies; the hounds, which fastened the rear axle to the reach and the front axle to the wagon tongue; and the bolsters, which supported the wagon bed. Dangling from the rear axle was a bucket for grease or a mixture of tar and tallow to lubricate the wheels.

The cover, made of canvas or cotton, was supported by a frame of hickory bows and tied to the sides of the bed. It extended beyond the bows at either end of the wagon and could be closed by drawstrings.

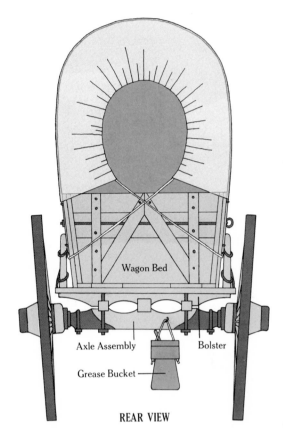

Wagon Bed

Axle Assembly   Bolster

Grease Bucket

REAR VIEW

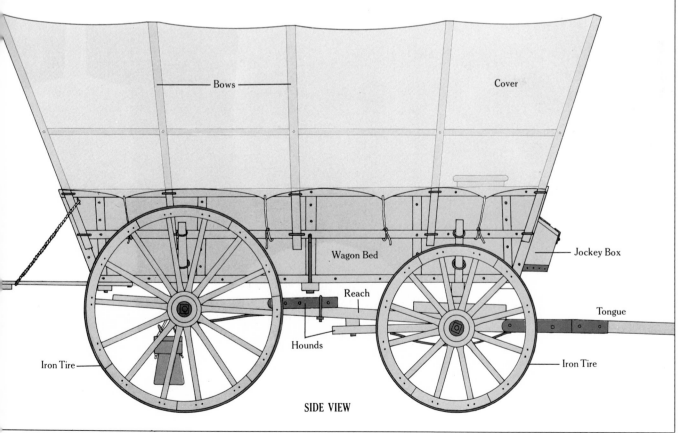

Bows   Cover

Wagon Bed   Jockey Box

Reach   Tongue

Hounds

Iron Tire   Iron Tire

SIDE VIEW

101

A PRAIRIE SCHOONER'S VARIED CARGO

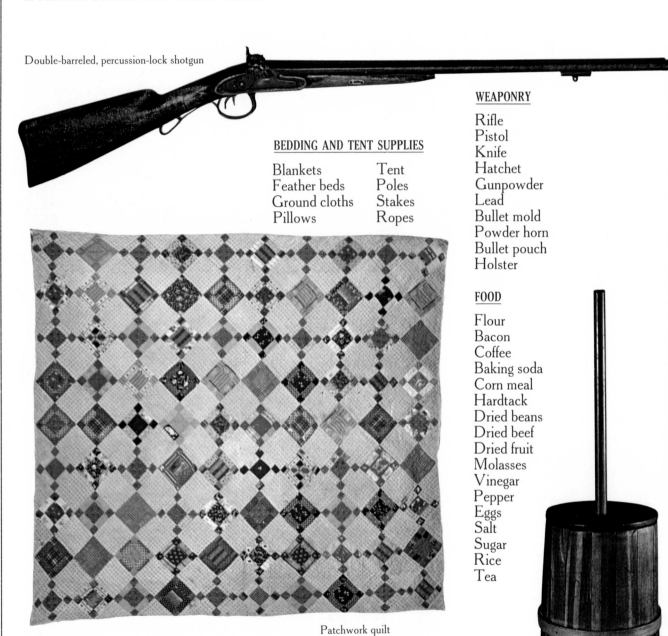

Double-barreled, percussion-lock shotgun

BEDDING AND TENT SUPPLIES

Blankets	Tent
Feather beds	Poles
Ground cloths	Stakes
Pillows	Ropes

WEAPONRY

Rifle
Pistol
Knife
Hatchet
Gunpowder
Lead
Bullet mold
Powder horn
Bullet pouch
Holster

FOOD

Flour
Bacon
Coffee
Baking soda
Corn meal
Hardtack
Dried beans
Dried beef
Dried fruit
Molasses
Vinegar
Pepper
Eggs
Salt
Sugar
Rice
Tea

Patchwork quilt

COOKING UTENSILS

Dutch oven	Butcher knife
Kettle	Ladle
Skillet	
Reflector oven	
Coffee grinder	Tin tableware
Coffeepot	Water keg
Teapot	Matches

Spider, or three-legged skillet

Butter churn

1851 kit of herbal medicines

HANDY ARTICLES

Surgical instruments
Liniments
Bandages
Campstool
Chamber pot
Washbowl
Lanterns
Candle molds
Tallow
Spyglasses
Scissors
Needles, pins, thread

Clock with brass works

CLOTHING

Wool sack coats	Duck trousers	Boots
Rubber coats	Cotton shirts	Felt hat
Cotton dresses	Flannel shirts	Palm-leaf sun hat
Wool pantaloons	Cotton socks	Green goggles
Buckskin pants	Brogans	Sunbonnet

Oxhide-covered trunk

LUXURIES

Canned foods
Plant cuttings
Schoolbooks
Musical instruments
Dolls
Family albums
Jewelry
China
Silverware
Fine linens
Iron stoves
Furniture

TOOLS AND EXTRA EQUIPMENT

Set of augers	Oxbows
Gimlet	Axles
Ax	Kingbolts
Hammer	Linchpins
Hoe	Oxshoes
Plow	Spokes
Shovel	Wagon tongue
Spade	Heavy ropes
Whetstone	Chains

Ox yoke

A favorite campsite along the Sweetwater lay beside a granite monolith known as Independence Rock, so called because, by a coincidence of scheduling and timing, many wagon trains reached it around the Fourth of July. Phoebe Judson celebrated the Fourth there in 1853 by whipping up a "savory pie, made of sage hen and rabbit, with a rich gravy; and a crust, having been raised with yeast, was as light as a feather." Fruitcake, poundcake and spongecake rounded off the feast, though Phoebe said that she would have concocted something more lavish back home.

Independence Rock was famous. Thousands of names, dates, monograms and initials were chiseled or painted on it during the emigration years, and few pioneers passed up the chance to add one more inscription. As early as 1841 a missionary who spotted some names carved there by fur traders foresaw the rock's future and called it the Great Record of the Desert.

The travelers shivered in the July nights and mornings along this part of the trail. At a place called Ice Slough, 77 miles west of Independence Rock, a bed of ice lay about a foot underneath the sod even in the heat of noontime, and travelers would chop out big chunks for their water casks. The presence of ice in midsummer indicated the altitude that the emigrants had attained—some 7,000 feet. They had, in fact, reached the crest of the trail—the Continental Divide—at the spot called South Pass, in the Wind River mountains.

Many pioneers found South Pass a disappointment, for it was nothing like the dramatic gorge they had envisioned. Instead, the trail arched gracefully over a broad grassy meadow, then dipped down toward the Pacific. Travelers could not even be sure that they had reached this milestone until they went another four miles to a landmark called Pacific Springs. There they would celebrate their arrival at the eastern boundary of the Oregon Territory (later to become the western border of Wyoming). Rugged mountains—the Sierra Nevada on the route to California, the Cascades of Oregon—still lay between them and their destinations, but for the moment they put the thought out of their minds.

A night's rest at Pacific Springs and the trains rolled on again. In a day or two the emigrants would have to make a choice of trails. Some of them took a safe, well-watered, roundabout route that dropped southwest to Fort Bridger. To Joel Palmer, who passed it in 1844,

Fort Bridger seemed "a shabby concern built of poles and daubed with mud." But it was home to the mountain man Jim Bridger, a leathery wilderness veteran who had roamed the Rockies ever since he answered a fur company's help-wanted ad in 1822. He had built his fort in 1843 to settle down, more or less, and to make a dollar or two by providing emigrants with fresh supplies and recruited oxen. (In pioneer parlance, a recruited ox was one whose strength had been restored by rest and good pasture; for a cash consideration, Bridger would exchange such an ox for a broken-down animal coming off the South Pass.)

Though it offered good water and forage, the Fort Bridger route seemed to many emigrants a needless detour. They chose a shortcut—Sublette's Cutoff, which ran straight across a grassless, sun-dazzled, 50-mile tableland. The only water available was on its far western side in the Green River. The bolder pioneers who took the cutoff made their way through gravelly rifts, ravines and dried-up alkali lakes. Their route was not always clearly delineated in the guidebooks of the day, though few of them lost the way: the trail was clearly marked by the bleached bones or bloated carcasses of abandoned animals. But the melted-snow water of the Green River had a magnetic attraction for the tired oxen that survived the trek; they would break into frenzied, clumsy gallops for the last few miles to this oasis. And when travelers on the cutoff rejoined the main trail coming up from Bridger's place, they had an 85-mile, seven-day jump on those who had gone the long way.

From the point at which the cutoff merged with the main trail, the wagons moved northwest. Seventy miles and seven days onward they passed Soda Springs, where the naturally carbonated water was potent enough to raise bread. To some travelers the water tasted like beer and, said Alonzo Delano, it made a good lemonade when mixed with citrus syrup and sugar.

Fifty-five miles beyond Soda Springs, at Fort Hall, built by Nathaniel Wyeth but now operated by the Hudson's Bay Company, the wagon trains prepared to split up once again—this time for good. A few miles west of Fort Hall, at the Raft River, the trail to California branched off the main Oregon Trail. Pioneers who took the California Trail veered southwest through an arid, rocky landscape of sagebrush and greasewood, and into the fearsome Great Basin of Utah and Ne-

along the Snake River's high, boulder-strewn south rim. Just getting water to drink meant clambering down a precipice into the gorge of the river, then toiling back up again; by the time a pioneer had returned to the trail he generally needed another drink. Beyond lay the steep Blue Mountains, a formidable barrier. Once past the mountains, the emigrants still faced either a dangerous 230-mile-long trip on rafts or boats down the Columbia River or the exhausting road trip 250 miles by wagon over the Cascades to the Willamette valley.

It was on this final leg of the journey that the Oregon emigrants, like their California-bound counterparts, often tested the limits of their endurance. The multiple trials along these last stretches of the trail had to be faced by even the best-planned expeditions, including the so-called Great Emigration of 1843, the first large emigrant train to come all the way from Missouri to western Oregon with its wagons intact. In the huge contingent of 1,000 pioneers and 120 wagons was seven-year-old Jesse Applegate, traveling with his parents, four brothers, one sister and numerous cousins, aunts and uncles. One Applegate uncle, also named Jesse, had charge of the expedition's livestock, and later wrote a vivid account of a day on the trail *(pages 90-91)*. The younger Jesse's own recollections, which were set down years later, provide a small boy's perspective to the ever-increasing hardships that the emigrants encountered as they neared their goal.

The earlier stretches of the trip, across the prairies and over the Rockies, had been one long lark for the boy, and at first his reminiscences bubble with wonder and excitement. The plains Indians, "gay and savage looking," had awed but not frightened him. Chimney Rock had seemed to "touch the sky." With unquenchable high spirits, he had bartered trinkets with Indian children; he and other emigrant youngsters had engaged in a mock snowball fight, using buffalo chips as missiles; and along the Snake River they had rolled rocks down a precipice to the riverbed, ending the game only after one boulder hit a calf and killed it.

But when the wagons left the Snake River to climb west over the Blue Mountains, Jesse remembered, he began to grasp the grimmer aspects of the trek. "The timber had to be cut and removed to make a way for the wagons," a tedious, backbreaking job for everyone. The weather closed in: "We were overtaken by a snow-storm which made the prospect very dismal. I remember wading through mud and snow and suffering from the cold and wet." Once out of the Blue Mountains, Jesse's spirits picked up briefly. The travelers found a grove of black haw trees bearing a succulent fruit and Jesse "ate about all I could get my hands on."

On the first of November, the expedition reached Fort Walla Walla. The trip was almost over. Only the snow-capped Cascades lay between the travelers and their destination, the Willamette valley — but the main bulk of the range rose a mile above sea level, and its most prominent peak, the white cone of Mount Hood, nearly another mile higher. There was no feasible wagon route across this barrier in 1843. But the mighty Columbia River flowed not far from Fort Walla Walla, and the Applegates and others prepared to tackle the water route. They abandoned their wagons, built large wooden boats and embarked on the river.

This voyage proved to be the worst ordeal of all. By the time the emigrants began the river run they had been on the trail from Missouri for almost five months; ahead lay four weeks more of travel, no less rugged for being on water. Their energies were sapped; their provisions were almost gone. Though they managed to trade with local Indians for vegetables, roots and river salmon, they never seemed to get enough. "Emigrants were hungry all the time," Jesse remembered. "Children seated in the boats would enjoy themselves for hours gnawing off the fat coating from the dried salmon skins. An emigrant not hungry was thought to be ill."

Several horrendous sets of rapids interrupt the flow of the Columbia, and in running these rapids many pioneers met disaster.

Tragedy struck the Applegates after they had been floating downstream for several days, as they were approaching the first set of rapids. Jesse was in one boat with his parents, his Uncle Jesse and Aunt Cynthia, and a hired Indian pilot. In a second boat rode Jesse's 11-year-old brother, Elisha, another brother, Warren, and a cousin, Edward Applegate, both about nine, two strapping pioneer men in their 20s, and a pioneer of about 70, Alexander McClellan. As the two boats rounded a bend of the river, Jesse caught sight of "breakers ahead extending in broken lines across the river, and the boat began to sweep along at a rapid rate." A short distance behind them, Jesse and his companions saw

Reflecting the strain of their journey, westbound pioneers
pause in the foothills of the Rockies. In the heat of the day,
after a morning of five hard hours on the trail, emigrants
often unhitched their wagons, watered their stock, ate the
noonday meal, rested — and sometimes posed for the camera.

Enchanted by the exotic wildlife of the plains, an unknown emigrant artist depicted an improbably busy scene in which prairie dogs scurry for cover, owls scout for prey and a snake slithers past a buffalo skull.

the second boat, with no pilot, veering into dangerous water near the opposite bank.

"Presently there was a wail of anguish, a shriek, and a scene of confusion in our boat that no language can describe. The boat we were watching disappeared and we saw the men and boys struggling in the water. Father and Uncle Jesse, seeing their children drowning, were about to leap from the boat to make a desperate attempt to swim to them, when mother and Aunt Cynthia, in voices that were distinctly heard above the roar of the waters, commanded, 'Men, don't quit the oars, if you do we will all be lost.' The men returned to the oars just in time to avoid, by great exertion, a rock."

The other boat went under, surfaced briefly, then was swept to the bottom by a whirlpool. Jesse's brother Elisha swam to safety and the two men in their 20s floated ashore, buoyed up by bed ticking. Old Mc-Clellan had placed cousin Edward on a pair of oars and tried to swim him ashore. But after a few moments Mc-Clellan's strength gave out, and both man and boy disappeared under the water. "The brave old soldier could

have saved himself by abandoning the boy," wrote Jesse, "but this he would not do." As for Jesse's brother Warren, he was never seen again.

Battered and sorrowful, the survivors continued downriver without further mishap. They arrived at Fort Vancouver in late November, 1843, and paused to gather their strength before turning to the formidable task of building their future homes in the brand new world of Oregon's Willamette valley.

Many other pioneers came to grief on the Columbia River, and many attempts were made to open alternate routes across the Cascades. In 1845, Stephen Meek, a onetime fur trapper, persuaded about 200 emigrant families to take an abandoned Indian trail through mountains south of the Columbia, presumably a shorter route to their goal. By the time the expedition emerged almost two months later, about 75 pioneers had paid for the passage with their lives; some died of starvation, others were poisoned by drinking alkali water. Their disastrous shortcut went down in history as Meek's Terrible Trail. But the very next year, workers under

Samuel Barlow of Illinois completed a wagon road over the mountains south of Mount Hood that became the standard emigrant route to western Oregon.

Like the main branch of the Oregon Trail, the fork to California remained uncertain for years, with one group or another constantly trying to find a better way west. In 1846, about 300 pioneers took the California Trail south from Fort Hall, along the Humboldt River and over the Sierra Nevada to the Sacramento valley. Though hunger, thirst and exhaustion beset them, most reached their destination without serious misfortune. One now-famous pioneer group, however, did not.

George Donner, the party's nominal leader, was no ordinary emigrant. A well-to-do farmer from Illinois, he had married three times, sired 13 children, and now, at the age of 62, was headed for California on a last great adventure. Donner traveled with his third wife, the 45-year-old, petite Tamsen, his five youngest children and a retinue of three wagons, 12 yoke of oxen, five saddle horses, numerous milk and beef cattle, several hired hands, a dog and $10,000 in bank notes sewn into a quilt. His older brother, Jacob, aged 65, had a similarly affluent train. An Illinois neighbor, merchant James Reed, with his wife, mother-in-law and four children, rounded out the group. Reed, a vigorous 46, also believed in traveling first class. He stocked two support wagons with an assortment of fancy foods and liquors, and fitted his living wagon with such lavish appointments as built-in beds and a stove.

The Donners and the Reeds made every mistake that travelers could make. Not only did they overload their wagons, but they started late and had to rush to catch up with the tail end of the 1846 migration across the plains. Then, at Fort Bridger, they decided to take an untested shortcut to California.

The party made the decision on the basis of a guidebook published the year before by Lansford Hastings, a zealous California booster. Hastings was trying to overthrow California's weak Mexican government; he hoped to bring in enough emigrants to start a revolution and found an independent republic with himself as president. His guidebook, written as a spur to emigration, was the first step in his plan. It made the trek to California seem as easy as a jaunt to market.

The shortcut Hastings recommended left the main Oregon Trail at Fort Bridger, well before the usual Cal-ifornia turnoff at Fort Hall. It went directly west across the Wasatch mountains, down into Salt Lake valley and across the Great Basin, and rejoined the standard California Trail along the Humboldt River, thus saving some 400 miles. Hastings had not taken his own short-cut to California; he had gone west by the standard Oregon Trail in 1842. He never doubted his judgment, however. In 1846 he came eastward along the proposed California route, carrying his gear and provisions on pack mules. He had no trouble. Arriving at Fort Bridger a few weeks before the Donners, he persuaded a company of 200 emigrants and 66 wagons, headed by an old Indian-fighter named Captain George Harlan, to follow him back to California. He was sure that wagons traveling westward would have no more difficulty on the trail than his mules had traveling eastward.

Cutting across the Wasatch mountains, Hastings led the emigrants through the narrow gorge of the Weber River, a passage so cramped and treacherous that the wagons had to be pushed and dragged along the riverbed. The travelers heaved boulders aside and hacked away brush; when the riverbed became totally impassable, they hoisted their wagons over the adjoining bluffs by windlass. On the average, the wagon train labored forward at a rate of a mile and a half a day.

Beyond the mountains, in the Great Basin, the going got even worse. The wagons moved for two days across the waterless desert. "Such a sight!" wrote an emigrant named Samuel Young. "The sun rose in full splendor, reflecting his rays on this vast salt plain, as white as snow, and as far as the eye could reach not a thing to be seen, not a spear of grass or a drop of water. Oxen gave out and lay down, some to rise no more; others, from extreme thirst, became crazy and nothing could be done with them, and finally they would become exhausted and drop down dead. Wagons were abandoned until it seemed as if all were lost."

The company reached the Humboldt River three weeks behind the pioneers who had taken the longer route by way of Fort Hall. The group crossed another dry stretch to the foot of the Sierra Nevada, hauled the wagons over the mountains by windlass, and arrived in California's Sacramento valley as the first snows started to fall. Miraculously, only one life was lost.

The Donners were less lucky. When they arrived at Fort Bridger and heard that Hastings himself had start-

A pioneer party struggles up a slope in an effort to cross the Rockies before the first snow. One man urges the oxen ahead with a whip, two others push the wagon and a watchful horseman counsels from the rear.

ed down his shortcut with another emigrant train, they saw no reason not to follow. By now a large number of other pioneers had joined their group, and on July 31, 1846, they set out, a contingent of 74 men, women and children, with 20 overloaded wagons.

The party followed the wagon tracks of the Harlan company into the Wasatch where they were joined by 13 other pioneers and three wagons, bringing the travelers' total to 87. Almost immediately the caravan got into trouble. They lost four days trying to penetrate the Weber River gorge, decided it was impassable and turned back to find an alternate path over the mountains. It took them 28 days to reach Great Salt Lake, a distance of about 50 miles. They pushed on.

The desert exacted a terrible toll of the Donner party. It ate up six precious days of traveling time, killed off almost 100 oxen and forced many emigrants—including the luxury-loving James Reed—to abandon their wagons and supplies. By the time the caravan reached the Humboldt River on September 30, the Harlan group was at least 300 miles farther on.

Time was running out for the disintegrating Donner party. Short of food, near the end of their endurance, growing desperate as they realized how far they still had to go, the emigrants added to their woes by constant bickering and feuding. On October 5, at the end of a blazing hot day along the Humboldt, the enmities boiled over. The wagons were stretched out in two units, and in the rear unit John Snyder, a young, well-liked teamster, was lashing furiously at some tangled oxen. James Reed, also in the rear, told him to stop. Snyder's anger shifted to this new adversary and he threatened Reed with his bull whip. Reed drew his hunting knife, a move that prompted Snyder to reverse his whip and to flail at Reed with the handle butt. Reed plunged the knife into Snyder's chest. Snyder sank to the ground and died in a few minutes.

Those who witnessed the incident were stunned. Snyder had been popular. Reed, though tacitly acknowledged as a leader, was considered arrogant and aloof. Several people wanted to hang him on the spot. After further deliberation the company decided to expel Reed from the train, making him leave his wife and four children with the group.

Reed rode ahead to the lead unit, picked up a friend there and struck out for California. Traveling light, the two men sped down the trail in an effort to catch up with the Harlan company. In the high slopes of the Sierra their food ran out. Weak with hunger, the two men struggled on over the mountains. Finally, on October 25 in the western foothills, they staggered into the circle of wagons of the encamped Harlan party, having subsisted only on wild onions, a bit of tallow from an abandoned tar bucket and a few beans that had been dropped along the trail. Four days later they reached the haven of Sutter's Fort in the Sacramento valley. Here Reed paused to recoup his strength and began organizing an expedition to fetch his family and to bring food to the rest of the Donner company.

Far back on the trail, the emigrants were now close to starvation. Two days after Reed's ouster, a man named Hardkoop, who was over 60, fell far behind the train. By then many of the wagons had been abandoned, and Hardkoop, along with other men, had been walking across the desert. Too feeble to keep up, and unable to find anyone who would carry him in a wagon, he had simply dropped out. No one had the energy to go back and look for him. After some discussion, the emigrants decided that he was expendable and left him to die. A few days later, Patrick Breen, the father of seven children, refused a cup of water to William Eddy, who wanted it for his three-year-old son and his infant daughter. Threatening to kill Breen, Eddy took the water by force. Two days later Eddy applied to Mrs. Breen and a Mrs. Graves for food for his famished children. They turned him down.

Eleven weeks after heading out from Fort Bridger on the Hastings shortcut, the battered remnants of the Donner party reached the lush meadows along the upper Truckee River, in the eastern shadow of the Sierra Nevada. It was now October 20—and early winter snow glinted on the high Sierra ridges ahead. The travelers grazed their emaciated cattle for five days, then prepared for the final push over the mountains.

The trail led about 50 miles into the hills, then, just beyond Truckee Lake, climbed to its highest and most difficult point at Truckee Pass—the last major barrier between the emigrants and the Sacramento valley. It was absolutely vital to cross this pass before further snowfalls made travel impossible.

The first three families to arrive at Truckee Lake were the Patrick Breens, the William Eddys and the

Recovered from the Donner tragedy, Margaret Reed sits reunited with her husband, James. Reed was ousted from the Donner group before its disaster; he later made a fortune speculating in California real estate.

Lewis Kesebergs. On October 31 they camped near the lake, in an inch of snow, and next morning made an assault on the pass. By afternoon they were wallowing through five-foot snowdrifts and could climb no higher. The three families turned back to the lake and set up camp, the Breens moving into a deserted cabin built by earlier pioneers. A chill rain began to fall.

All through the next day, the rain continued to come down in torrents. After dusk a second group of wagons reached the lakeside encampment. With it came Charles T. Stanton, a diminutive and doughty 35-year-old bachelor who, weeks earlier, had ridden ahead to Sutter's Fort and returned with food, mules and two Indian cowboys as guides. On the morning of November 3, Stanton led a second assault on the pass. But the storm that had brought rain to the lake had clogged the trail higher up with still more snow and soon after setting out the wagons bogged down in drifts. The party struggled forward on foot, almost every adult carrying a child. Only Stanton and an Indian reached the summit of the pass, but they descended again when they saw the others could not make it. That evening another storm blew up. Pelted by snow and sleet, the party spent the night around a tree they had set afire. Next day they retrieved the wagons and retreated to Truckee Lake.

It was plain that they would have to dig in, and a frenzy of building began. A lean-to was erected against the old cabin—which the Breens continued to claim as their own—and two double cabins went up nearby, small log shelters with oxhides for roofing.

Meanwhile, the tail end of the wagon train was enmeshed in its own troubles five miles back at Alder Creek. In this group were George Donner, his brother Jacob, their families and hired help, and a widow, Mrs. Wolfinger — 21 people in all. George Donner's wagon had broken an axle. Pausing to carve a new one, he had gashed his hand with a chisel; he shrugged off the injury but it refused to heal. The storm that had swamped the vanguard campers at the lake also hit the Donner group at Alder Creek. They hurriedly erected two tents, two lean-tos of brush covered with blankets and clothing, and a tipi. Huddled in these fragile shelters, they decided to stay put.

The snow continued falling, off and on, for two weeks. When it ended, the emigrants at Truckee Lake made several desperate attempts to get through the pass. An ominous truth became apparent to everyone: they were imprisoned on the back side of the California mountains and would probably have to stay there all winter. Eighty-one people were now mired in at the two camps; 41 of them were children.

It was snowing, too, on the west face of the mountains, where James Reed, now leading a rescue party, was trying to get eastward over the pass with food from Sutter's Fort. As the rescuers worked their way through the accumulating drifts, their Indian guides deserted with three pack horses. Soon all the other pack horses dropped from exhaustion and died in the snow; then the saddle horses gave out. For a while, the men pushed ahead on foot, with a single mule carrying their remaining supplies, but they soon realized it was useless to go on. They made their way back to the fort, where Captain John Sutter—who had no other men to send—consoled them with the assurance that the Donner party could survive on ox flesh and beef.

But by December, the outlook in the two camps was grim. The oxen and cattle, unwatched, had wandered off and perished in deep snow. Their carcasses could not be found. The meat that was left would not last through Christmas. A few cupfuls of flour were hoarded to make a thin gruel for infants, and a little sugar, tea and coffee remained, but no salt. Trout in the lake would not bite. The deer had disappeared. Eddy, a 28-year-old emigrant from Illinois, shot a coyote one day, an owl the next. Then he wounded a bear, and, when it fought him, clubbed it to death. Most of it was soon devoured. The campers began boiling hides—even those used as roofing—and eating the resultant glue. In

Wagons forsaken, members of the Donner group struggle upslope in a second vain attempt to surmount a snow-clogged Sierra pass. Two men reached the top, but they turned back rather than leave the others.

Near Truckee Lake, the forward section of the Donner party prepares to withstand winter's siege in three hastily built log-and-oxhide shelters and a fourth cabin (*far right*) erected by some earlier emigrants.

one cabin, children cut up a fur rug, toasted it and ate it. At the creek camp, water continually dripped into the tents and brush shelters, putting out fires that were intended to keep the occupants warm.

The deepening winter brought more storms and less to eat. Gradually, death began to stalk the marooned travelers. Baylis Williams, a 24-year-old hired hand of the Reeds, was the first to go, on December 15. The following day some of the campers at Truckee Lake embarked on one more frantic effort to conquer the pass.

Ten men, five young women and two boys set out on snowshoes fashioned from rawhide and the wagons' hickory oxbows. They had a blanket apiece, one gun, a couple of pistols, a hatchet and finger-sized strips of meat — enough to last six days if each person ate only two strips three times a day. Stanton and his two Indians led, accompanied by Eddy, "Uncle Billy" Graves — who was 57 — and the others. They managed to travel only four miles the first day. One boy, Billy Mur-

phy, 11, and a teamster, "Dutch Charley," turned back, but Billy's brother Lemuel, 12, struggled on.

Miraculously the group got over the pass to an open downward slope. But the clear skies and treeless expanse only brought the travelers another hardship: the sun on the snow blinded them. Stanton, worst affected by the glare, began to lag. On the morning of the sixth day — the last for which they had food — Stanton sat by the campfire as the party prepared to move on. Asked if he was ready, he replied "Yes, I am coming soon." In fact, he could not go on and did not want to delay his companions. He died by the fire's embers.

The others kept going, Eddy subsisting on a half-pound of bear meat that he discovered secreted in his pack along with a note from "Your own dear Eleanor." Eddy's wife had deprived herself and their children to provide this extra food for him.

Back at the lake, where the last of the livestock had been slaughtered and eaten, the huddled families gnawed

116

on boiled hides and bones seasoned with pepper. Margaret Reed, aged 32 and accustomed to the comforts of life, killed the family dog, Cash, to feed her four children. The Reeds ate "his head and feet & hide & every thing about him," 13-year-old Virginia reported. "We lived on little Cash a week."

Meanwhile, the snowshoe party groped down the west face of the mountains through a succession of blizzards. For several days, they were totally without nourishment. And now began a gruesome series of events that stood in bleak contrast to Stanton's quiet act of heroism on the trail, and to Mrs. Eddy's sacrifice of food to help her husband. Through these events the Donner expedition would earn a unique place in the annals of emigrant travel.

On Christmas Eve, during a snowstorm, two members of the snowshoe party died of cold and starvation. With his last words one of them, Uncle Billy Graves, urged his daughters to eat his body. The next day, Christmas, Pat Dolan died. The 11 survivors huddled under blankets, half-crazed with hunger but still unable to bring themselves to eat human flesh.

The storm lifted the following afternoon, and the dreaded step was taken. Averting their eyes from one another, the survivors began to roast and eat strips of flesh from Dolan's body. Only Eddy and the two Indians abstained. The others dried what they could not eat, to save for later. Within four days, Eddy and the Indians, hunger gnawing at their bellies, gave in and consumed some of the dried strips.

The group struggled on. On December 26 young Lem Murphy died; and soon after New Year's Day Jay Fosdick followed him. The remaining travelers carved up the bodies and ate them. Even earlier, William Foster had proposed murdering the two Indians for their flesh. Eddy, horrified, warned the Indians and they disappeared. Foster then suggested killing one of the women. Before he could carry out this threat, Eddy was able to shoot a deer. The travelers cut and dried the meat over a fire, and kept going. Beside the trail they found the two Indians lying near death. Foster, now obviously deranged, barely hesitated before shooting them and butchering their bodies. After that Eddy and three of the women camped apart from Foster.

On January 17, 1847, Eddy, emaciated beyond recognition, limped into an American settlement on the eastern edge of the Sacramento valley. His boots had long since given out, and his feet were torn and frozen. His remaining companions had lain down to die miles back on the trail. A rescue party from a nearby ranch went to find them—Eddy's bloody footprints provided a clear trail to follow—and brought them in. Of the 17 people who had left the lake camp a month earlier, only two men—Eddy and Foster—and the five women had made it out alive.

A massive rescue operation was now begun to reach the emigrants still encamped on the other side of the mountains at Alder Creek and Truckee Lake (later renamed Donner Lake). On February 4 the first of a series of relief parties struck east over the mountains. Eddy, whose wife and two children had remained at the lake, started out with the rescuers; but his ordeal had left him so weakened that he had to turn back. Two weeks later the relief team reached the encampment by the lake with packs full of food. A woman staggered from a cabin and cried, "Are you from California or Heaven?"

The situation at the two camps was hideous indeed. Thirteen people had died, including Eddy's wife and daughter. At the creek camp, Jake Donner and three of the four hired men were dead. George Donner was dying; his gashed hand had turned gangrenous. Many of the living seemed to be teetering on the verge of lunacy. At the lake camp, the idea of cannibalism had become so commonplace that Patrick Breen noted it as a brief aside in his diary, between comments on the weather: "Mrs. Murphy said here yesterday that thought she would commence on Milt and eat him, it is distressing Sat 27th beautiful morning."

The rescuers headed back with 21 people, as many as they could safely take. Plucky Tamsen Donner refused to leave her dying husband, George. Mrs. Reed had to go without her son, Tommy, who was as yet too weak to travel. Little Patty Reed stayed behind to care for him. "If I do not see you again, Mother," Patty said, "do the best you can."

Halfway down the west slope of the Sierra the first relief party met a second band of rescuers, this one led by James Reed. After embracing his wife and the two children that she had managed to bring out with her, Reed continued on east. The second relief team gathered up 17 more survivors from the creek and lake camps, most of them children. But almost as soon as they had crossed the pass, a storm struck and immobilized them for two days and three nights. The fire they built sank 15 feet into the snow. Then the food gave out, and Reed penciled this anguished entry in his diary: "'Hunger hunger,' is the cry with the children and nothing to give them. 'Freezing' was the cry of the mothers. Night closing fast and with it the hurricane increases." Five-year-old Isaac Donner died. And when the storm at last abated, Reed could not get the Breen family and the Graves family to move. He had to leave them behind in the snow, where they stayed for six days until they were found by a third rescue team from California. By that time, Elizabeth Graves and her five-year-old son Franklin had died too. Parts of their bodies were found boiling in a pot when the rescuers finally arrived, and Elizabeth's infant daughter was wailing beside her mother's half-devoured corpse.

In this rescue party were Eddy and William Foster, now recovered from their terrible journey to Sutter's Fort. Both had left young sons at the lake camp—but they had come back too late to save them. Lewis Keseberg, a big, blond, bearded German who had emigrated to the states only two years earlier, and who was by far the best-educated member of the entire Donner party, told the two men what had happened to their boys: he had, he said, consumed them. Eddy and Foster collected George Donner's three children and quickly departed. Donner, unable to walk, stayed behind to die, Tamsen still with him. Lavina Murphy, almost blind, stayed with Keseberg, whose wife had gone out with the first relief team.

When a fourth relief party arrived at the lake cabins in mid-April, the only survivor they found there was the spectral Keseberg, lying beside a pot in which simmered the liver and lungs of a young boy. Keseberg was living exclusively on human flesh—while whole legs of oxen, dug up from the melting snow, lay untouched not far away. The ox meat, he explained to his rescuers, was "too dry eating."

Of the 81 travelers who had made camp east of the pass on the night of October 31, a total of 47 survived. One of the survivors was young Virginia Reed, who later wrote to a cousin back home, offering this poignant bit of advice for future westbound travelers: "Never take no cut ofs and hury along as fast as you can."

Survivors of the Donner ordeal emerge from a snow-buried cabin as the first of four rescue teams arrives at the lake camp. Some of the sufferers were almost past caring. One diary noted matter-of-factly: "Froze hard last night 7 men arrived from California yesterday evening with provisions."

4/Settling in at last

Their running battle with deserts, rivers and mountains ended at last, emigrants changed into settlers and sought to claim the rewards of the promised land. But the benefits were a long time coming, and many a harsh reality gave the lie to such idyllic visions of the settlers' life as the scene at left—the work of an Easterner who stayed East.

The first problem faced by the newcomers was the selection of a prime homesite, a task that became an increasing scramble as more and more emigrants swarmed in off the trail. Most of the pioneers who headed for Oregon arrived at the start of the rainy season and had to conduct their search through miles of mire. The tedious quest was slowed by the weakened condition of their draft animals, whose strength had been sapped by the cross-country trek. Families, grown heartily weary of their covered wagons, nevertheless had to spend weeks more living in them while building their log cabins—itself no easy matter. Food was scarce, for weather discouraged hunting and the men could spare little time for it anyway. Having shed their excess baggage on the trail, the settlers owned few garments other than those they wore—and cloth for replacements was in short supply at Oregon's few stores.

For all the adversities, however, a brighter side could always be discerned. Wrote one pioneer, "I never saw so fine a population as in Oregon. They were honest, because there was nothing to steal; sober, because there was no liquor; there were no misers because there was no money; they were industrious, because it was work or starve."

Home from the hunt, settlers carrying an improbably full litter of game are greeted by impossibly well-dressed children in this Currier & Ives lithograph, the pleasant fantasy of a lady artist back in New York.

Resourceful tamers of a new frontier

On a bright Sunday morning in April 1843, an Oregon settler named Gustavus Hines took a stroll along the wooded south bank of the Columbia River. Hines, aged 34 and a member of a Methodist mission in the nearby Willamette valley, was beset by loneliness and doubt. He sat down to rest under a wild apple tree that leaned over the river and let his imagination carry him back to the New York home he had left four years earlier. His thoughts, he later confided to his journal, were not just of distant family and friends but of the joys and comforts of civilization a continent's breadth away: "of bustling cities, with wheels rattling and hoofs clattering over their pavements; of smiling villages and towns, with their splendid turnpikes and McAdamized roads; of railroad cars and steamboats; of temples erected to the God of heaven."

Gus Hines returned to the present with a shudder. "I found myself," he wrote, "surrounded with the stillness of death, save the murmuring of the turbid waters of the Columbia that rolled beneath where I sat." He was "a voluntary exile in a land of darkness."

The same sense of isolation that gnawed at Gus Hines also oppressed other early residents in the Pacific Northwest. While the handful of Americans living in California were a tiny minority compared with the established community of Spanish-speaking cattle ranchers who were their neighbors, the first pioneers in the sprawling Oregon country had virtually no neighbors at all. The region's population in 1840, not counting Indians or fur men, numbered only 200.

But new American settlers were beginning to arrive. Soon there would be thousands of them. The unearthly stillness of the Pacific forests would give way to the ring of axes, the rasp of saws, the lowing of cattle and the creak of plows. Before the decade was over, the pioneers would cover the landscape with wheat fields and dairy farms, build sawmills, lay out towns, organize a government and transform the Northwest into one of the richest and most bountiful of American provinces.

The immense vacancy of the Oregon country attracted by far the greatest influx of pioneers in those early years of the 1840s. In size alone, the region seemed overwhelming: some 250,000 square miles of virgin forest, mountains, plateaus and prairies. Its only settlements consisted of the Hudson's Bay Company headquarters at Fort Vancouver, a few company trading posts in the interior and a scattering of Protestant and Catholic missions. Unlike California, where 300 years of Spanish habitation had shaped the land to the ways of men, the Oregon country was a place untouched by civilization. Nowhere else did the wilderness seem so raw or remote. Nowhere else was the act of pioneering so fundamental — or so dramatic.

The setting could not have been more spectacular. Most newcomers headed for the great Willamette valley (pronounced Wil-LAM-ette), a broad tract of prairie and timberland south of the Columbia River, cupped between the lofty spine of the Cascade Range to the east and the coastal mountains on the west. The valley's rich alluvial topsoil and gentle climate produced an extraordinary abundance of crops, and inspired some equally lush prose from the settlers. "Picture an evergreen valley 150 miles long and 40 miles wide," said one, "a navigable river running the whole length through its middle, with numerous branches on each side, the smaller rising in the foothills, the larger emerging from the forest covered mountains, the rich agricultural surface of the valley interspersed with timber and prairie in profitable proportions, and innumerable springs of pure,

A robust Oregon settler pauses to quench his thirst in this 1868 idealization of a pioneer father and child working together to clear the land around a wilderness home.

soft water." In sum, it was "the best poor man's country on the globe." The Willamette River, flowing from the Cascades to a junction with the Columbia River opposite Fort Vancouver, bore white swans, and seals rode its tidal currents. Deer, grizzly bear and wolverine roamed the forest; grouse and quail nested in the brush; and salmon, trout and sturgeon thronged the waters.

Never did the summers grow oppressively hot, nor the winters too cold. Light snows fell in January and February, but quickly melted. More frequently it rained —a penetrating drizzle that started in late October and never seemed to stop. "Sometimes the sun would not be seen for twenty days in succession," wrote Peter Burnett, a 36-year-old self-taught lawyer from Missouri who migrated to Oregon in 1843. But the dampness of the climate was a blessing for farmers. "The copious rains fertilize the soil of the fields and keep them always fresh and productive," Burnett observed.

The fecundity of the soil had been tested even before the 1843 settlers arrived. For almost two decades the Hudson's Bay Company had been raising crops and cattle around Fort Vancouver to feed its fur trappers. So productive were the results—5,000 bushels of wheat were harvested in 1837 alone—that the company exported surplus flour, salted beef, hams and butter to the Russians in Alaska. When the emigrants began pouring in, most of them arriving with the October rains and most having used up all their provisions on the trail, the company was able to tide them over until the next summer's harvest with loans of food as well as supplies.

Other help for the new arrivals came from the Methodist missions in the Willamette valley. Jason Lee, the strapping minister who had trekked overland in 1834 with the first missionary group, now presided over a thriving Methodist colony near a place called French Prairie, 45 miles up the Willamette River. The mission had opened a store downriver at Willamette Falls, where settlers could buy grain, clothing and a few tools. By 1843 Willamette Falls also included a tin shop, a blacksmith shop, a sawmill, a gristmill and a dozen houses—making it Oregon's largest town and requiring a grandiose new name: Oregon City.

Even so, a city of 12 houses and a philanthropic Hudson's Bay Company could not fulfill all the needs of the 1,000 or so pioneers who flooded into Oregon

Settlers send a log up a pair of skids, adding the final tier to a wall of a new Idaho home. Neighbors from miles around helped in such cabin-raisings, and could finish the job in a day — though the owner had to spend weeks on the preparatory work of chopping logs and hauling them to the site.

Yoked oxen, veterans of the journey west, are put to work in the raw Oregon wilderness, pitting their brawn against a stubborn boulder as their pioneer owners clear a field in preparation for spring planting.

in 1843, or the 2,000 who came the next year, or the 3,000 the year after that. For the most part the newcomers were on their own. One overwhelming fact weighed in their favor, however: they were Americans with a pioneering past. What they were doing their parents had done before them.

Anyone with sense knew that an Applegate boy, for example, understood pioneering inside and out — one of the reasons that Jesse Applegate had been elected to head the cow column in the 1843 migration (*pages 90-91*). His father, Daniel Applegate, had played a fife for George Washington's soldiers during the Revolutionary War. When the war was over, the lad's family emigrated to what was then America's western frontier — Kentucky. In 1820, Daniel moved his own family on to St. Louis. Presently, his sons — Jesse, Charles and Lindsay — started farming on the western edge of Missouri. Now here they were, with wives and children, settling into Oregon's Willamette valley.

But the Applegates, like other Oregon pioneers, faced a challenge far greater than any they had met before. Cut off from civilization by 2,000 miles of wilderness, they had to rely on themselves and make do with what the land provided. At first the land provided them with precious little. For lack of tools and equipment, tasks that normally took a week or two might stretch into months of backbreaking labor. The challenge was not so much to build a glorious future in a fine new place; it was simply to survive the first winter.

The Applegates were luckier than most pioneers during that first winter in 1843, for they found a ready-made shelter. Twenty miles south of Willamette Falls they discovered three empty log cabins that had been built almost a decade before by Jason Lee for his first mission headquarters. Lee had long since abandoned the site and constructed a larger compound at Salem. So the Applegates moved in. A few other settlers were already living in the vicinity, and Lindsay Applegate got a job building a boat for one of them.

Lindsay took his pay in provisions, which consisted mostly of pork and peas. His seven-year-old son, Jesse, later remembered "wading around in a large bin of peas for an hour or more," and noted that his neighbors seemed to live on nothing else.

The following autumn Lindsay moved his family upriver, built his own cabin and cleared some land. He brought with him some wheat grown in the fields of the abandoned mission, and now it had to be converted into flour for baking. Lindsay set out through the woods with three sacks of the wheat for the nearest gristmill, operated by the Methodist mission at Salem. It took him a week to reach the mission, grind his grain and return with three sacks of flour. The next morning young Jesse awoke to the fragrance of pancakes. "This was my second realization of perfect bliss," he later wrote. The first had occurred the previous fall, when Jesse inhaled the delicious odor of frying bacon in the house of a missionary who had fed the Applegates their first indoor meal in the Willamette valley.

Most settlers, before they could savor such luxuries, faced the elemental task of building a house. They had only the most basic tools, coupled with an infinite willingness to expend huge quantities of sweat. "Weeks of hard labor were required to fell the trees, clear away the brush, and prepare the site," reminisced Charlotte Cartwright, who arrived in 1845. "Trees were cut the proper length, one side of the log hewed smooth with a broadax, and fitted so they would join at the corners and lie compact. Logs for the floors were split and smoothed with an adze." Rough-hewn timbers set on log rafters provided the roof. Then came the finishing work on the structure. "The fireplace and chimney was built with sticks and plastered inside and out with a thick coating of clay. Windows were a sort of sliding door in the wall, without glass." The door consisted of hewn planks pegged together and hung on wooden or leather hinges; sometimes a buffalo hide was draped over the door to help keep out the winter cold.

With the same kind of ready ingenuity, the pioneers built rudimentary furnishings. An Ohio rocking chair might have survived the overland trip, but the oak dining table had probably been abandoned on some uphill stretch. A new table would be hewn out of logs and fastened together with wooden pegs. A bed was commonly built into a cabin corner, with one leg for support. "Large quantities of moss stripped from the trees made good mattresses," one settler reported. "With buffalo robes and blankets we had comfortable beds."

Dishes were usually the same tin plates that had been used on the way west. They were almost irreplaceable. Matilda Sager Delaney, an 1844 emigrant, recalled that one man, "to avoid the risk of loss, nailed his dishes to the table. When he wanted to wash them he would turn the table on its side, take the broom and some hot water and wash them well."

One frustrating problem, the settlers discovered, was clothing. No cotton grew in Oregon, and there were as yet no sheep to be sheared for wool. Cloth for making garments was scarce and costly. Young Jesse Applegate's Aunt Melinda tried with limited success to spin yarn from the hair of wolves and coyotes. "Wolves could not be fleeced so long as they were alive," Jesse noted, "and a man could not kill a sufficient number, in a month, to make a sweater."

More commonly, settlers cut up tents and wagon covers into overcoats, lining them with skins or rags. Or else they turned to the old standby of the mountain men—buckskin. Even this proved less than ideal in the soggy Oregon climate, young Jesse was to remember in later years: "Trousers after frequent wettings and dryings would assume a fixed shape that admitted of no reformation. This malformation did not appear when a man was sitting, which was, for this reason, his favorite posture; but when he arose the appearance to an inexperienced eye was that he was not yet up."

Pioneer children went barefoot in Oregon, and so did many adults when their trail-tattered footwear proved beyond repair. Peter Burnett recalled that after he had plowed three acres of land, sown them with wheat and fenced in the field, "my old boots gave out entirely, and I had no time to look for a substitute. During the first week my feet were very sore: but after that there came a shield over them, so that I could work with great ease, and go almost anywhere except among thorns." Eventually Burnett decided to make some shoes for himself and his family. The cowhide he used

had been tanned on the surface only, leaving the leather raw in the middle. "To keep the shoes soft enough to wear through the day," he noted, "it was necessary to soak them in water every night."

Given the time and the money to pay the premium prices demanded for imported goods, Burnett might have traveled to Fort Vancouver or Oregon City to buy shoes, cloth, tools or foodstuffs. But for a backwoods family a trip to market meant a journey of 30 miles or more each way. A housewife who lost her last sewing needle might have to wait months before her husband could find time to fetch another.

So the pioneer woman learned to improvise. She manufactured soap from animal fat and lye. She extracted dye from tree bark, brewed tea from sage leaves, and boiled carrots with sugar syrup to make jam. Onions mashed in sugar became cough syrup; gunpowder dissolved in water turned into a serviceable eyewash; and the juice squeezed from an onion, after it had been wrapped in tobacco leaves and baked in the hearth, was administered for earache. When children caught cold or fever, a pioneer mother rubbed their skin with goose grease and turpentine, which seemed to be a standard salve for almost any disorder. "It was all you could smell in a schoolroom," one settler remembered.

These home remedies must have worked at least part of the time. William Allen, a doctor, arrived in Oregon City in 1851, well after the first wave of emigrants, hoping to set up a practice. But no one ever seemed to need his services. "In Oregon there is very little sickness," Allen lamented. "I take it that a man must die here with old age. It is said that they have to go East of the mountains to die at all." To eke out a living, the doctor made it known that he was also available to play his violin at barn dances.

At some point, even the most self-sufficient backwoods settler had to go to town. There he would sell surplus wheat or barter it for tools, dry goods and food staples. And even in the early days he found prices appallingly high—often three or four times the going rate back in the States. Joel Palmer, the Indiana emigrant who captained a wagon train along the Oregon Trail in 1845, visited Oregon City before heading east again to get his family. A thrifty man, he nodded with approval when he saw a craftsman melting down broken cannons into kitchenware. But Palmer felt dismay that

"a common coarse cotton flag handkerchief, which can be had in Cincinnati for five or ten cents, was *fifty* cents." A few years later, Dr. Allen registered amazement at the prices in Oregon City: flour $75 a barrel, butter $1 a pound, eggs $1 a dozen.

Few settlers had cash enough to pay. Indeed, hard money was so scarce that everyone bartered—the most common items of exchange being wheat and blankets. Often the items a settler sought were simply not available. Peter Burnett, in his capacity as frontier lawyer, had earned a $49 credit with the general store at Oregon City; he decided to take his fee in goods since the storekeeper, like everyone else, was short of cash.

"Judge, my stock is now very low," the storekeeper told Burnett. "I would suggest to you to wait until my new goods shall arrive from Honolulu."

Burnett agreed and, when the shipment arrived three months later, returned with a list of the things he needed. He recorded the colloquy with the merchant:

"I asked him if he had any satinets? None. Any jeans? None. Any calico? None. Any brown cotton? None. I then asked what he had. He said tools."

Burnett reluctantly bought $13 worth of tools—none of them on his shopping list—and noted that they cost double the amount charged at Fort Vancouver. At this point he "became tired of paying such prices for articles I could do without," and asked the storekeeper if he "had any brown sugar, and at what price. He said plenty, at 12½ cents a pound." The price seemed fair, so Burnett took the balance of his credit in sugar and "went home knowing that he had sugar enough to last for a long time"—288 pounds of it.

Beyond the material needs, there was something else that every settler in the lonely Oregon forests craved: the society of other people. A pioneer family might hike miles through the woods on a Sunday to attend church at one of the missions—an occasion that combined piety with a chance to talk crops and exchange gossip with other pioneers. As the valley grew more populous, families within reasonable traveling distance of one another would gather at a settler's house after chores on Saturday nights for a round of Virginia reels and other square dances. These frontier cotillions were exuberant, the women decked out in calico dresses, the men with beards trimmed and hair slicked down with a pomade of bear grease and lavender.

More essential to building a sense of community was the formation of a government. Oregon's first civic body started as a kind of impromptu town meeting and, like everything else about the settlers' lives, it took a rough-and-ready shape that reflected the needs of the moment.

The meeting evolved out of a funeral held at the Methodist headquarters in Salem in 1841. An early settler, Ewing Young, had died leaving a considerable amount of property but no known heirs. As the pioneers tried to figure out what to do with the property, which included a large tract of land as well as livestock, the discussion moved to broader issues. At the urging of the missionaries, who were determined to protect American interests in the valley, a resolution was passed calling for "drafting a constitution and code of laws for the government of the settlements south of the Columbia River." (North of the river the British-owned Hudson's Bay Company held de facto jurisdiction.) Jason Lee was elected president and Gustavus Hines secretary of the project.

The following day the meeting continued, its membership swelled by a contingent of French-Canadian fur trappers, retired employees of the Hudson's Bay Company who had settled at French Prairie. With them came a group of Catholic priests from a mission in the French settlement. A batch of new titles was handed around and everyone agreed to draw up a constitution at some unspecified time in the future.

For the next two years, the settlers went about their business. Then, early in 1843, they assembled again, this time to organize a vendetta against wolves, bears and mountain lions, which were menacing their livestock. The Wolf Meetings, as they were called, led to a gathering in May near Willamette Falls at Champoeg, a shipping point for wheat grown in the valley. Again the American settlers raised the issue of founding a government. The French settlers, with their past allegiance to the Hudson's Bay Company, held back. Two factions emerged, pro government and con. After much argument, Joe Meek, a burly, black-haired mountain man with a reputation for wrestling grizzly bears, called for a vote. According to one witness, Meek drew a line in the dirt with a stick and shouted, "All in favor of an organization, follow me!" Of the 102 men present, 52 crossed the line and thereby established — with a

Two pioneer lads stand outside their sturdy wilderness home, complete with windows, a roof of cedar shingles and a massive stone fireplace. The sticks used to make the chimney were held together with clay.

In praise of the pioneer woman, an Eastern magazine illustrated just a few of her many chores. Her complaints about her lot were rare and terse. "Churned & baked, washed & ironed," one wrote, adding "Very tired."

PLOWING

PLANTING CORN

majority of one vote—Oregon's first formal government.

The settlers proceeded to draw up a bill of rights, a constitution and some rough-hewn laws. Among the key provisions were freedom of religion, the right to trial by jury and a ban on slaveholding, public buildings and taxes. Eventually taxes had to be levied, but since money was scarce, payment in wheat was sufficient.

Of supreme importance to every settler, rules were drawn up for claiming land. Most early pioneers, on arriving in Oregon, had simply cleared a likely spot in the wilderness and started farming. No boundaries were laid out, no deed was filed, no limitations were placed on the amount of land a man could claim. Now, to legitimize their holdings, the pioneers enacted their own extremely generous land law. Each man was allotted a square mile—640 acres—provided he staked out his land, filed a claim and built a cabin within six months.

At the Champoeg meetings and subsequent gatherings, the owner of the missionary store at Oregon City, George Abernethy, was elected the first Provisional Governor. Jesse Applegate, after his arrival with the 1843 cow column, became a member of the legislature, as did Peter Burnett. Later, Burnett took a seat on the supreme court.

One problem the new government seemed unable to solve was trouble with Indians. At first a genuine friend-

liness had prevailed between most settlers and their Indian neighbors. An Indian would appear at a cabin door to offer pelts and salmon in exchange for tobacco and gunpowder. Indian children gradually began to attend mission schools. Young Jesse Applegate and his brother Elisha learned to carry on conversations in Chinook dialect with Indian playmates.

But as more and more pioneers moved into Oregon, pushing back the wilderness and laying claim to the land, frictions and animosities inevitably arose. The peace grew fragile and uneasy, and settlers in the back country, cut off from the protection of other whites, became increasingly edgy. A Mrs. Comstock living in the Umpqua valley was considerably shaken one noontime in the 1850s when she looked up to see an Indian staring fixedly at her through the open door of her cabin. She was alone with her infant daughter, Mary Lettie. Thinking fast, she moved the dining table near the door and set it for four places. Then, "without paying the least attention to the sullen fellow outside, I walked to the front door and yelled 'Dinner!' " The Indian, she said, loped off "faster than any horse I ever saw."

Simple curiosity may have brought the Indian to Mrs. Comstock's door, and most Indian scares that occurred west of the Cascades ended just as uneventfully. But in the remote, scattered settlements east of the Cas-

cades a sudden orgy of bloodshed had erupted several years earlier. In the 1840s there were only three isolated American enclaves in the desolate plateaus of this area. All three had been established by the American Board of Commissioners for Foreign Missions for the express purpose of bringing the ways of God and civilization to the Indians. One of the settlements, located near what is today the southeast corner of the state of Washington, was supervised by the energetic Dr. Marcus Whitman and his wife Narcissa.

After his trailblazing wagon trip to Oregon in 1836, Whitman had picked a mission site among the Cayuse Indians, on the north bank of the Walla Walla River 22 miles upstream from its junction with the Columbia. Compared with the lush valleys west of the Cascades the country was bleak — sage flats, scattered cottonwood groves and grass prairies. The Cayuse called it Waiilatpu, "The People of the Place of the Rye Grass." Marcus built a crude log lean-to containing a kitchen with a fireplace, two small bedrooms and a pantry. Then he and Narcissa settled in for the winter. On March 14, 1837, Narcissa gave birth to a daughter, Alice Clarissa.

The Whitmans' trail companions, Henry and Eliza Spalding, built their mission 110 miles to the east at Lapwai, in country just as unpromising, and proceeded to spread God's word among the intelligent and receptive Nez Percé Indians. Two years later, in 1839, the missionary board in Boston sent another group of evangelists to establish a third mission, among the Spokane Indians far to the north of Waiilatpu.

The main outpost, however, was always the Whitmans' mission at Waiilatpu, closest of the three to the main Oregon Trail. By the time other emigrants started trekking past on their way to the Willamette valley, Marcus had constructed a larger mission house, one and a half stories high, out of sun-dried adobe brick; he had set up a gristmill and blacksmith shop, and built a number of outbuildings. A school had been started for Indian children. The mission seemed to be thriving.

But the whole missionary enterprise had a major flaw — its continuing failure to Christianize the Indians. The Cayuse had seemed eager at first to learn about the white man's God; but the lessons never seemed to stick. "Some feel almost to blame us for telling them about eternal realities," Narcissa noted in her diary. "One said it was good when they knew nothing but to hunt, eat, drink and sleep; now it was bad." For one thing, the missionaries kept urging the Indians to glorify God by becoming farmers and homemakers — a dreary prospect to the Cayuse, fiercely independent tribesmen who hunted and fished when they had to, and in between these exertions did little but smoke their pipes.

The Cayuse may also have detected a certain hypocrisy in the white man's ethics. Joel Palmer, who passed through the area in 1845, was flabbergasted when a Cayuse chief, Tiloukaikt, appeared at his campfire one night and chided him for playing cards. "No good, no good!" said Tiloukaikt, who had learned rules of proper behavior at the Whitman mission. Palmer, chastened, inwardly resolved to quit cards forever.

Another barrier to understanding arose from the fact that some missionaries tried to teach the intricacies of Christianity without bothering to learn the Indian language. Mary Walker, who had traveled more than 3,500 miles from her home in Baldwin, Maine, to the Spokane mission, admitted candidly: "Instead of engaging with interest in learning the language, I am more ready to engage in almost anything else, & as I do not like others to excell so I feel a wicked satisfaction in seeing them as little interested as myself."

Mary Walker found plenty of other things to engage in, including the basic struggle to survive. The stringencies of pioneering taxed the missionaries' strength and considerably eroded their evangelical zeal. In 1840, Mary's husband, Elkanah, tried to explain the situation in a letter to the missionary board. He wrote that they were so hard pressed by their day-to-day duties—digging wells, herding livestock, gardening, making shoes, butchering meat, dipping candles, making soap, baking bread, washing clothes, sewing, milking cows and rearing children—that they often lost sight of what they had come West for in the first place. "Am up again till 12 ironing, cooking &c.," Mary noted in her diary on November 26, 1840. She had an even greater vexation one rainy March day when the roof and chimney of the Walkers' cabin collapsed.

Mary acknowledged some good times, though. In the cabin one day in 1843 she and Elkanah put on a splendid wedding for a certain Mr. McPherson and Miss Charlotte. The newlyweds were toasted "with cake and cold water" by their teetotaling hosts. The wedding party might have had music, too, but for an earlier calamity. Before leaving the East Coast, a fellow evangelist at the Walker mission had sent his bass viol to Oregon by ship. The instrument arrived at Fort Vancouver in good condition, though not until two years after the missionary himself reached Oregon. But dur-

This sketch of the Waiilatpu mission, scene of the Whitman massacre, was drawn by a child survivor. It shows (1) the adobe mission house, (2) the blacksmith shop, (3) emigrants' quarters, (4) gristmill, (5) stream and (6) orchard. The mission's Indian workers lived in the tipis at right.

A drawing of the assault on Marcus Whitman, more dramatic than correct, shows the victim calmly reading while his wife Narcissa tries to stay the arm of his Indian attacker. Actually, Narcissa was not present.

ing a rest stop, as the viol was being carted overland to the Spokane mission, an Indian helper tethered his horse to the crate that contained it. The horse took alarm at some disturbance and went crashing off, crate in tow. The bass viol was never heard from again.

At the Place of the Rye Grass, as more and more emigrant trains rolled past along the nearby Oregon Trail, Marcus Whitman gradually turned his energies away from converting Indians and toward helping the newcomers. His mission became an important stop where exhausted travelers could find food and clothing, lodging in one of the missionary buildings, and medical care from the doctor himself. The Indian school was expanded to take in emigrant children. Narcissa's own daughter, at the age of two, had fallen into the Walla Walla River and drowned; heartbroken, Narcissa now started adopting orphans whose parents had died on the trail and any other waifs who needed mothering. The mountain man Joe Meek left his half-breed daughter with Narcissa. So did his comrade, Jim Bridger.

The Cayuse Indians viewed the influx into the mission with alarm. They began to suspect that the white men had come not simply to preach to them, but to take permanent control of their ancestral hunting grounds. Adding fire to the Indians' resentment, the pioneers brought a new and terrible scourge — the measles. White children seemed to survive the disease without much difficulty, but the Indians — adults as well as children — lacked natural immunity and died with dreadful predictability.

A measles epidemic struck the Place of the Rye Grass in the autumn of 1847. At the time 74 people were living there, most of them in transit on their way farther west. They crowded the buildings almost beyond capacity: 23 people in the mission house, eight in the blacksmith shop, 29 in a house built for the transients and 12 in a cabin at the sawmill, half a day's journey away. Two half-breeds lived in lodges on the mission grounds.

The measles spread quickly to the nearby Cayuse villages and took a horrendous toll. Four or five children died each day at the height of the epidemic, and by the middle of November more than half of the tribe of 350 Cayuse had perished. Marcus Whitman tried desper-

Whitman's Cayuse killers, Tomahas and Tiloukaikt, posed for artist Paul Kane before the 1847 massacre. Of Tomahas, Kane wrote: "His appearance was savage and by no means belied his character."

Tomahas

Tiloukaikt

ately to relieve the suffering, but his efforts were in vain.

According to the custom of the Cayuse tribe, any medicine man who failed to balk death might be required to pay with his own life; by tribal rumor, Dr. Whitman was not only a powerless medicine man but one who was causing sickness on purpose, poisoning the Indian children even as he pretended to treat them. He had to be stopped.

The night of November 28 was sleety and cold. Whitman rode 25 miles through the miserable weather, visiting Indian encampments and treating the measles sufferers. Then the doctor returned to his own household, where 11 of the 42 mission children were ill. He stayed up the rest of the night, attending them. The dawn of November 29, a Monday, brought a low fog and drizzling rain. Whitman fried a steak for his breakfast.

Other men at the mission set out for various tasks: three to the butcher's shed to dress a carcass of beef, one to conduct class at the children's school, one to run the gristmill in the mission yard, one to sew a suit of clothes for Whitman. Whitman himself spent the morning performing various chores and reading.

At noon an Indian appeared at the kitchen door with the disturbing news that three more measles deaths had occurred—one of them thought to be a child of Chief Tiloukaikt—the same man who had admonished Joel Palmer for card-playing. Two of the chief's other children had already succumbed to the disease. Whitman picked up his King James Bible and hurried through the gloom to the mission burial ground.

Later that afternoon, when he had returned home and eaten a delayed lunch with Narcissa, the grieving Tiloukaikt himself arrived at the mission with several other Indians, one of them named Tomahas, and asked

to speak to the doctor. Whitman met the men in the kitchen. While Tiloukaikt engaged him in conversation, Tomahas stepped behind the doctor and brought a bronze tomahawk thudding down on his skull. Tiloukaikt hacked and slashed at his face. Then another Indian pressed a rifle against Whitman's neck and fired. Jim Bridger's daughter, Mary Ann, whom the Whitmans had adopted, was also in the kitchen. She ran from the room, crying "They're killing Father!" But Whitman was still breathing when Narcissa rushed in a moment later.

Indians elsewhere on the grounds were murdering the miller, the teacher, the tailor and the three butchers. People were fleeing in all directions, some to the main house where they barricaded themselves in the upstairs bedroom, some to other hiding places, some off into the fog of darkening afternoon. Even as Narcissa watched her husband lapse into unconsciousness, a bullet fired into the house through a window struck her in the breast. Badly wounded, she staggered upstairs to the attic bedroom and began to pray for the children and Indians. Presently, more Indians broke into the house and ordered the people huddling in the bedroom to come downstairs. An old Indian friend of the Whitmans then appeared, telling them that the house was about to be burned down and offering to help them get away. Faint from loss of blood, Narcissa allowed herself to be carried outside on a settee. Suddenly a fusillade of bullets struck her body, and she was shoved off into the cold mud. The Indian friend had led the whites into an ambush, and another Indian, who once had attended mission church services, dragged Narcissa's corpse upright and whipped the lifeless face with a riding crop.

Throughout that night and the next few days the Cayuse warriors picked off the white survivors until

A mere hamlet in the 1830s, Oregon City in 1857 reflects its growth as a hub of pioneer commerce. Dozens of artisans and shopkeepers plied their trades on Main Street, the rutted thoroughfare running along the east bank of the Willamette River and past the steepled Methodist Church.

On farmland wrested from wilderness only a few decades earlier, 32 horses draw a thresher through a sea of wheat — affirming an old settler's dictum that Oregon was "one of the most fertile spots of earth."

the death toll numbered 11 men, one woman and two children. Three other sick children, bereft of attention, died of the measles. A Cayuse brave sexually assaulted several of the surviving women and older girls. About a month later officials at a Hudson's Bay Company outpost 20 miles away on the Columbia River were able to ransom the 47 remaining captives. When they and all other missionaries in eastern Oregon had been escorted down the Columbia to safety, the Cayuse first set fire to the buildings at the Place of the Rye Grass, then, to avoid reprisals, left their tribal land — and children's graves — and dispersed into the mountains.

The news of the Whitman massacre reached the settlers in the Willamette valley with thunderous impact. The Provisional Governor, George Abernethy, called for volunteers to punish the Cayuse. Five hundred pioneers showed up, rifles in hand. A party of emissaries set out for Washington, D.C., to seek federal help. At its head rode Joe Meek.

Meek had powerful friends in Washington. For all his crude frontier ways and blustering manner, the 37-year-old retired fur trapper belonged to a patrician Virginia family; his cousin, Sarah Childress, was married to the President of the United States, James Polk. Meek arrived in Washington on May 28, 1848, ragged, bewhiskered, still wearing his trail-stained buckskins. Without bothering to change, he strode up the White House steps and demanded to see his cousin-in-law, the President. Proclaiming himself Envoy Extraordinary and Minister Plenipotentiary from the Republic of Oregon to the Court of the United States, he told Polk the story of the massacre. He then presented a request from the settlers that Oregon be made a U.S. territory, a status that would entitle it to U.S. protection. The next day Polk referred the request to Congress.

Congress debated, considered, weighed issues and generally shuffled its feet. By now the U.S. had legal title to the vast Oregon country, secured two years earlier in a treaty with Great Britain terminating the prior agreement of joint occupancy *(page 51)*. The acquisition of such an immense region understandably posed political and administrative problems that would require time to solve. But on August 14 — less than nine months after the Whitman massacre — a law was enacted establishing Oregon as a U.S. territory. Joe Meek, appointed U.S. marshal, headed back west to his post

An 1866 *Harper's Weekly* cartoon pokes fun at Asa Mercer and his shipload of marriageable New England women recruited for the Northwest. Another journal twitted the project as a Mercer-nary Adventure.

IS WASHINGTON TERRITORY IN DANGER?
THE MODERN ARK, THE MODERN NOAH, AND THE MODERN "WATERFALLS" THAT ARE ABOUT TO DESCEND UPON WASHINGTON TERRITORY.

THE MODERN NOAH (*loq.*). "There, my dear young ladies, I think I see something."
CHORUS OF 400 UNMARRIED WOMEN. "Oh! please, Sir, is it a Man?"
THE MODERN NOAH. "No, bless ye! not a Man: it's a Gull."
MARY ANN (*aside.*) "Oh, dear! I wonder when we'll see **a Man!**"

with the new territorial governor, a Mexican War general named Joseph Lane.

In the interim the pioneer militia of about 500 men had pursued the remnants of the Cayuse into the mountains. The hunt was to last for two years, off and on. Then, to buy peace for the tribe, five Cayuse warriors—including Tiloukaikt and Tomahas—gave themselves up. All five were summarily tried and hung. Before the executions Tiloukaikt was reportedly asked why he had surrendered. He gave this reason: "Did not your missionaries teach us that Christ died to save his people? So we die to save our people."

With the Indian problem temporarily brought under control, and with proud new status as a territory, Oregon began to acquire a gloss of civilization. Little more than a decade after the first settlers had arrived, the hamlets along the Willamette River were growing into bustling towns with well-stocked general stores, tanneries, blacksmith and silversmith and tailor shops, hotels and white-steepled churches. Portland, which had been a tract of virtually untouched forest in 1844, within six years boasted 821 residents, making it the region's most up-and-coming community.

The log cabins of the early settlers were giving way to neat frame houses with glass windows, painted woodwork and papered walls. Oregonians exchanged their moss-filled mattresses and buffalo robes for feather beds, and they bought dressers and easy chairs from local cabinetmakers. A small steam-powered riverboat puffed up and down the Willamette, hauling goods and people. Mail arrived regularly by ship around Cape Horn and was distributed to the territory's 40 post offices. Franklin's Book Store on Front Street in Portland guaranteed delivery of a score of local newspapers, as well as the *New York Tribune, Harper's Monthly,* the *Saturday Evening Post* from Philadelphia and even the *Dispatch* from Keokuk, Iowa. The settlers gobbled up reading matter with ravenous delight. (Books and newspapers had been so scarce in the early days that one old pioneer boasted he had studied the family Bible until the pages wore thin; another confessed to reading Webster's dictionary from cover to cover, though he complained that the subject matter changed too abruptly.)

In 1850 settlers in Oregon numbered more than 13,000, which—compared with the population of 200 a decade earlier—must have seemed like rank over-

crowding. Some 7,000 more people arrived overland in 1851, the *Oregon Spectator* estimated, and 11,000 more a year later.

This inundation would have been totally welcome except that an overwhelming percentage of it was male. Like most frontier regions, Oregon was desperately short of women. Bachelors, faced with the dismal prospect of a life alone in the backwoods, went to considerable lengths to avoid such an outcome. Sometimes the solution was to marry an Indian girl, paying a dowry of blankets to her father. According to a visitor from Boston, Theodore Winthrop, the going rate in blankets per bride was: "five, a cheap and unclean article, a drudge; ten, a tolerable article, a cook and basket-maker; twenty, a fine article of squaw, learned in kamas-beds; fifty, a very superior article, ruddy with vermilion and skilled in embroidering buckskin with porcupine quills."

Women of almost any age were deemed acceptable as mates. "Soon after my arrival in Oregon in 1851,"

Pupils at an Oregon school in the 1860s interrupt their lessons to have a picture taken with their teacher and a male visitor. At this time fewer than half the Northwest's youngsters received any formal schooling.

recalled one settler, "I formed the acquaintance of an interesting girl of apparently eight or nine years, whom I caressed and petted as a child. I enquired, 'Have you left home to attend school?'

" 'La, no!' was her reply. 'I'm married.'

"Amazed, I let her down from my knee, saying, 'I thought you were a child.' Before that child was eighteen, she had been several times married and divorced."

After Oregon achieved territorial status and was subject to U.S. laws, females became more precious than ever. In 1850 Congress passed the Donation Land Act, which cut the permissible size of a land claim from 640 free acres per man to 320 acres. But the new law also allowed a pioneer to claim another 320 acres for his wife, if he had one, thus bringing his potential landholdings up to the pre-act level.

The demand for brides, which was already high, promptly skyrocketed. Fails Howard, for example, a cheeky bachelor who lived in the Willamette valley, was not about to let a good claim slip through his fingers. Hearing of a certain Greenstreet family with several daughters, he went to their place, introduced himself and inquired of the first daughter he encountered—Marilda—if she would marry him and help him claim 640 acres. Marilda, a romantic soul, rejected his passionless courtship out of hand. Undaunted, Howard then turned his attention to Marilda's sister Parmelia, who was considerably more businesslike. Howard had hardly finished restating his proposition to her when Parmelia said, "Sure, I'll marry you; a farm like that looks good to me and so do you."

Nowhere was the dearth of females so oppressive as in the area north of the Columbia River, which in 1853 split away from Oregon to become the separate U.S. territory of Washington. Here the male population outnumbered the female by a dreary ratio of nine to one, giving rise to a popular saying that in Washington "men are wondrous cheap and women are so dear." By the late 1850s the situation had improved so little that bachelors called open meetings to publicize their plight. In 1858 the *Puget Sound Herald* issued an open letter to single women in the East, holding forth on the deep matrimonial hunger of Washington males: "Many who are wretched for want of comfortable homes would lose no time in allying themselves with the fair daughters of Eve if they would but deign to favor us with their presence." This poignant appeal produced no visible result.

At this juncture a 22-year-old bachelor named Asa Mercer arrived in Seattle, fresh from college in Ohio. Brainy, well-mannered and supremely self-confident, Mercer spent his first few years building and serving as the first president of tiny Territorial University — later renamed the University of Washington. Then he turned his enterprising talents to solving the female question.

Mercer perceived that the imbalance of men and women was a problem afflicting both edges of the continent. For while Washington Territory had far too many men, there was an estimated surplus of at least 30,000 unattached women in the Northeastern United States, many of them Civil War widows. The solution, Mercer decided, was to rearrange the population somewhat, and bring the Eastern women west. So in 1864 he set sail for Massachusetts to test his theory by means of a discreet dry run.

To avoid ruffling prim Eastern sensibilities, which might have been offended at the idea of a wholesale export trade in marriageable women, Mercer couched his proposal in terms of a recruiting drive for teachers. "*School teachers* and *music teachers* are in short supply in the new Washington Territory," he assured lecture audiences in New England, and if the ladies present wished to do something for their country as well as for themselves, they should sign up. Eleven young ladies felt so inclined, and allowed Mercer to shepherd them to Seattle that spring. All but one or two were soon teaching — and happily married.

Statesmanship of that order deserved recognition, the delighted Washingtonians felt, and they quickly elected Mercer to the territorial legislature. Brandishing a letter of reference from the Territorial Governor, Mercer in 1865 set out on another female-foraging expedition. This time he was bluntly explicit. What Washington needed was wives, he said, as many as it could get. In due course several hundred young ladies enrolled in the cause. For the benefit of any purse-lipped critics, Mercer noted that the enlistees were "selected with great care, for intelligence, modesty and virtue."

Despite all such assertions, Mercer's matchmaking schemes struck some Easterners as dangerously unorthodox. The *New York Herald* printed a defamatory column, "a long, scurrilous article," Mercer labeled it, "slandering me, stating that all of the men on Puget Sound were rotten and profligate; that the girls would all be turned into houses of ill-fame. The old saying that a lie will travel a thousand miles while truth is putting on its boots was true." Many of Mercer's recruits read the article and had second thoughts. By sailing time, scarcely 100 ladies showed up to board the steamer S.S. *Continental* for the trip west.

During the voyage, Mercer tried his utmost to enforce propriety, but with little success. To guarantee the virtue of his wards, he banned any contact between them and the ship's crew — an injunction frequently violated by both sides. When he decreed a 10 p.m. curfew, the ladies paid not the slightest attention, but promenaded past him on the deck chanting, "Go to bed! Go to bed!" And when Mercer, though mercilessly taunted by his charges, proceeded to fall in love with one of them, she coldly rejected his suit, loudly calling the 25-year-old swain "Old Pap" in the presence of her tittering companions.

But when the S.S. *Continental* finally reached Seattle, Mercer's project became an instant success. To witness the arrival of "Mercer's belles," nearly all of the town's 300 inhabitants turned out on the dock. "Conspicuous were the young gallants of the town," a certain Ida May Barlow of New York delightedly observed. "One of the young men stepped forward and assisted me to land."

Only a single small detail marred the otherwise universal jubilation. One of Mercer's belles, older than the rest, had lost her dentures overboard in a bout of seasickness, and had to greet her prospective suitors minus teeth. Everyone else seemed blissfully happy. Most of the belles found husbands in short order. Mercer, rebounding nicely after his earlier rebuff, married another young woman from among the passengers aboard the S.S. *Continental,* Annie Stephens of Baltimore.

Ida May Barlow married the man who helped her off the boat, Albert Pinkham from Seattle. The wedding was held on August 14, 1866, at Seattle's Occidental Hotel, with most of the young people in town as guests. She and Albert built a home beside Lake Union near Seattle and raised 11 children. Most of Ida May's shipmates also settled down to domestic bliss, and within a few years a new generation of Americans would come to know the Pacific Northwest as their native land.

A club devoted to collecting eyewitness accounts of Oregon's settlement summons members to a get-together. The Latin motto below the poster's eagle translates roughly as "One flies with one's own wings."

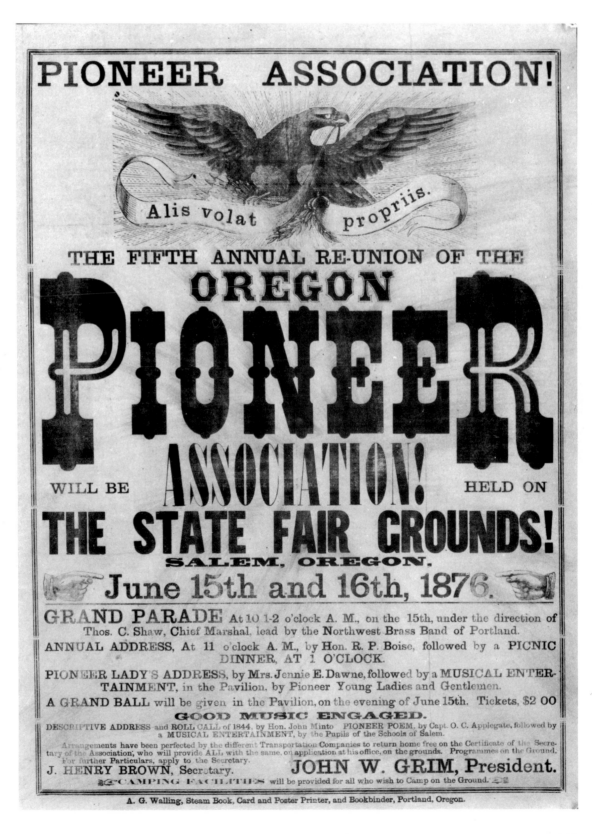

PIONEER ASSOCIATION!

Alis volat propriis.

THE FIFTH ANNUAL RE-UNION OF THE
OREGON
PIONEER
ASSOCIATION!

WILL BE   HELD ON

THE STATE FAIR GROUNDS!
SALEM, OREGON.
June 15th and 16th, 1876.

GRAND PARADE At 10 1-2 o'clock A. M., on the 15th, under the direction of Thos. C. Shaw, Chief Marshal, lead by the Northwest Brass Band of Portland.

ANNUAL ADDRESS, At 11 o'clock A. M., by Hon. R. P. Boise, followed by a **PICNIC DINNER, AT 1 O'CLOCK.**

PIONEER LADY'S ADDRESS, by Mrs. Jennie E. Dawne, followed by a **MUSICAL ENTERTAINMENT,** in the Pavilion, by Pioneer Young Ladies and Gentlemen.

A **GRAND BALL** will be given in the Pavilion, on the evening of June 15th. Tickets, $2 00

GOOD MUSIC ENGAGED.

DESCRIPTIVE ADDRESS and ROLL CALL of 1844, by Hon. John Minto PIONEER POEM, by Capt. O. C. Applegate, followed by a MUSICAL ENTERTAINMENT, by the Pupils of the Schools of Salem.

Arrangements have been perfected by the different Transportation Companies to return home free on the Certificate of the Secretary of the Association, who will provide ALL with the same, on application at his office, on the grounds. Programmes on the Ground. For further Particulars, apply to the Secretary.

J. HENRY BROWN, Secretary.   JOHN W. GRIM, President.

CAMPING FACILITIES will be provided for all who wish to Camp on the Ground.

A. G. Walling, Steam Book, Card and Poster Printer, and Bookbinder, Portland, Oregon.

5 | The odyssey of the Saints

Of all the motive forces that drove families to seek a better life in the West, none was stronger than the urge to be free of religious persecution. And no group of pioneers suffered more — and in the end won more — than the adherents of the Church of Jesus Christ of Latter-day Saints: the Mormons.

The sect was founded in 1830 by Joseph Smith, a farm-bred Yankee who claimed direct contact with the Almighty, and it rapidly attracted followers. But it also drew the hostility of nonbelievers to whom the Mormons' theocratic government, communal economics and practice of plural marriage seemed threats to American values.

The Mormons' hegira began as early as 1832 when mobs tormented them in a community they had established in Ohio. The next year, violence flared around Independence, Missouri, where some 1,200 Saints had moved with the peaceful aim of transforming the frontier settlement into their own religious capital. Forced to flee after a series of attacks by Missourians *(right)*, the Saints sought refuge in Illinois, where they built the model city of Nauvoo, a stronghold that boasted its own Mormon army. But the very success of Nauvoo aroused a wrathful countryside once more. After Joseph Smith was jailed on a flimsy pretext and then murdered by militiamen in 1844, the Saints resolved to move on westward into the unknown. Three years later, they reached their ultimate sanctuary in the Salt Lake Valley.

A decade afterwards, Carl Christensen, a Danish painter and Mormon convert, traveled the same trail taken by those first pioneers. To instruct subsequent generations of Saints in their heritage, he dramatized the early Mormon trials and triumphs in a remarkable series of canvases, five of which follow.

A Missouri rabble sacks a settlement of Mormons near Independence in 1833, putting a brutal

end to the hope of the Saints' prophet, Joseph Smith, that the site would someday become "the chief city in the Western Hemisphere."

149

Outside the thriving city of Nauvoo on the Mississippi, Joseph Smith and his church elders review the private Mormon army. In 1844, the

Illinois Governor ordered the disarming of the legion — then 4,000 men strong — and a few months later the charter of Nauvoo was revoked.

An assassin recoils as a shaft of unearthly light falls on the body of Joseph Smith. The murder of the Mormons' leader took place on the afternoon

of June 27, 1844, after a mob stormed the jail in Carthage, Illinois, where he and his brother Hyrum were being held on a charge of treason.

153

In the spring of 1847, wagons prepare to roll out of Winter Quarters, the Mormons' staging area on the Missouri River, for the long journey

west. Some 600 of the 3,500 migrants at the encampment succumbed to cholera and other diseases; they were buried on the hill above the site.

En route to their western Zion, members of a Mormon wagon train break camp as a vanguard crosses the Platte River in Nebraska. The new

leader of the Saints, Brigham Young, answered their queries about their final destination by saying only that he would know it when he saw it.

Laying claim to an unlikely paradise

ost emigrants, bound for green pastures of California 750 miles farther west, hurried through the Salt Lake Valley as fast as they could. But the party of pioneers who reached that silent, sunscorched expanse on the morning of July 23, 1847, were there to stay. By 11:30, scarcely two hours after choosing a campsite, the first Mormons to set foot in Utah had hefted three plows and a harrow from their wagons, hitched up trail-weary oxen and begun to chisel furrows in the earth.

But this attempt at instant agriculture was to no avail. The soil of the valley, cupped high on the western slope of the Rockies, was baked so hard that it broke the iron-tipped plows. So while the men searched for shade in which to repair their equipment—"I don't remember a tree that could be called a tree," a member of the pioneer band said later—their brethren cut willow brush and moved rocks to dam a creek fed from the snowy heights of the mountains they had just descended.

As the meltwater backed up and flooded out onto the valley floor, the soil, steaming in the 96° heat, relented. By noon the next day, a Saturday, the men had plowed five acres and planted potatoes, corn, turnips, beans and buckwheat. Just as they were finishing, a sprinkling of summer rain settled the seeds and cooled the backs of the newcomers—143 men, three women, two boys, 66 oxen, 93 horses, 52 mules, 19 cows, 17 dogs and an unrecorded number of chickens. Most of the people lifted dirt-streaked faces toward the clouds to offer thanks to God for blessing their labor.

Pious, industrious, puritanical—and sometimes polygamous—the Mormons, members of the Church of Jesus Christ of Latter-day Saints, had one supreme desire. When their wagons clattered down the Wasatch mountains into the blistering barrens of the Salt Lake Valley, what they wanted was to be left alone. Already, in the brief 17-year history of their church, they had known persecution and martyrdom. Perhaps here they might find at last the isolation in which to realize their dream: to erect the kingdom of God on earth.

Since their prophet and first leader, Joseph Smith, had founded the sect in 1830, that dream had been frustrated three times. In Ohio, Missouri and Illinois, mob fury had routed the Saints from their homes and farms. But far from discouraging them, their torment had bound them into a union so strong that their emigration to the West would be the best executed in American history; so strong that they could dare to plant the forbidding valley; so strong that a decade later they could jut out righteous jaws and challenge a U.S. President and his Army to a showdown.

But during those first days in Utah in July of 1847, the Mormons' struggle was simply to stay alive. The fate of the entire church hung on their efforts. Following in the wheel ruts of the advance party, 1,800 more of the faithful plodded in bands of 10, 50 or 100 people each. In addition to those already on the way, some 13,000 well-disciplined Mormon refugees huddled in a series of encampments on the Iowa and Nebraska prairies, waiting patiently for the word from the west that would signal their time to get moving.

In Utah, members of the advance guard, too, needed patience. Having plowed and seeded, they now awaited the results of their labors. Often the outcome seemed in doubt as they looked beyond their plantings to a sea of knee-high sagebrush, where the sole signs of activity were a host of thumb-thick crickets gnawing on wilting yellow wild flowers. One determined optimist could only express his "happy disappointment" with the place,

---

Brigham Young, photographed in 1853, held absolute power as president of the Church of Latter-day Saints and governor of the recently organized Utah Territory.

In a portrait made two years before his murder in 1844, Joseph Smith exudes assurance. Founder of the Mormon Church, he was designated "a Seer, a Translator, a Prophet, and Apostle of Jesus Christ."

and a woman became immediately "heart sick" when she beheld her new homeland. "Weak and weary as I am," she confided to her diary, "I would rather go a thousand miles farther than remain in such a desolate and foresaken place as this." When the Mormons explored the valley that extended 20 miles east and west and twice that distance north and south—sizzling here in beds of sand and salt, reeking there in fetid flats of mud, bubbling elsewhere in hot springs of sulfur—the prospect for survival seemed grim.

However, Brigham Young—Joseph Smith's successor as head of the church—never doubted the suitability of the site. According to tradition, while Young was still in the mountains overlooking the region, he experienced a vision of the future city of God. "This is the right place!" he declared confidently.

The dynamic, 46-year-old Yankee was also a thoroughgoing pragmatist. *New York Tribune* editor Horace Greeley would one day describe him as "frank, good-natured, a rather thick-set man, seeming to enjoy life and in no particular hurry to get to heaven." Young had not led his flock into the valley on faith alone. Back in Illinois, he and other Mormon elders had carefully studied an 1845 report on the area by the Army explorer John Charles Frémont. They were particularly impressed by his conclusion that the Salt Lake Valley, harsh though it was, had "valuable, nutritious grass" and might be adapted to "civilized settlement."

And, indeed, within a week after the vanguard's arrival, the wilderness did begin to quicken. Seedlings soon stood two inches tall above the irrigated soil, and the Saints allowed themselves to hope that this was truly their promised land. "We have been thrown like a stone from a sling," the epigrammatic Young was moved to say, "and we have lodged in this goodly place just where the Lord wants his people to gather."

But as the Mormons had learned from their first day's effort, the Salt Lake Valley was a goodly place only to the degree that it could be nourished with water. Young and his companions were keenly interested,

therefore, in its potential for irrigation. More than enough water, they knew, existed to the east and south in the Wasatch mountains. There 11,000-foot peaks methodically raked moisture from the winds blowing in from the Pacific and sent it gushing down through scores of canyon creeks to the parched plains. But as matters stood when the Saints arrived, the creek waters either petered out soon after leaving the hills or made their way weakly to a shallow river draining the eastern side of the valley. The river, flowing northward from a large freshwater lake (Utah Lake), dissipated through a briny marsh into the Great Salt Lake. The Biblically oriented Saints were quick to recognize the similarity to Palestine's water system, in which the fresh waters of the Sea of Galilee make their way down the Jordan River to the salty Dead Sea. They named their river the Jordan of the West.

The Great Salt Lake—a shrunken remnant of a prehistoric body of water that once rose halfway up the surrounding mountainsides—lay about 20 miles northwest of the Saints' first campsite. When a 16-man exploring party reached the lake shore, the powerfully built Brigham Young was the first to plunge into the water. The whole company thereupon "had a fine bathing frolic." "The water," one of them later wrote, "was warm and very clear and so salt those who could not swim at all floated upon the surface like a cork and found it out of their power to sink." (In a few days some of their number would return with kettles to boil off the water. Four barrels of lake water, they found, produced one barrel of table salt.)

Previous forays had taken the explorers into sterile deserts and timbered mountain canyons. Just four days after the Mormons' arrival in Utah, Brigham Young sat down with his advisers to assess their findings. The Great Basin, the immense depression in which the Salt Lake Valley lay, was 95 per cent desert and mountains. And the valley itself, Young noted accurately, contained very little game (even the Ute Indians came there only to harvest crickets for food). But the first

crude attempts at irrigation had shown that the valley was fertile. Most crucial of all, it was "coveted by no other people." The vote was to stay. Young had known all along, he said, that "If the Lord should say by his revelation this is the spot, the Saints would be satisfied if it was on a barren rock."

Early in the evening after the vote, Young led his advisers on a walking tour of the area close by the tents and wagons of the vanguard camp. At a spot midway between the north and south forks of the creek the Saints had dammed up, he struck the ground at his feet with his cane, Moses fashion, and said: "Here will be the temple to our God." The Temple Square *(pages 184-187)* would occupy 40 acres—a figure Young reduced to 10 a few days later. The rest of the city would stretch away in all directions, covering an area two miles square.

Young's idea of the city plan was no less specific. The settlement would be divided into 135 blocks of 10 acres each, and each block would be divided into eight lots, one and one quarter acres each. The streets would run north-south and east-west, and they would be splendidly wide—eight rods, or 132 feet. The sidewalks themselves would be 20 feet wide. All houses would be set back 20 feet from the sidewalk, and everyone's front yard would be adorned with fruit trees and other beautiful greenery. Canals would provide water for the vegetation and the household needs of every family. The farmlands would lie outside the town limits —a plan borrowed from New England, where both Joseph Smith and Young had been born.

Young also specified how lots outside the city were to be distributed. Closest to the city would be five-acre parcels for mechanics and artisans. At the outer edges of the area would be 40- and 80-acre parcels for farmers. Young felt that his plan would make the most productive use of the land, but he also foresaw a problem and simultaneously its solution: in order to "prevent any hardness that might occur by any method of dividing the land, it shall be done by ballot, or casting lots, as Israel did in days of old."

From the advisers who surrounded him in respectful silence that night, Young appointed a committee of 12 to begin laying out the City of the Great Salt Lake. They could, the president allowed, wait until the morrow to start. There being no questions, the men retired.

A measure of Young's extraordinary power to lead was that he could with equal fervor launch grand schemes and deal with the minutiae of day-to-day existence. In later years, when Salt Lake City had become a major Western metropolis and the hub of the Mormon nation-within-a-nation, he continued to set aside one hour each day to listen to the cares of individual Saints, advising a farmer on the most propitious time to breed a prize cow or asking by name after the health of a woman's eighth child.

Having chosen the Temple site and delineated the future city, the Mormon president turned his attention to the problem of providing shelter for the coming winter. Though some of the work force would continue to irrigate and plow, all remaining hands were to immediately begin the construction of a fort. Their first task would be to open a wagon road to City Creek Canyon, seven miles north of the camp and the nearest source of lumber. Along this road oxen would draw pine and fir logs to be used for the walls of the fort and for framing and roofing the houses. Clay would be used to mold adobe bricks, the chief building material.

Soon 92 men were engaged in making the bricks and setting them out by the thousands to bake hard in

the fierce August sun. Within a month a massive fort enclosing 29 cabin homes, a smithy, a corral and a communal storehouse had risen near the center of the city-to-be. So much was accomplished that on the morning of August 26, less than five weeks after his arrival in Utah, Brigham Young felt free to march out with a company of 106 men and retrace hundreds of arduous miles over the trail that had so recently brought them west. Their mission was to report back favorably on the Salt Lake Valley to the 13,000 Saints camped expectantly in Iowa and Nebraska, and then to point this vast flock toward their new kingdom of God on earth.

What the Mormons confidently acclaimed as an earthly Eden was, in fact, the most inhospitable environment ever to confront American pioneers. Yet a foothold had been gained there with a remarkable economy of effort, and a no less remarkable orderliness was to attend the subsequent influx and settling in. Only the strictest discipline—a basic tenet of Mormonism —made all this possible; consciously or not, the Saints had been girding for their epic leap westward ever since the founding of the sect less than two decades earlier.

Mormonism was born in a period when religious fervor was beginning to run high in America. It was a time when a Hall Jackson Kelley could unequivocally assert that Jesus had appeared to him and bade him Christianize Oregon. A time when such missionaries as

Narcissa and Marcus Whitman felt a personal call to spread the light of the Bible to the dark corners of the Pacific Northwest. And a time when the civilized East seethed with the feuds of rival Protestant sects.

Joseph Smith, a poor Vermont-born farm boy raised in New York State during the early 1800s, was keenly sensitive to the surcharged religious atmosphere around him. His mother encouraged this tendency; she firmly believed that her children had inherited mystical powers from her side of the family.

Her hopes seemed to be borne out when, at 17, Joseph reported that he had had a visitation from an angel sent by God. The angel was named Moroni, and he directed the youth to dig beneath the sod on a hillside not far from the Smith home in Palmyra, New York. In the hole, Joseph said, he discovered a set of tablets, about the size of book pages and the thickness of light sheet metal. They were bound together with rings of wire, and they were made of pure gold.

Moroni forbade Joseph to remove the tantalizing tablets for four more years. When at last he took them out of the ground, he found that they were engraved with hieroglyphics that he identified as "Reformed Egyptian." The spot where the tablets had been buried also yielded a pair of crystal spectacles. Looking through them, Joseph saw the Reformed Egyptian symbols dissolve into 17th Century English—a language familiar to readers of the King James version of the Bible.

Only Joseph, Moroni had cautioned, was permitted to view the tablets. So he dictated their contents in his own words to his young bride, Emma, and other believers who sat out of sight of the tablets on the far side of a strung-up blanket. The story that evolved was as extraordinary as the discovery of the golden plates. According to the narrative, God had dispersed certain of his faithful from Israel some 600 years before the time of Christ, commanding them to colonize the region that came to be known as North America. In time they divided into two tribes: one a "fair and delightsome people," the other a "wild and ferocious and bloodthirsty people" whom God cursed for their savagery by turning their skins a reddish brown—which explained the presence in America of the Indians. In the ensuing wars between the two tribes, the barbarians annihilated the fair-skinned people. The golden plates were hidden away by Moroni, the sole fair-skinned survivor of the final

awful battle. Whoever found them was directed to restore the true church of Jesus Christ, and build up God's kingdom on earth before Christ reappeared to begin a 1,000-year reign.

When the dictation of the tablets had been completed, Joseph Smith published the work as the Book of Mormon—so titled because the golden plates were said to have been engraved chiefly by Mormon, Moroni's father and the historian of the fair-skinned people. On April 6, 1830, eleven days after the book had left the bindery, Smith and five converts, including his brother Hyrum, established the Church of Jesus Christ. The words Latter-day Saints were added four years later.

Joseph preached that individual rights must bow to the good of the organization—in this case a Mormon theocracy with Joseph as its absolute, if benevolent, dictator. In return for total obedience, prospective Saints were assured of their election as a chosen people who would reap the double benefits of living in an earthly city of God before inheriting the inner circle of the heavenly hereafter. Within a year Joseph and his five disciples had won more than a thousand converts.

Brigham Young—then working as a carpenter, house painter and glazier in western New York—was first introduced to the Mormon message in 1830, but he did not join the fold immediately. He considered the Book of Mormon for two full years before making his commitment. Then there was no wavering. "I knew it was true," he recalled, "as well as I knew that I could see with my eyes, or feel by the touch of my fingers." Promptly he was baptized by total immersion and "was ordained to the office of Elder before my clothes were dry upon me." It was an auspicious day in Mormon history, for when Joseph Smith was murdered 12 years later, Brigham Young would almost singlehandedly save his church from extinction.

A violent death for Smith was all but assured by the mission he had set himself. Quite apart from his unorthodox religious teachings, he openly challenged many of America's most cherished beliefs—the separation of church and state, for instance, and the inviolability of individual freedom. Moreover, Joseph Smith had become fascinated by communal economics. Early in 1831 he announced a revelation—later modified—that made the property of any one Saint the common property of the church. To a young nation exuberantly pursuing

A wagon train of trail-weary Saints enters Echo Canyon on the last leg of its journey to Utah in 1867. By then a heavily worn trail, flanked by the poles of the transcontinental telegraph system, wound through the rugged Wasatch mountains that lay between Fort Bridger and Salt Lake City.

free enterprise, the man was spouting utter nonsense.

The distaste of nonbelievers for the Saints and for the ideas of their prophet steadily deepened. Meanwhile the Saints, aloof in the conviction of their own divine election, rejected outsiders—the gentiles, they called them, borrowing Biblical parlance for members of pagan tribes. Inevitably, the outsiders retaliated.

In Kirtland, Ohio, 11 miles from Lake Erie, where the prophet had established the first small settlement of Saints in 1831, anti-Mormon feeling was confined for a year to private mutterings and newspaper editorials. Then one Saturday night in March 1832, a mob from several nearby towns dragged Joseph from his bed.

"God damn ye, call on yer God for help; *we'll* show ye no mercy," a frenzied farmer spat at him. Joseph was mauled, choked, cut, scratched, stripped, tarred and feathered; he escaped castration only because no one would volunteer to hold the knife. Despite this ordeal,

he managed to stagger back into his house, and endured the pain of being scraped clean of the tar and feathers. The next morning he stood in his pulpit and preached a gentle sermon without mentioning the attack.

Some Mormons hung on in Kirtland for six more years, but others sought to establish more secure colonies farther west in Missouri, only to be harried by mobs there as well. In 1838, the governor of Missouri, Lillburn Boggs, decreed: "The Mormons must be treated as enemies and exterminated or driven from the state." He mobilized the state militia to do the job.

Abandoning all they owned, the Saints once again took flight, this time eastward into Illinois. To command the exodus Smith chose Brigham Young, who had risen rapidly in the Mormon hierarchy to become president of the church's Council of 12 Apostles.

Many of the dazed but dogged Mormons crossed the Mississippi River at Quincy. A resident of the town

named Mary Jane Selby, in her "Recollections of a Little Girl in the Forties," would remember them distinctly but disdainfully. "There were several not very desirable events that occurred in Quincy," she wrote. "One was the advent of a large number of refugee Mormons, driven out of Missouri. Another unwelcome visitor that I remember was the invasion of cholera."

Contempt was gradually tempered with grudging admiration as the gentiles watched the Mormons build up the nondescript Mississippi River town of Commerce, which they renamed Nauvoo—a Hebrew word conveying the idea of a beautiful and restful place. No "profane or indecent language" was tolerated in Nauvoo. Its enterprises thrived, and by 1844 it was the largest city in Illinois, with a population of almost 15,000. But to Smith it was more than just a flourishing city; it was his fiefdom, and he became a law unto himself. In exchange for the votes that he could deliver in Illinois elections,

the legislature granted Nauvoo the autonomy of a city-state, empowered to raise its own home guard, equipped in part with weapons supplied by the state.

But even as the Saints prospered, the old antagonisms festered, erupting in 1844 when Smith announced his candidacy for President of the United States on a platform of "Theodemocracy." As if that threat to the constitutional separation of church and state were not enough, an even graver menace to American values was surfacing: whispers about the many wives of the prophet and of his closest councilors were heard everywhere.

Some years earlier, the prophet had experienced his last revelation—that a man had a spiritual duty to marry as many wives as he could support. The revelation was not committed to paper until 1843, and even then it was communicated only to the elders of the church. Its public proclamation would not come for nine more

167

Mormon farmers from southern Utah arrive at Salt Lake City's Deseret Store and General Tithing Office to fulfill their annual obligation of contributing a tenth of their income to the church. Since cash was scarce, the Saints generally paid the tithe in produce, livestock or handicrafts.

years. But the practice of polygamy at the highest levels of Mormondom was an open secret. According to one estimate, Smith himself had as many as 60 wives.

What others called polygamy Smith preferred to call celestial marriage, a term derived from the Mormon doctrine that in the hereafter families would be reunited, and each husband and all his wives would resume connubial relations in order to propagate spiritual progeny. In this world, however, the practical and immediate goal of the system of plural wives was the production of as many Mormon children as possible.

Smith's reluctance to let the practice be widely known was understandable, for it struck at the very basis of conventional society — the monogamous family unit. Even some of his fellow Mormons disapproved of it, and Smith found himself beset by reform-minded members of his own church as well as by gentiles. The Mormon dissenters established a newspaper — the *Nauvoo Expositor* — that attacked not only the prophet's polygamy but his pretensions to national office.

Smith ordered the paper's press demolished, and the decree was swiftly seen to. The gentiles needed no clearer cue. The issue now became freedom of the press, and with this battle cry ringing in the air, Smith and his brother Hyrum were thrown into jail in Carthage, Illinois, for violating the Constitution. On June 27, 1844, state militiamen, their faces daubed with lampblack, invaded the jail and shot Joseph as he was poised to jump from a second-story window. Hyrum was killed as he tried to fight off the assassins.

The Mormon community in Nauvoo swayed but did not topple. At the public funeral for Joseph and Hyrum the caskets were half-filled with sand; their bodies had already been secretly buried under the city's temple to prevent their possible desecration. Brigham Young, later to be elected president of the church, was able to shore up the people again and hold them together. Indeed, they lived in relative peace in Nauvoo for another year, unmolested because the gentiles themselves were shocked by Joseph Smith's violent death and were weary of violence. But by the summer of 1845, when it became apparent that the vines of the church had not died with its root, the gentiles demanded that the Mormons leave Illinois before the next spring. It was at this point that Mormon history took its most decisive turn: Young and his advisers concluded that removal to the Far West was the only hope for the Saints.

During the winter every house in Nauvoo was turned into a workshop for the production of wagons, tents and other traveling gear, and property was bartered to the gentiles in exchange for animals, food and ammunition. Under relentless pressure, groups of Mormons began leaving Nauvoo early in the spring of 1846. But 500 of them, not quite prepared to go, were still in the city in September. By then, despite the Mormons' conciliatory decision to depart, Illinois gentiles had entirely lost patience. Mobs, entering the city to steal arms and loot homes, finally drove the remaining Saints across the Mississippi into the southeastern corner of Iowa.

The 1,400-mile journey from Nauvoo to the Salt Lake Valley was the most superbly planned migration by any westering pioneers. Slowly the Saints made their way across Iowa, moving in small, manageable segments. Each detachment was meticulously divided and subdivided in military fashion. Duties were clear-cut. The first groups plowed fields and planted crops. Later groups harvested the food and left behind new plantings for those in the rear. By mid-fall of 1846, several thousand of the refugees had traveled 400 miles to Winter Quarters, a way station that Brigham Young established in Indian country on the Missouri River, just west of Council Bluffs. There the migrants encamped for what was to prove a winter of sheer misery. Despite the careful planning, food and fuel supplies dwindled, and cholera and other diseases claimed some 600 victims. But by the spring of 1847, Brigham Young and his advance party were ready for the final push to the Rocky Mountains.

The vanguard of 148 left Winter Quarters on April 17, to be followed by a much larger body of emigrants later that summer. The Mormons prudently plotted a course that was north of the Platte River to separate themselves from possibly hostile Missourians trudging along the Oregon Trail on the south bank.

The pioneers in the lead suffered no casualties, nor was there any confusion concerning permissible and impermissible conduct en route. Brigham Young kept everyone straight on that. One thing he liked was dancing; another was prayer. Many a night the travelers danced; every night they prayed. The worst part of the journey, all agreed, was the last precipitous stretch of 36 miles

"Let them gird up their loins and walk through"

Of all pioneer journeys across the West, none tested human mettle more than the treks undertaken between 1856 and 1860 by 3,000 Mormon converts from Europe who walked 1,300 miles from Iowa to the Salt Lake Valley hauling their possessions in two-wheeled handcarts.

This bruising mode of travel was Brigham Young's idea. A crop failure had left the church short of funds to buy wagons and oxen to bring the converts west. So Young decreed: "Let them come on foot with handcarts or wheelbarrows; let them gird up their loins and walk through and nothing shall hinder or stay them."

The first groups to heed this advice, in 1856, paid a heavy price for mistakes in planning. At the assembly point in Iowa City, the Mormon ar-

tisans who made the carts used green lumber and dispensed with iron axles and tires to save expense and time. Most carts were heaped with the maximum load of 400 to 500 pounds of goods, and the pilgrims set out in military-style companies. Families divided labor, father and mother pulling and children pushing.

The cart's wooden axles were soon ground down by sand, and the summer heat cracked them. Exhaustion began to take a heavy toll. Archer Walters, an English carpenter, kept a grim diary of the passage: "June 15th: Got up about 4 o'clock to make a coffin for my brother John Lee's son named William Lee, aged 12 years. Meetings as usual and at the same time had to make another coffin for Sister Prator's child. . . . June 17th:

Travelled about 17 miles. Made a little coffin for Bro. Job Welling's son and mended a cartwheel."

Some of the pilgrims defected: two girls in one company dropped out to wed a pair of tipsy miners who lived in a cabin along the way (one of the girls showed up later in Utah with her spouse—newly converted). Two companies, starting out late in the season, were caught in winter storms, and cold and hunger took 200 lives before rescuers reached them.

But the great majority of the handcart travelers survived to hear Salt Lake City's welcoming bands. As it turned out, many had made the grueling trip faster than if they had gone in ox-drawn wagons—although one six-year-old child calculated she had taken a million steps to attain the goal.

Mormons hauling handcarts ford a prairie stream and prepare to make camp on a stretch of level terrain that belies the rigors farther ahead.

before they reached the valley of the Great Salt Lake. This was the same narrow, nearly impassable trail across the Wasatch mountains from Fort Bridger that had been broken by the Donner party the summer before—the trail that had broken them in turn.

Yet before the Saints' first autumn in the valley was over, the torturous canyon trail leading to it had been smoothed and worn by the passage of hundreds more Mormon wagons. This second wave of emigrants came down the final difficult miles full of assurance and determination. There was a reason: they had passed Brigham Young working his way back eastward along the trail. He had greeted his people by their first names and given them good tidings. The valley awaiting them was already growing Mormon crops; it would hold and support them all, he assured them. Press on!

Young's optimism, however, had been premature. No real harvest had been possible before cold weather set in. Famine soon forced the Saints to grub for roots. The family of Lorenzo Young, Brigham's brother, was reduced to boiling ox hides for soup. His wife Harriet had brought along a good set of china, and Lorenzo was glad she did. "I never knew more need of an inviting looking table," he recalled long afterward, "than in those days of glue soup."

The Saints barely managed to get through another starvation winter—it was as bad as the one near Council Bluffs—but when the spring of 1848 arrived their hopes rose anew. Again they set their seeds into the ground and looked forward to a bountiful summer—only to face a new crisis. Soon after planting time, the crickets that swarmed everywhere in the valley got into the corn and wheat fields, threatening to destroy the crop. "This morning's frost in unison with the ravages of the crickets for a few days past," one woman noted in a diary entry of May 28, 1848, "produces many sighs and occasionally some long faces with those that for the moment forget that they are Saints." But sea gulls off the Great Salt Lake swung in daily during June to feast on the crickets, and some of the plantings survived. Although gobbling up crickets was a reasonable thing for hungry gulls to do, the Saints saw the Lord's handiwork in all that transpired, and the "miracle of the gulls" quickly became part of Mormon lore.

Most of the Saints' success that second summer and during the years that followed was won by communal muscle. Indeed, nearly all that the Saints accomplished in Utah depended upon their readiness to pull together. Looking beyond the Salt Lake Valley to other reaches of the Great Basin, Brigham Young intended not to ignore a single acre of it that was possible to settle and cultivate. And as he well saw, the more hands that could be turned to the task, the sooner the kingdom of God on earth would be built.

Ever the brilliant planner, Young promptly set about finding the desired help. Mormon missionaries were already at work in England and northern Europe. He ordered them to step up their proselytizing among the poor and oppressed, and to send on the converts as quickly as possible. By the mid-1850s, English, Scandinavian and German families were coming by the thousands, eager to dwell in a realm that promised each of its loyal subjects a new beginning and a happy ending.

As the devout streamed into the Salt Lake Valley, they were put to laying out new settlements north and south of the lake region. Each arriving group was quickly integrated into the fabric of Mormon society. If a recruit knew a trade, his parish elders would encourage him to follow it. If he was a farmer, he would be assigned land, and his neighbors would house and feed him and his family until he could build his own cabin, plow his fields and sow his crops.

Whatever work the newcomer chose, part of his labor had to go into communal projects. As one pioneer expressed it, they were "to put their mites together for that which is best for every man, woman and child." No project was more impressive or more crucial during the early years than the Mormons' irrigation systems—vital to all and requiring the effort of all.

Some rain did fall in the Salt Lake Valley, but the quantity was hardly sufficient for crops that need as much as 40 inches of rainfall a year. The water supply had to be augmented by irrigation, with which the emigrants had almost no experience. But they soon learned by trial and error how to tap the streams in the surrounding mountains.

The first consideration was where to put the dams, flumes and canals. The higher up in the mountains the work began, the more water could be caught and the farther afield it could be channeled. But high-level dams meant months of canal building and a longer wait until the water could reach the thirsty farmlands. And so the first systems built were low-level, serving only those fields that lay close to the canyon mouths.

Damming the fast-moving mountain meltwater was a feat in itself, though help on at least one occasion came from an unexpected source. "The creek was full of Beavers," one dam builder remembered, "so as soon as the Beavers understood that there was going to be a dam built, they would work at night. They would cut willows into three- or four-foot lengths, sometimes longer, weave these together in the water where the dam was to be, and plaster the thing up with mud; the Beavers ran the night shift, so they were a great help."

If a dam held—and there was always the possibility it would not—work on canals would begin. Plowmen would first cut several parallel furrows in the soil, following the contour of the valley's slope in a gradual descent. A weighted, A-shaped sled—called a go-devil —was then dragged through the loosened soil, heaping it up in high banks on either side of the furrow. A typical canal was four feet deep, five feet wide at the bottom and eight feet wide at the top.

The slope of the canal had to be carefully controlled. If the slope was too gradual, the canal would quickly fill up with silt; and if it was too steep, the canal water would wash out in a torrent of muddy spray. Folk wisdom held that the optimum declination was a drop of half an inch for every sixteen and a half feet of canal. For this hairbreadth measurement the Mormons used a

On an 1870 tour of Mormon colonies on the Colorado plateau, a top-hatted Brigham Young (in a chair, at center) and his party take time out

crude but serviceable gauge called a Jacob's staff. It was a frame of three planks that were shaped into a wide and squat letter H. One of the two upright legs was a half inch longer than the other. When the canal bed had been roughed out, the Jacob's staff was set on it longitudinally, its longer leg on the downslope side; the workmen then packed and scraped the canal bottom until the sixteen-and-a-half-foot crossbar of the H-shaped frame was seen to be level — a matter that could be determined by simply placing a full pan of water on the crossbar. If the water did not spill, that meant the canal sloped precisely as desired — one half inch.

Once a system was working properly, irrigation water was supplied to the valley homes and farmlands on a metered basis, each acre being allotted enough water annually to cover it to a depth of two feet. When the Saints began to fan out from the Salt Lake Valley to establish new settlements, their company always included those who knew how to bring the water down from the mountains and regulate its use. By 1865, two hundred seventy-seven canals — whose total length added up to 1,043 miles — had been constructed, irrigating 154,000 acres of formerly arid terrain.

Setting up irrigation systems was just one of the Mormons' cooperative endeavors. A concourse of willing hands worked at building roads, bridges and even an extensive telegraph system: In the summer of 1876, Americans all across the nation first learned of General

for a group portrait. The Saints established hundreds of outposts, some as far afield as San Bernardino in California and Fort Lemhi in Idaho.

George Custer's defeat at Little Big Horn by means of the Saints' private telegraph wires.

Nor was industry neglected. "Produce what you consume," was Brigham Young's dictum. So his people built gristmills and sawmills, ironworks and tanneries, and by 1853, Salt Lake City hummed with the manufacture of flannels, linseys, jeans, pottery and cutlery.

There were some notable exceptions to the Saints' imposing record of successful efforts to exploit the resources of their new domain. Young dispatched 309 families to southern Utah with specific orders to grow cotton, but the alkaline soil and alternating inundations and droughts, as well as infestations of grasshoppers and crickets, doomed that enterprise. His attempt to launch a silk industry also met with failure.

For the most part, the Saints thrived. But all that they achieved was threatened by problems arising from the church's commitment to multiple marriages. The potential of polygamy for peopling the Great Basin was awesome. A Mormon newspaper in England published an arithmetical exercise intended to show that a conscientious Mormon with 40 wives—Mr. Fruitful, the paper called this hypothetical man—could, by age 78, have added 3,508,441 Saints to God's kingdom. On the other hand, a gentile with one wife and five sons would have produced only 152 descendants by the time he reached that age.

Presumably Mormons were as temptable as other humans, and it is undoubtedly true that marrying motives were sometimes more libidinous than liturgical. But to a devout Mormon the taking of more than one wife was an act of faith as sacred as baptism. Before the marriage ceremony—called sealing—was celebrated, a man's first wife was expected to give her consent.

Even when the church was firmly established in the Great Basin and its leaders felt safe in encouraging polygamy, fewer than 20 per cent of Mormon husbands had multiple marriage beds, and at least two thirds of these were merely bigamous. Many Mormon wives were opposed to polygamy—an attitude that had been shared by Joseph Smith's first wife, Emma. When she read the paper enunciating the revelation, she flew into a rage and flung the document into the fire.

Brigham Young had no such domestic difficulties. With the Rocky Mountains to insulate him from gen-tile disapproval, he took 27 wives; he was also sealed to perhaps 50 more women "for eternity only" (that is, he would see them later in heaven but did not take them to his earthly bed); and he was sealed to another 150 who had already passed into the spirit world. Of all of Young's earthly spouses only one, his 19th, defected. However, he fell short of the hypothetical Mr. Fruitful's achievement. Mr. Fruitful had 400 children; Young sired but 56—31 daughters and 25 sons.

Meanwhile, outside the Western fastness of the Mormons, the rest of the country regarded their polygamy with increasing outrage. Rumors about the plural wives of the Saints were confirmed by the forty-niners who passed through on their way to seek California gold. And Army explorers dispatched to survey the valley in 1849 sent back further reports on the marital system. One of them, Captain Howard Stansbury, wrote:

"It is in their private and domestic relations that this singular people exhibit the widest departure from the habits and practice of all others denominating themselves Christian. I refer to what has been generally termed the 'spiritual wife system,' the practice of which was charged against them in Illinois, and served greatly to prejudice the public mind in that State. It was then, I believe, most strenuously denied by them that any such practice prevailed, nor is it now openly avowed, either as a matter sanctioned by their doctrine or discipline. But that polygamy does actually exist among them cannot be concealed from any one of the most ordinary observation who has spent even a short time in this community. I heard it proclaimed from the stand, by the president of the church himself, that he had the right to take a thousand wives, if he thought proper; and he defied any one to prove from the Bible that he had not."

Predictably, the plural marriage system became a constant source of tension between the Mormons and the U.S. government. When the Saints applied for statehood in 1849, polygamy proved to be a major argument against acceptance. A second problem was the prodigious extent of the lands that the Mormons wanted to include in their state.

The boundaries, as drawn by Brigham Young and his council, would have included nearly all of Utah, Nevada and Arizona and some of Oregon, Idaho, Wyoming, Colorado and southern California—in all, about one sixth of the nation's land area. Young viewed the

California portion as particularly vital. It would have
given the Saints a seaport city in San Diego; without
it, they felt, they would always be economically de-
pendent upon gentile America. The Saints proposed to
name the resulting state in honor of that heroic insect,
the honeybee — a symbol of unremitting industry. In the
Book of Mormon the busy little worker is called deseret, and the Mormons thought that "The State of
Deseret" would eminently fit their society.

In Washington, Congress had other ideas. In 1850,
after due deliberation, the legislators voted not for statehood but for territorial status. Instead of the immense
domain that the Mormons had envisioned, the new
U.S. territory was to cover a considerably lesser area:
all of present-day Utah and Nevada and half of Colorado and Arizona. No seaport was included, nor was
the name Deseret approved. Congress preferred the
name of Utah, after the Ute Indians who lived there.

All this dealt a severe blow to the Mormons' hopes.
Statehood would have guaranteed them representation
in the national capital. Territorial status, on the other
hand, created a master-servant relationship between
Washington and Salt Lake City. Millard Fillmore, then
President of the U.S., had the good sense to appoint
Brigham Young as territorial governor, but most other
federal appointees — specifically the judges — were gentiles sent from the East.

In Mormon eyes these guardians of the law seemed
to be trying to outdo one another in injudiciousness, ras-
cality and anti-Mormonism. In consequence, Mormons
shunned the federal courts, settling their difficulties
among themselves. The judges, in turn, went fuming
back to Washington, charging that the Mormons were
disloyal to the federal government, scornful of the Congress and disrespectful of the Presidency. By 1855 the
press was insisting that Brigham Young ought to be
shorn of authority.

Young now had been ruling both church and secular
government for 10 years. His reaction to his prospective dismissal, expressed in a sermon to his people, was

emphatic: "I am, and will be governor, *and no power can hinder it, until the Lord Almighty says, 'Brigham, you need not be governor any longer.'*"

In 1857 the newly elected U.S. President, James Buchanan, took it upon himself to act on behalf of the Lord Almighty. Trouble enough beset Buchanan at that time: an increasingly bitter national debate over slavery, and growing tensions between North and South, which in four short years would erupt in civil war. He came to the politically popular decision to replace Young as governor partly on the advice of friends. One of them, Robert Tyler—himself the son of a former U.S. President—wrote Buchanan a letter:

Phila: April 27, 1857
My dear Sir:

The Public mind is becoming greatly excited on the subject of *Mormonism*. The Popular Idea is rapidly maturing that Mormonism (already felt slightly in our large Northern cities) should be put down & utterly extirpated.

I believe that we can supercede the Negro-Mania with the almost universal excitement of an Anti-Mormon Crusade. Should you, with your accustomed grip, seize this question with a strong, fearless & resolute hand, the Country I am sure will rally to you with an earnest enthusiasm & the pipings of Abolitionism will hardly be heard amidst the thunders of the storm we shall raise."

ever your friend
Ro: Tyler

A few months after receiving Tyler's letter Buchanan designated Alfred Cumming, former mayor of Augusta, Georgia, as the new governor of the Utah Territory. Anticipating the Mormon reaction (one spokesman for the Saints declared that the 240-pound Cumming had "more chops than brains"), Buchanan decided to apply some military muscle. He dispatched an Army force of 2,500 soldiers from Fort Leavenworth, Kansas, to Utah to ensure that the Mormons received their new governor with proper respect.

Remembering the militia mobs of Missouri and Illinois, no Mormon could be sure what the federal soldiers—many of them recent recruits from among the dregs of Eastern cities and the Western frontier—might do when they reached the Salt Lake Valley. For his part, Brigham Young reacted with thunderous fury.

"Woe, woe to those men who came here to unlawfully meddle with me and this people," Young told a congregation assembled in Temple Square in August 1857. "I swore in Nauvoo, when my enemies were looking me in the face, that I would send them to hell . . . if they meddled with me; and I ask no more odds of all hell today."

As for the claim that Cumming and his supporting army were merely bent on enforcing peace, Young roared, "I would not trust them any sooner than I would a wolf with my dinner." He promptly mobilized the Mormon militia but also made plans for the general evacuation and burning of Salt Lake City. A realist, he had no intention of engaging in a face-to-face confrontation with the U.S. Army.

Meanwhile other Mormons living in the isolation of southern Utah acted on their own—with tragic results. Into Utah and its emotional chaos that autumn of 1857 had come a party of 137 California-bound pioneers. Mostly family groups, they were all gentiles from Arkansas and Missouri. Like scores of other emigrant trains that year, they had passed through Salt Lake City in early August after forking off the Oregon Trail at Fort Bridger. Because they were running late, and aware of the Donner party's disaster, they had gone down into southern Utah to steer clear of a possible snow trap in the more northern passes of the High Sierra.

As often happened on the trail, certain riffraff elements had attached themselves to this wagon train, and so the emigrants left a string of enemies behind them as they rolled through the territory. Reports flew that they had sold poisoned beef to some Indians and had fouled an Indian well. Moreover, they had insulted the Mormon settlers they met as they traveled. They dubbed their oxen Brigham and said that Mormon wives were whores; one Missouri man was even heard to boast that he had had a hand in ridding the world of Old Joe Smith back at the Carthage jail.

When Mormons farther along the route refused to sell supplies to these emigrants, their mirthless humor ceased. Now preoccupied with trying to eke out rations, they at first ignored the band of Indians dogging their tracks. There was no overlooking the Indians, though, on the Sunday afternoon of September 6, when the emigrants set up camp at a spot called Mountain

Brigham Young's official residence, named Beehive House for the Mormon honeybee symbol, flaunts a wooden eagle atop the main gate.

Adjoining the Mormon leader's abode, this building housed his wives in apartments marked by the 20 gables on the top story.

Wolves forage among human remains in this *Harper's Weekly* sketch of the aftermath of the 1857 massacre at Mountain Meadows, where 120 emigrants were shot by a joint force of Mormons and Indians.

Meadows. Some 200 warriors encircled the camp, and at daybreak on Tuesday attacked. The emigrants threw up earthworks and the Indians sniped at any movement within the circle of wagons. The following night three of the whites ventured out of the camp to look for help but were ambushed and killed by a force of Mormons working in concert with the Indians.

The next day, sucked into a kind of madness that later would make no sense to the Saints or anyone else, the Mormon men in the area devised a brutal plan. It would cover traces of the shooting, it would avenge the insults, and it would also atone for the sins of those gentiles who had killed innocent Saints back east. The motives were complex but the plan was simple: the Mormons and the Indians would kill every emigrant at Mountain Meadows who was able to talk. The Saints would then claim the tribesmen had acted alone. After praying for guidance and strength, two of the planners, under a white flag, went to the emigrants' camp and made this proposal: if the pioneers would leave their wagons, their cattle and their weapons as an appeasement for the Indians, and if certain of the men would stand trial for their transgressions along the Utah route, the Mormons would escort the other campers — men, women and children — out of the Indian trap.

Apparently under intense strain as a result of the siege, the emigrants accepted these harsh terms. As they filed out of their makeshift fort — women and children first and the disarmed men last — a shouted Mormon signal was given: "Halt! Do your duty!" With that the Indians sprang from the roadside underbrush — "like a howling tornado," one Mormon eyewitness later recalled — and knifed and hatcheted the women and children to death. Mormons posing as escort guards turned and shot the male emigrants in their tracks. When the dust had settled, 120 bodies lay strewn about; the only survivors were 17 children deemed too young to give an account of what had happened.

Brigham Young had heard reports that trouble was brewing in Mountain Meadows — which was a distance of 350 miles from Salt Lake City—and he had dispatched a letter to the local Mormons expressly forbidding any interference with the emigrants. It arrived two days after the carnage. Though the details did not emerge until years afterward, the Mountain Meadows massacre proved to be the worst single episode of violence in the Mormon War, as it came to be called.

As the U.S. Army contingent sent by President Buchanan marched toward the valley, the war went on as a contest of nerves, feints and parries in which Young persuaded his foes of one unequivocal fact: the Saints would, if necessary, emulate the Dutch—who flooded Holland in 1672 to save it from the French—by reducing the Mormon settlements to ashes. As one man said, "We must destroy our property joyfully to disappoint our enemies."

Preparations for this eventuality began during the fall of 1857. Church records, livestock, farm implements, other possessions and 20,000 bushels of wheat were stockpiled in the Mormon town of Provo, 45 miles south of Salt Lake City. A detachment of Mormon militia raced eastward to burn down two Mormon settlements on the far side of the Rocky Mountains—Fort Bridger, which the Saints had bought from Jim Bridger, and Fort Supply—before the U.S. Army could get there. They also burned all grazing sites where the Army might try to camp. When the column of federal soldiers approached, Mormon guerrillas operating from nearby hills harassed them by stampeding their livestock and setting fire to their supply trains. Though very little blood was shed, the assault created total disorder in the government ranks. The disheartened troops were forced to spend the winter huddled near the sooty remains of Jim Bridger's old fort.

By early spring a compromise was effected, to the enormous relief of practically everyone. American public opinion, impressed by Mormon readiness to sacrifice everything in defense of their faith, had swung in favor of the Saints. President Buchanan thereupon "forgave" them for the incipient insurrection. Brigham Young's response was spirited: "I have no vanity to please. If a man comes from the moon and says he will pardon me for kicking him . . . I'll accept his pardon. It won't affect me one way or the other."

In exchange for the forgiveness, Young accepted Albert Cumming as governor of the Utah Territory and reluctantly agreed that the Army might enter the Salt Lake Valley—but on condition that no troops be quartered in Salt Lake City itself. To emphasize his resolve to raze the city if this proviso were flouted, he ordered his people to evacuate it. The only Saints left were those who would put the place to the torch if the troops stopped there. On June 26, 1858—as it happened, the eve of the 14th anniversary of the murder of Joseph Smith—the wide streets of Salt Lake City resounded to the footsteps of 2,500 U.S. soldiers. No smoke issued from kitchen chimneys and not a Mormon face was to be seen.

Some 30,000 Mormons had abandoned their city of God while the detested soldiers headed toward it. Watchful and waiting, the Saints were camped in wagons and lean-tos outside Provo. If, as they feared, the U.S. Army had come with the purpose of abolishing the Mormon Church, they were ready to flee again, perhaps even to Mexico or Canada. But the troops, as arranged, marched ceremoniously into Salt Lake City and then out of it to a camp 44 miles distant. The Saints began to return from the desert by the first of July.

The U.S. Army remained in the valley for three years. The Mormons would certainly have preferred to see the soldiers gone, but by an ironic turn of fate the military supply requirements added measurably to the region's prosperity. When the troops left in 1861, it was more precipitately than they had come. Abraham Lincoln had succeeded James Buchanan as President and the Civil War was on. Other issues were more pressing than how many wives a Saint might wed. Although Congress and the Supreme Court would periodically attempt to ban polygamy, that matter was not to be resolved until 1890, when the Mormon Church revoked its endorsement of the practice.

A few months after Lincoln took office T.B.H. Stenhouse, the Mormon representative in Washington, visited the White House to inquire after Lincoln's intentions toward the Saints. "Stenhouse," Lincoln answered after an extended pause, "when I was a boy on the farm in Illinois there was a great deal of timber which we had to clear away. Occasionally we would come to a log which had fallen down. It was too hard to split, too wet to burn, and too heavy to move, so we plowed around it. That's what I intend to do with the Mormons." That was all the Saints had ever asked for.

A clothing factory built at Parley's Canyon in 1863 formed part of Brigham Young's campaign to "become independent of our enemies."

Monuments to Mormon faith and zeal

Granite blocks, weighing up to five tons each, await removal from the quarry to the Temple.

A few days after his arrival in the Salt Lake Valley, Brigham Young marked off a 10-acre tract for the Temple Square, the future spiritual core of the kingdom of God on earth. Here, Young decreed, two monuments would arise —the Temple for religious ceremonies, and the Tabernacle for public gatherings and singing.

Work on the edifices was put off while the Mormons built homes, factories and irrigation canals — tasks that helped prepare them for their president's most cherished project. Manpower for this herculean effort was provided by a feature of the Saints' tithing system that allowed a man to contribute every tenth workday to a common enterprise in place of donating a tenth of his income or produce to the church. By the time ground was broken for the Temple in 1853, a large, efficient and rigorously monitored labor force was available.

Young had glimpsed the future Mormon Temple in a vision and had communicated its general outlines to an architect with the happily appropriate name of Truman O. Angell. The massive granite blocks that translated Angell's drawings into reality came from a quarry 20 miles away in the Wasatch Range. Each was inspected and numbered before being hauled to the city, since the dimensions of every block were specified in the Temple plans.

When the walls of the Temple were barely showing aboveground, the indefatigable Saints began work on a second monument. The Tabernacle, with its huge roof resting like an inverted bowl upon 44 sandstone piles, took seven years to complete. But one phase of its creation was simplicity itself. The design, according to Young, was inspired "by the best sounding board in the world ... the roof of my mouth."

In this northward view of Temple Square in

The Tabernacle's roof, arched to achieve optimal acoustics, required almost a million board feet of lumber. The maze of timbers was joined together with long wooden pegs and rawhide bindings, since the beams were too massive to be fastened by nails.

1880, the completed Tabernacle looms beyond the unfinished Temple. The Tabernacle, seating 10,000, was the structural wonder of its day.

185

A crowd of 40,000 Mormons gathered on April 6, 1892, to watch the emplacement of the Temple's capstone. They shouted "Hosanna!"

Officials prepare to set the capstone in place.

then pledged themselves to finish the Temple's interior by the following spring — a promise kept.

Building the Temple preoccupied the Mormons for 40 years, cost nearly four million dollars and required an incalculable amount of human labor. Some 10,000 man-days were needed just to excavate the foundation. Even more strenuous was the task of transporting the granite from the quarry at Little Cottonwood Canyon. During the first 20 years of the project, huge carts, drawn by four yoke of oxen, hauled the blocks — one at a time — to the city. This system was so wasteful of time and energy that the Saints tried digging canals so that barges could float the granite to Temple Square, but the porous soil absorbed the canal water. Although the work quickened in the 1870s when they began freighting the granite to the city on railroads, Brigham Young did not live to see his vision realized: he died in 1877, sixteen years before the Temple rose in all its finished splendor.

On a homestead set in the immensity of western Kansas, pioneers present their Sunday best outside a house built of sod.

6|Sodbusters in the heartland

Thousands upon thousands of emigrant wagons had traveled through the great central prairies and plains before pioneers thought of actually settling there. And, indeed, the vast region — stretching from the Missouri to the Rockies and from the Canadian border to the Texas Panhandle — abounded in reasons for pressing on. It was treeless, matted with dense sod in its eastern reaches, arid farther west, and everywhere possessed of a climate that ran to brutal extremes of hot and cold. But after the Civil War, pioneers swarmed onto this desolate expanse — and stayed. In two decades, more new U.S. terrain was brought under cultivation than in the previous two and a half centuries.

The conquest was spurred partly by the growing shortage of arable lands elsewhere and partly by intense propagandizing. Newly built railroads, eager for business, wooed settlers with promotional campaigns. They were joined in their hard-sell tactics by transatlantic steamship companies hoping to tap a huge pool of land-hungry foreigners.

For newcomers from abroad, the plains offered the chance to rise from peasanthood to proprietorship, and the land was surely no worse than what they left behind on Russia's steppes or in Sweden or Ireland or Germany. However, many an American-born wife from the East wept when she first saw her husband's choice of a homestead. In the absence of wood and stone, the only building material for a house was sod stripped from the soil. The only fuel was the dried manure of buffalo or cows. Droughts and grasshopper plagues brought havoc to crops. But, as on earlier frontiers, most pioneers lustily accepted the challenge. As one young Nebraska settler wrote his mother back East: "Ma you can see as far as you please here and almost every foot in sight can be plowed."

An obstinate ocean of grass

On the huge central prairies west of the Missouri River, the tall grass heaves and plunges in shimmering, wind-driven billows. "Like an ocean in its vast extent, in its monotony, and in its danger," wrote a sportsman hunting antelope there in the 1850s; "like the ocean in its romance." No traveler could fail to be awed by the sight. But to the pioneers who toiled west along the Oregon Trail in the mid-19th Century, the ocean of grass seemed anything but inviting. It was desolate, without shelter or respite, infinitely lonely and unforgiving. Who would ever want to live there?

Who indeed? The prairies and the plains beyond presented challenges and hardships unlike any the pioneers faced elsewhere. For thousands upon thousands of square miles, from roughly the Missouri River in the east to the Rocky Mountains in the west, and from Canada in the north to the Texas Panhandle in the south, the land offered only two natural resources in generous portions: soil and grass. It was poor in almost every other essential, including timber and sometimes water. Though relatively moist along their eastern fringes, the prairies grow progressively drier until, in western Kansas and Nebraska, annual rainfall drops below the 20 inches needed to grow most crops. The stands of cottonwood, ash and oak seen in the eastern river bottoms give way to stunted willows and plum bushes, and then to no trees at all. People foolhardy enough to settle here had to learn to dig for water the way other men in other parts of the West sank shafts for gold. They had to build houses without timber, burn fires without wood and carve furrows in a soil so matted and tough that an ordinary plow would often snag in the

sod or skitter across its surface like a stick over ice.

All the elements seemed to conspire against human habitation. Summer droughts, when the thermometer rose well above 100° and hovered there for weeks on end, could char a pioneer's corn crop as effectively as a blowtorch. In winter, when temperatures sometimes plunged to 40° below zero, horrendous snowstorms struck so suddenly that a man might lose his way between his house and barn and freeze to death. And then there was the wind. It blew ceaselessly — winter and summer, night and day — a low, stupefying moan that drove many pioneers to distraction. One woman commented that, in this land without trees, the Rocky Mountains provided the nearest windbreak.

Settlement of the grasslands did not begin until the decade before the Civil War, and then only hesitantly. But after the war pioneers surged into the region by the tens of thousands — farmers from the increasingly crowded Mississippi valley, disappointed gold seekers returning from California and the Rockies and wave after wave of immigrants from Europe. The first newcomers built their homes in the lush, well-timbered river bottoms of eastern Kansas, Nebraska and Minnesota. In the late 1870s, after the choicest lands had been filled, settlers spread out into the surrounding prairie. And finally, they moved westward into the semiarid uplands of Colorado, Wyoming and the Dakotas. These pioneers would not merely survive; they would convert the bleak expanse into some of the most productive farmland the world has ever known.

One man who flourished on the grasslands was a young sodbuster named Howard Ruede. On the summery day in 1877 when Howard moved into his new prairie shelter — a freshly dug hole in the ground of central Kansas — he could barely contain his high spirits. "Hurray!" he exulted in a letter to the anxious kinfolk he had left in Bethlehem, Pennsylvania, six months ear-

A railroad advertisement offers settlers easy credit for the purchase of company-owned prairie land. Unscrupulous sales agents often touted the region as a Garden of Eden.

Swedes who succumbed to "America fever" — as the lure of the West was called back home — record their arrival on the Kansas prairie. Some 17,000 countrymen joined them there by the century's end.

lier. As he wrote by the flickering light of a coal-oil lantern, he admitted that the atmosphere in his underground cell seemed a trifle close: "The sweat runs off of me, and some of the drops wet the paper; so if you can't read it you'll know the reason." To get a drink of water he had to hike to a stream a good quarter-mile away. Still, he insisted that he had built a mighty fine dugout, all things considered. Certainly it was far snugger than the dwellings of some of the first Kansas settlers who had lived in tents fabricated of tree bark or in houses made of hay bales.

At 23, Howard Ruede was particularly well suited for life on the prairie: he had the resilience of youth, an unflappable disposition and enormous energy. His house beneath the sod was the second he had built in only half a year in Kansas. His first subterranean dwelling had collapsed in a rainstorm a few months earlier. The new dugout — bigger, sturdier and more comfortably furnished than its predecessor — filled him with intense pride of ownership. "I took inventory this morning," he wrote his mother and brothers on the family farm back in Bethlehem, "and give it for your benefit: Stove, tin wash boiler, 2 iron pots, teakettle, 2 spiders [three-legged skillets], 3 griddles, 3 bread pans, 2 tin plates, a steamer, coffee pot, coal oil can, gridiron, 4 tincups, wash basin, pepper box and 2 lb. nails." He went on to list the domestic purchases he had made that day in town, 13 miles away — knives and forks, a lamp, a bucket, sugar, rice, salt and coffee.

Howard managed to find a place for everything in the tidy and compact 14-by-16-foot dugout, and a few days later he sent his family a little pencil-drawn floor plan. The oblong sketch contained numbers around its perimeter. According to the attached key, #10 was the bed made of hay, #7 the sack of flour, #1 the front door and #3 — Howard's special pride and joy — a pile of potatoes stacked on the dirt floor in the northeast corner. He had grown those potatoes himself, and bragged: "Nobody need tell me now that the upland is worth little for raising potatoes, as I got some that weighed over a pound a piece, and would make enough for a meal for two."

In raising potatoes as in everything else, Howard Ruede thrived on challenges and hard work. As a staunch member of the Moravian Church in Bethlehem, he had grown up thoroughly imbued with the virtues of

thrift and industry. "Tired?" he wrote home after spending three sweltering August days threshing wheat in a neighbor's field. "You better believe it!" He was not complaining, but expressing satisfaction at a job well done. He scoffed when an admiring letter came from his Aunty Clauder in the Allegheny foothills. "She tries to make me out a hero," he told his mother, "but for the life of me I can't see anything heroic in coming out here to do farm work." Things were none too luxurious, perhaps, but he voiced only one regret. He had forgotten his mother's recipe for johnnycake and would be much obliged if she would send it soon by train mail — along with some pumpkin seeds and maybe a cigar or two.

Not all settlers faced life on the prairies and plains with the same breezy equanimity. For some the conditions seemed intolerably severe, the land hopelessly unyielding, the need for toil incessant. "We wanted to be in a free state," wrote an antislavery farmer from Missouri, who arrived in Kansas shortly before the Civil War, "but I reckon there ain't no freedom here except to die of thirst." A later Kansas homesteader, whose crops were gobbled up by insects in 1874, packed his family into a wagon and hastened away from this land "where it rains grasshoppers, fire and destruction."

Yet the settlers kept coming. They were impelled by the same complex passions that had sent earlier pioneers to the Pacific Coast and the Great Basin: a hunger for land, an urge to escape poverty or persecution at home, a thirst for adventure or simply for a fresh start in life. But for the prairie settlers there were certain propitious new circumstances at work. The most important of these was the government's increasingly active interest in populating the region west of the Missouri River. In 1854, Senator Stephen A. Douglas of Illinois had persuaded Congress to pass the Kansas-Nebraska Act *(page 201),* which created two U.S. territories out of Indian lands. Treaties with the Indians opened these lands to white ownership, but many Northerners who might have settled there were put off by a provision of the act that allowed slavery in the territories until the settlers themselves could vote on the issue. In the wake of this controversial legislation, the violence between the supporters and opponents of slavery that swept the region — and that soon engulfed the entire nation — prevented any real influx into the grasslands. Yet even while the Civil War raged, Congress pro-

A government receipt formalizes Daniel Freeman's ownership of 160 acres of free land. He was the first Nebraskan to meet the Homestead Act's requirement that a claim be occupied or farmed for five years.

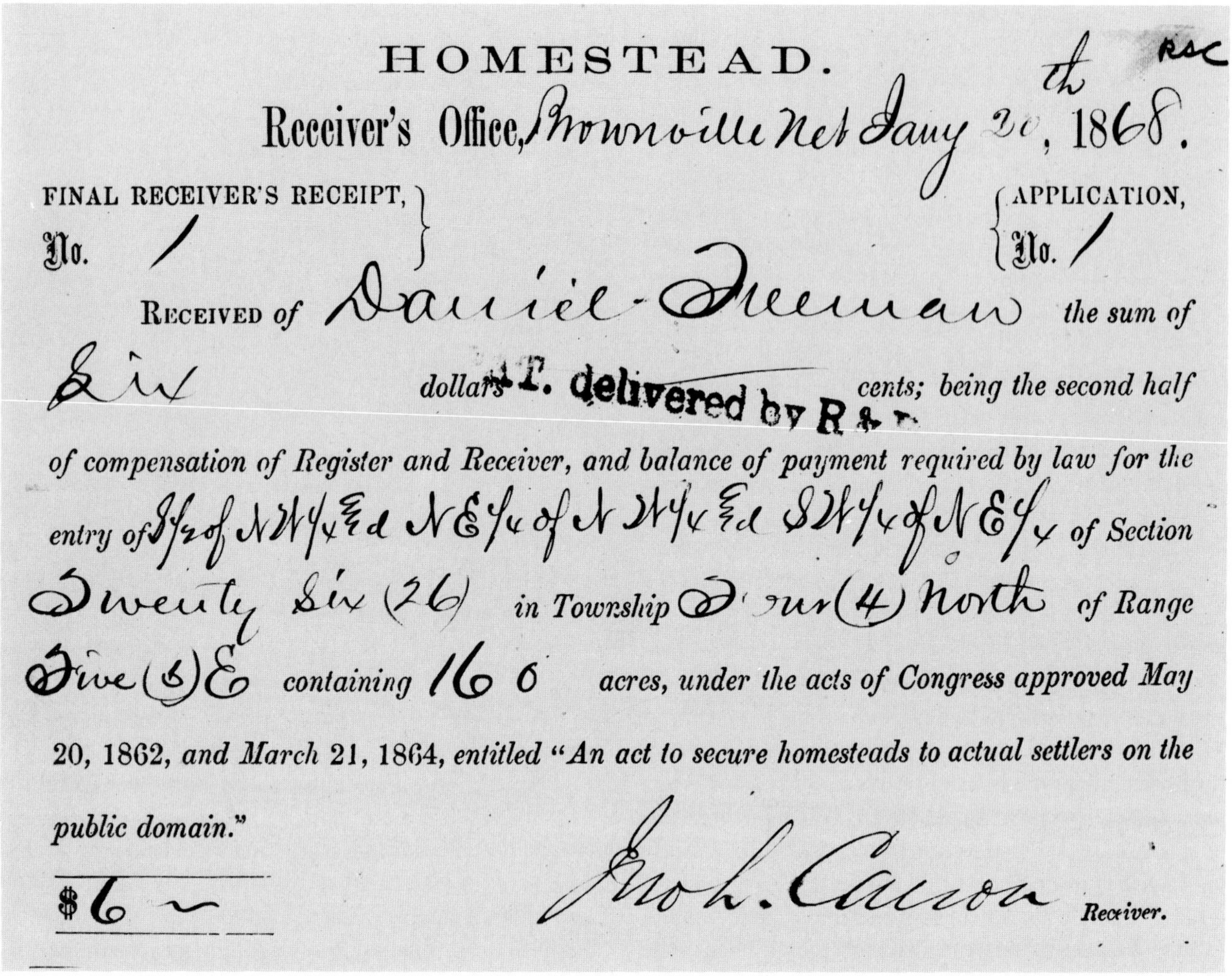

HOMESTEAD.

Receiver's Office, *Brownville Neb* Jany 20th, 1868.

FINAL RECEIVER'S RECEIPT,
No. 1

APPLICATION,
No. 1

RECEIVED of *Daniel Freeman* the sum of *Six* dollars *T. delivered by R & r* cents; being the second half of compensation of Register and Receiver, and balance of payment required by law for the entry of *S½ of NW¼ & d NE¼ of N W¼ & d SW¼ of NE¼* of Section *Twenty Six (26)* in Township *Four (4) North* of Range *Five (5) E* containing *160* acres, under the acts of Congress approved May 20, 1862, and March 21, 1864, entitled "An act to secure homesteads to actual settlers on the public domain."

$6 ~

Jno L. Cannon Receiver.

duced a more constructive law that offered an almost irresistible incentive for settlement.

Under the terms of the Homestead Act of 1862, a man could stake a claim to a piece of unoccupied public land by living on it and cultivating it for five years—after which he could file for ownership. By limiting these homesteads to 160 acres, Congress hoped to favor small, independent farms rather than plantation-like spreads worked by slaves or tenants. The fact that 160 acres of dry and recalcitrant prairie barely sufficed to sustain a single family bothered no one. Settlers claimed 224,500 acres in Kansas and Nebraska within six months after the act was passed.

An equally strong impetus to settle the prairies came later in the decade, as the new transcontinental railroad began laying track across the West. With empty boxcars available for profitable freight and with countless uninhabited acres along the right of way, the railroad barons began selling farmland at $2.50 an acre. In an all-out campaign to lure settlers, railroad land offices churned out reams of propaganda that painted the prairies and plains as a veritable paradise. To inject a note of authority into their pitch, salesmen frequently cited the words of William Gilpin, a soldier-explorer who had traveled across the grasslands as early as 1843 and returned there many times. Gilpin vigorously attacked the common notion that the region lacked rainfall and was in places virtual desert; he compared it to a "vast amphitheater," its face lifted "towards heaven to receive and fuse harmoniously whatever enters its rim."

Thus, Gilpin concluded grandly, "The PLAINS are not *deserts,* but the OPPOSITE, and the cardinal basis of the future empire."

The call for settlers resounded throughout the East, and reached across the Atlantic to northern Europe. Millions of pamphlets and posters, printed in a variety of languages, were circulated through Sweden, Holland, Norway, Denmark, Germany, England and Wales. Local boosters in the prairie country lent support to the clamorous promotion activities of the railroads. "Land for the Landless! Homes for the Homeless!" advertised the Nebraska Immigration Association, and the Dakota Territory voted a $3,000 annual appropriation to finance the establishment of a bureau of immigration to attract settlers from abroad.

The response was overwhelming. Swedes and Norwegians arrived in Minnesota in such numbers in the 1860s that the editor of the St. Paul *Pioneer* declared: "It seems as if the Scandinavian Kingdoms were being emptied into this State." So many Germans moved to Kansas and Nebraska during the late 1860s and early 1870s that one tribe of Kansas Indians spoke German, not English, as a second language.

The immigrants themselves were often the region's most avid promoters, touting the virtues of prairie life in letters home. "I advise everybody in Norway who lives under unhappy and straitened circumstances to come to Minnesota," wrote one man who arrived in 1866. He went on to extol the fertility of the soil and to express wonder at the American farmer's knack for doing things quickly and efficiently. "They have machines for taking up potatoes," he marveled, "machines for milking and churning, for washing clothes and wringing them dry." Another Norwegian immigrant, Paul Hjelm-Hansen, claimed that a tour of Dakota's Red River valley in 1869 cured his rheumatism and improved his disposition; he recalled mile after mile of beautiful farmland with rich black soil and "not as much as a stone or a stump in the way of the plow."

Some correspondents balanced their praise with hard, practical advice. Percy Ebbutt, an Englishman who arrived in Kansas in 1870, cautioned his countrymen in a pioneering guide:

"You must make up your mind to rough it. You must cultivate the habit of sleeping in any kind of surroundings, on a board and without a pillow, indoors or

out. I have been to sleep on horseback before now.

"You must be prepared to cook your own dinner, darn your own socks if you wear them, and think yourself fortunate if you are not reduced to the position of a man I knew, who lay in a bed while his wife mended his only pair of trousers. Learn to ride as soon as you possibly can; a man or boy who cannot ride is, in a new country, about as valuable as a clerk who cannot write in a city office."

As the railroads began to reach across the grasslands in the 1860s and '70s, most prairie settlers, whether European immigrants or native Americans, were able to travel to their destinations in relative comfort. Getting there became far easier than it was in the days of wagon caravans, and so families would arrive on the

A dugout carved into a prairie knoll—and about to undergo roof repairs—shelters a family new to Nebraska.

Nebraska prairie sod, peeled off in rows with a special plow and cut into blocks, is loaded onto a wagon for use as the basic home-building material. An acre of turf was needed to construct an average house.

prairies piecemeal. Fathers or older sons would come first, stake out a claim and put up a house before the rest of the clan followed.

Such was the case with Howard Ruede, who set out for the prairies well in advance of his parents, his two younger brothers and his sister, intending to pick a homestead site near the village of Osborne, Kansas, where a number of Pennsylvania neighbors had already located. He left his hometown of Bethlehem in March 1877, after closing out his $75 bank account and using part of it — $23.05 — to buy a train ticket West. Accompanied by a friend, Levin Brunner, he traveled by rail almost all the way — first to Buffalo, New York, from there to Kansas City, Missouri, then switching to the Kansas-Pacific line for the final leg of the journey.

The first day out of Kansas City, the train stopped at Manhattan, where Howard got a glimpse of the casual ways of land developers on the prairies. Manhattan had been founded by speculators who had simply bought up some uninhabited acreage in the middle of nowhere, laid out a few building plots and announced the birth of a new metropolis. The founders, Yankees from Massachusetts, initially named their town Boston. Then an-

other band of would-be colonists happened by on their way elsewhere. The speculators persuaded them to stay — and gratefully changed the town's name to suit the preference of its first inhabitants.

Manhattan, 126 miles west of the Missouri River, was in the middle of the flatlands of eastern Kansas. Such was the flatness, Howard reported home, that a fellow train passenger decided to throw in the towel the day he arrived. After staring at the monotonous scenery, the man declared that he had seen enough to convince him the place was irremediably "Godforsaken," and that he was going back East. Many other travelers had the same reaction, and so did some settlers. One day a Kansas woman watched her neighbors pull up stakes and head back toward Missouri, and wistfully noted in her diary that they were "traveling worldward, and every mile will bring them closer to civilization."

Howard Ruede was not so easily put off, even though the prairie wind flipped a prized worsted cap off his head, as he passed between train cars on his way from the smoker, and sent it scudding irretrievably over the sea of rippling grass. "That was a costly pipeful of tobacco," he concluded sadly. At Brookville he recovered his humor at the sight of a sign on a railroad water tank touting "Dan'l F. Beatty's pianos and organs, manufactured at Washington, N.J." Howard was pleased and surprised: "I didn't think he had got so far west with his advertising," he remarked in a letter to his family. Eventually—after a total of three days and three nights on the train—he and Levin Brunner disembarked at Russell, Kansas. They took a room at the Russell House (lodging and room $1) and slept soundly, "in spite of the lack of shaking to which we had become accustomed in the cars." Next day they hitched a ride to Osborne on a freight wagon, reaching it a day and a half later. Howard moved in temporarily with an old Bethlehem friend, Jacob Schweitzer, and promptly started looking for a plot of good farmland.

During the previous two decades, while most of the Kansas prairie still lay uninhabited, some townships had been arbitrarily divided into a checkerboard pattern of square-mile plots by federal surveyors. Each square contained 640 acres and was known as a section. The sections were further divided up into quarters of 160 acres each—the size that was subsequently allowed each settler free and clear under the Homestead Act. Howard Ruede staked a claim to a quarter-section outside Osborne, registering it with Squire Walrond, the local U.S. land office agent. In a letter home he reported that the land was "covered for the most part with buffalo grass," which, he assured his family, "was a sure sign of its being good." He also explained that he would have to work the claim for five years and "live 'off and on'—that is, we must sleep on it once in a while and make some improvements on it within 6 months, or it will be forfeited."

These provisions of the Homestead Act were intended to keep speculators from gobbling up huge tracts of free land and then selling off pieces at a profit. But in the remote reaches of the prairies, land laws were almost impossible to enforce. Land office agents were responsible for districts so vast that they could not always make firsthand inspections of settlers' claims. As a result, the laws were often ignored or adroitly bent by the claimants. A federal regulation, for example, required the settler to build a house on his claim that was at least 12 by 12, with windows. A number of Kansas land sharks managed to slip past this regulation by building cabins on wheels and rolling them from claim to claim. Another ploy consisted of erecting miniature "houses"—built with sticks and measuring exactly a foot high and a foot wide—and swearing, under oath, that a dwelling "12 by 12" had been constructed in accordance with the law.

There were other, more legitimate ways in which a settler could increase his holdings. By a process called preemption, he could purchase outright from the government as much as an extra quarter-section at $1.25 an acre. But preemption held a drawback that most settlers found insurmountable. The smallest unit they were allowed to buy, a paltry 40 acres, cost $50 plus a registration fee. This was simply too much money for most pioneers. The majority were as broke as Charley Wooster, a newly married pioneer from Hillsdale County, Michigan, who had arrived in Nebraska ahead of his bride, Nellie, to claim a homestead. He had to hold up construction on his sod house while Nellie, back home, tried to sell her favorite silk dress to get the money for a door and window.

Some pioneers secured extra land by filing a timber claim, which gave them another quarter-section in exchange for planting 10 acres in timber-producing trees. Howard Ruede considered but rejected the idea. Extra land was all well and good, he said, but it seemed very unlikely that the trees could take root in the prairie's hard-packed soil. Howard thought it was better to be content with the acreage he had, and to make it productive. "The curse of this community is land grabbing," he wrote. "Few men are satisfied with one claim; they must have a pre-emption, homestead and timber filing, and between the three they have so much work they don't know which end they stand on."

With his new homestead staked out and registered, Howard promptly set about improving it with a house. He admired the sturdy family home of his friend Jacob Schweitzer, who had taken advantage of a nearby source of white limestone. "Anybody, with a little practice, can lay up a stone house," Howard airily insisted. "The rock is soft and can be dressed square and hardens by exposure." But a stone house, he knew, took months to construct. He would build one later, he promised his mother; for the time being he needed something quick and easy. And so, like many other pioneers on the treeless prairie, he began with a dugout hollowed out of the earth. With the help of his friend Levin, and armed with an ax, a shovel and a borrowed pick, he set to work fashioning his first Kansas home.

On the sloping flank of a rise of ground — "where a patch of wild sunflowers had killed the grass" — Howard laid out a rectangle and began to dig a hole six feet deep, shaping a short flight of steps as he went down. The soil had the consistency of putty, and "Levin concluded that if we walked into the hole and then came out again and cleaned our shoes off, we could get the ground out a good deal sooner than if we used the shovel." When the hole was big enough, the two young men erected front and side walls with chunks of sod cut from the surrounding prairie. Howard raised these walls two and a half feet above the land's surface, then roofed the whole thing over with boards, straw and more sod. As the house took shape, settlers from nearby homesteads stopped by to offer Howard advice and muscle. His new neighbors included two former coopers, an ex-store clerk, a onetime gas-meter maker and a pawnbroker from England.

When the last chunk of dirt and matted grass had been fitted into place, Howard sprinkled seed corn over the scalped earth from which the sod had been cut. His house and garden were now complete. Altogether the project had cost just $10.05, he reported — $4.05 in cash for such items as nails, hinges and a window, and the rest in the form of labor he bartered to get firewood and lumber for furniture-making. Alas, it was an investment down the hole. This was the house that collapsed during a rainy spell not too many weeks later. Undeterred, Howard simply dug another home.

Underground living was, at best, a temporary solution to the problem of shelter. As soon as possible, most pioneers moved up to that classic of prairie architecture, the sod house — drier, sturdier and generally more comfortable than the lowly dugout. It offered so many advantages that settlers continued to build sod houses long after imported lumber became available for conventional frame buildings.

The building material for sod houses lay all about in limitless quantity, but it was stubborn stuff indeed. The buffalo grass of the prairies sprouted from densely tangled roots that filled the top three inches of soil like the roots of a tightly potted plant. Plowing such ground with a cast-iron plow — the kind that served perfectly well in other regions — was a slow and sometimes impossible task. By the 1860s, however, inventors had devised plows of tempered iron or steel that could turn the prairie soil efficiently. This advance in metallurgy was then applied to making a special plow that would cut sod for building purposes. The device shaved off a belt of roots and grass 12 to 18 inches wide and three inches deep; this ribbon of sod was then gently rolled over, in an unbroken strip, by means of parallel iron rods attached to the bit and extending outward like fingers. Since the rods vaguely resembled an insect's wings, the sod-cutting plow was sometimes called a "grasshopper." Howard Ruede, with his customary forthrightness, acclaimed the grasshopper a "tip-top invention," using an adjective he normally reserved for a bowl of ice cream on a summer's day.

As the grasshopper plow ripped through the earth it made a sound, the pioneers said, like the tearing of a heavy piece of fabric. Usually oxen were used to pull it because, unlike more wayward mules or horses, they walked almost as straight as they walked slow, producing a uniform strip of sod. Once the strips were turned over, the builder would cut them into two- or three-foot lengths with a broadax or a sharp spade. It was easiest to harvest the sod after a good rain or a snow melt had made the earth more pliable. Heavy with moisture, the sod blocks were hefted into a wagon or wheelbarrow and pushed to the building site — a task, said Howard Ruede, that "I tell you is no easy work."

Some builders staked out the rectangular foundation of their sod homes by moonlight, sighting on the North Star to get the desired alignment of walls — usually straight north and south, east and west. Thus oriented, they would set to work the next morning, with neighbors generally joining in for a building bee. Each block was laid with the grass side down, and the layers of blocks were staggered like brickwork. Two rows were usually placed side by side so that the finished walls were as much as 36 inches thick. At the corners, intersecting layers were lapped together and an iron rod or a pole made from a sapling was then hammered down from the top to pin the corners together.

As the walls of the sod house rose, the builder left spaces for window casements and door frames that were held in place by pegs driven into the sod mass. Since the walls were so thick, some of the casements were beveled outward to catch sunshine and funnel it into

"Bleeding Kansas": the price of an ill-conceived compromise

Two decades before emigration to the central grasslands reached full tide, a murderous ideological struggle broke out there—with bitter consequences for the entire nation. The trouble arose in 1854 when Senator Stephen A. Douglas of Illinois began to promote the building of a transcontinental railroad across the region. The first step in his plan was to get Congress to establish a territorial government that would help attract settlers. To win Southern votes for his bill, he baited it with a potential extension of slavery into the new territory.

Slavery had been prohibited north of latitude 36° 30' by the Missouri Compromise of 1820. The proposed new territory lay well north of this boundary, but Douglas felt that the limit could be conveniently ignored in the case of the vacant prairies. Anticipating Northern outrage, he devised an adroit formula. Not one but two territories, Kansas and Nebraska, would be created; initially both would be open to slavery; later the inhabitants would decide by vote—Popular Sovereignty, as Douglas called it —whether to retain or renounce slavery. He felt certain that Kansas would attract a proslavery majority from neighboring Missouri, and Nebraska an antislavery majority from such states as Ohio and Illinois; each side would thus win a state and a triumph.

After the Kansas-Nebraska Act slid through Congress on May 25, 1854, the scenario went as expected in Nebraska—but it unraveled catastrophically in Kansas. Both pro- and antislavery extremists began recruiting pioneers for Kansas to weight the voting lists. While the prospect of turmoil deterred most would-be settlers, 5,000 armed Missourians stormed in for the first election in 1855, seized polling places and installed a legislature that made even antislavery talk

In this 1858 cartoon, Douglas prepares to wage battle for the cause of Popular Sovereignty.

a crime. Next, an unknown assassin shot a proslavery sheriff visiting in the antislavery town of Lawrence. To avenge this act, 800 Southerners rode in and laid waste to the community. Then John Brown, a fanatical abolitionist, retaliated by murdering five Southerners in the hamlet of Pottawatomie Creek. In the three-month mini-war that ensued, 200 more people were killed, and the territory was stigmatized by the nation's press as Bleeding Kansas.

Appalled, Douglas broke with the leader of his party, President James Buchanan, when the administration upheld a proslavery constitution for Kansas. But the passions of the struggle had helped to set the stage for the Civil War—and not until that conflict had run its course did settlement of the plains get underway in earnest.

the gloomy indoors. And because the walls tended to compact about eight inches during the first years, a space stuffed with rags had to be left over windows and door openings to absorb the settling and keep the horizontal layers of sod reasonably in line.

In an optimistic effort to keep out the rain, prairie dwellers roofed their houses with a lattice of willow poles, brush, long grass, a layer of clay from the nearest creek bank and a final dressing of sod—grass side up. Even so, heavy spring downpours would cause a roof to leak water like an overloaded sponge. "Sometimes the water would drip on the stove while I was cooking," one prairie wife recalled, "and I would have to keep tight lids on the skillets to prevent mud from falling into the food. With my dress pinned up, and rubbers on my feet, I waded around until the clouds rolled by. Life is too short to be spent under a sod roof."

Even in the best of weather, various bits and pieces of matter came sifting down from the roof. To deal with this annoyance a prairie husband would tack cheesecloth to the rafters to catch the debris, and often he plastered inside walls with a mixture of lime and sand. ("It was a real temptation to write on those walls with a pencil," a Nebraskan who was raised in a sod house later recalled.)

There were other reasons for making the sod house as impervious as possible. Tight construction not only helped keep out the snow in winter, the rain in spring and the wind-blown dust in summer; it also helped deter mice and snakes. Even so, field mice were adept at tunneling through the walls, and garter snakes generally followed close behind. And nothing could ward off *Cimex lectularius,* the ubiquitous bedbug. Mollie Sanford, a Nebraska schoolteacher who sometimes boarded with her pupils' families, almost quit her profession after a stay in one sod house. "At this place I slept upon the floor," she wrote in her diary, "and festive bedbugs held high carnival over my weary frame the night through." Other forms of wildlife also abounded. A person did not "have to keep a dog," said Howard Ruede, "in order to have plenty of fleas, for they are natives too and do their best to drive out the intruding settlers. Just have a dirt floor and you have fleas sure. They seem to spring from the dust of the earth."

Despite all the inconveniences, most people grew to love their soddies, as the houses came to be called.

Pots of herbs and geraniums, set out on the deep, sunny window sills, gave sign that prairie wives were making a cheerful adjustment to their difficult lot. Eventually the sod house became a remarkably cozy haven in the midst of the rigors of prairie life. From Nebraska, Charley Wooster reassured his bride waiting in Michigan: "If we find any peace or happiness on this earth, I suppose 99 per cent of it will be within our own home."

Outside the home, however, there were still formidable obstacles to be surmounted. The sodbuster had to ensure himself of a water supply in a land that often lay bone-dry despite torrential spring rains. Some settlers collected rain in barrels and cisterns; others relied on water from a creek if one ran nearby. But most pioneers found water only by digging—often to incredible depths below the prairie surface. One man who each day carted his water in casks from a neighbor's well, a fair distance away, was asked why he didn't dig a well of his own. He replied that he would as soon go a mile in one direction as another. His estimate of a mile was an exaggeration, but some settlers had to sink shafts of 280 feet or more before reaching underground water.

Astonishingly, most of these wells were dug by hand. The sodbuster would scoop out the dirt, a shovelful at a time, throwing it over his shoulder for as long as he could. When the shaft got too deep, he rigged a windlass to crank up the dirt in buckets, stationing an assistant below to keep digging. Sometimes a rope would break and a bucketful of earth would come hurtling back down on the man at the bottom. Or subterranean gases, often mixed with deadly carbon monoxide, would seep into the hole and poison the digger.

Eventually well-digging became mechanized, a job for professional contractors who used steam-powered rigs that resembled oil derricks. But these men charged heavily for their services—as much as $1 a foot—and such fees were beyond the means of most pioneers.

There was one mechanical device that almost every sodbuster could afford—the windmill, which harnessed the grasslands' most reliable and handiest energy source to pump water from deep wells. Its stilt-legged tower, stark against the wide sky, became a lofty symbol of a homesteader's victory over the trials of prairie living.

The prairie windmill, like the tempered steel plows used to cut ribbons of sod, resulted from a special adaptation of an ancient tool to a harsh new environment.

Its principal designer was a mechanic named David Halladay. Tinkering in a Connecticut tool shop in 1854, Halladay perfected a mill that pivoted to face the wind and employed centrifugal force to adjust the pitch of the wooden vanes, allowing them to withstand the pressure of the high prairie winds. (A conventional windmill, without Halladay's governor, would have ripped itself to shreds in strong gusts.) A crankshaft transformed the mill's rotary motion to the water pump's up-and-down action. During a normal prairie day, the mill could lift hundreds of gallons from the earth. Most farmers needed such quantities to water livestock or, if they lived in the arid high plains of western Nebraska or Colorado, to irrigate their fields and keep crops alive.

Halladay's windmills made a tremendous hit with prairie settlers. Farm journals not only carried abundant advertisements for the Halladay Standard ("The *only* wind-mill awarded TWO MEDALS and DIPLOMAS"), but also published instructions for the frugal farmer who preferred to build his own. This, the directions said, could be done for as little as $1.50. Homemade windmills soon crimped the sales of the United States Wind Engine and Pump Company of Batavia, Illinois, manufacturer of the Halladay Standard.

A windmill was worthless, of course, if a farmer could not find a large underground pool of water. This elemental quest took on the same mingled aura of science, myth and instinct that attended man's search for gold or oil. The scientific approach entailed boring a test hole with a hand auger, which could be extended by the attachment of additional sections of rod as it went deeper. The trouble with the auger was that the

A Nebraska couple's cornfield covers every arable inch of land and almost engulfs their sod house. With the corn-hog ratio profitably figured at one bushel of feed to 12 pounds of pig, Nebraskans needed no urging when a state agriculturist wrote in 1876: "We cannot raise too much corn."

A windmill towers over a Nebraska homestead, providing power to pump water from a deep well. Ubiquitous by the 1880s, windmills harnessed the one source of energy that the prairies offered in abundance.

small test hole it made might miss an underground pool by inches. The alternatives were using sheer guesswork or engaging the services of a water witch. These individuals, in great demand on the plains, were said to possess the ability to divine underground water by mystical vibrations. They traced their skill back to Moses, who had caused water to bubble from a rock in the desert by smiting it with a stick. The water witch, usually an ordinary person in most other respects, would walk over a settler's claim with a forked, Y-shaped willow switch held in both hands. If the tail of the Y began to tug downward—or to bounce or vibrate—the witch would indicate that a water supply lay directly below.

Howard Ruede, in his solidly pragmatic way, did not believe in water witches. In digging his own well, he decided to use an auger, supplemented by a seat-of-the-pants guess. By this time it was November 1877, and Howard had been living in Kansas for seven months. He had finished his second dugout, and his father and a younger brother, Bub, had come west to join him. The water for the Ruede homestead came from a pasture pond frequented by cattle, and every mouthful made the men wish for a cleaner, cooler source. So, using a borrowed three-piece auger and with Bub to help, Howard drilled a test hole two inches in diameter and 23 feet deep. There the brothers struck shale.

Not a drop of water seeped into the hole, but Howard was undismayed. He felt so confident of his luck, in fact, that he began to dig out the well with a shovel. "It is possible," he said, "that in a hole 5 ft. in diameter we will be more likely to strike a vein of water than in a hole only 2 in. in diameter." But with winter coming on, Howard got sidetracked planting rye and winter wheat. When he turned back to well-digging in early December, the ground had frozen. His pick became so dull that he had to have it sharpened—which proved a mistake. On December 12, while digging in the dim light of the hole, Howard struck his head with the sharpened point. He took the rest of the day off.

Next morning he resumed digging. But at a depth of 25 feet he ran into the same plate of shale which had stopped his auger. Howard himself was unstoppable. "There are men in this neighborhood who have dug 4 and 5 wells, and still have no water," he wrote.

Reverting to the auger, he and his brother bored two more holes—both dry. Next, his father caused a brief

flurry of excitement with a hole he had dug, but hope quickly fizzled for a particularly frustrating reason. "I ran a sunflower stalk down," Howard reported of this venture, "and the auger hole was only four feet deep with about six inches of water in it. The misery of the thing is that it is not on my claim." The men tried still another spot—this one back on their own property—and on March 24, 1878, in gravel a mere eight feet from the surface, they met success. Water gushed up at last —after five months of searching.

The Ruedes dug their new well to a depth of 12 feet, and Howard shored up the interior with a circular wall of limestone blocks. Then he built a wooden framing at the top and attached a 65-cent iron pulley, around which he looped a rope and a pair of well buckets (costing 40 cents each). As one full bucket rose from the water, the empty one descended as a counterweight. The new well was clearly a triumph—except for one thing. It lay much too far from the dugout. Since the Ruedes were not about to dig another well, they decided to build another house and shut down the dugout. However, this time—because Howard's mother and the other children were expected to arrive any day—he constructed a proper, aboveground sod house. He built it just 100 steps from the well, and planted nine maple trees to provide shade.

Howard did not mention how much the new house cost, a departure from his usual preoccupation with dollars and cents. He once wrote home that a certain supper he had eaten had set him back five and three-eighths cents—about a half-pound of ham, five cents, and one ounce of beans, figured at three eighths of a cent—and his account books meticulously kept track of income and outgo to the half-cent. Such thriftiness was the key to survival; the Ruedes, like many of their neighbors, were forever skirting financial ruin. One reason was that money—at least the wildcat kind issued by banks in the form of paper notes bearing their own names—was not always worth its designated value. An insight into the loose financial practices of the region was provided by a local banker describing how he got started in business: "I didn't have much else to do and so I rented an empty store building and painted 'bank' on the window. The first day I was open for business a man came in and deposited one hundred dollars.

The second day another deposited two hundred-fifty dollars. And so, along about the third day, I got confidence enough to put in a hundred myself."

Where the money could be trusted it was hard to earn. Howard Ruede, who had experience as a printer's devil in Pennsylvania, got most of his cash from a part-time job in the print shop in Osborne. But he relied on barter for nearly all of his transactions—the same method used by pioneers who had settled farther regions of the West. As payment for the labor of plowing a neighbor's field, for example, Howard might receive so many bushels of wheat in exchange.

When he did have to tap his cash savings to make a major purchase, it was a matter to be approached in deadly earnest. One February morning he left home on such a mission, determined to return with a yoke of oxen and a wagon. He had $60 to spend for the oxen and another $30 for the wagon. He set off on foot at 6 a.m. and, according to his detailed account of the shopping venture, "arrived in Osborne about 9:30 and went to see Watson & Gillette, who had a wagon for sale. The price was $40. That was $10 more than I had. Then to Herzog's to see what Charley wants for his wagon. . . . He wanted $50 so that was no go. Back to W&G's to see if they would come down. But they would not. Next tried Ed Humphrey. He would sell for $30. . . . I went to see the vehicle. Found the tongue was broken, as well as the hind bolster, and the box was not much account."

Howard said he would take it anyway, but he promised himself that he would keep his eyes open for a better deal. Then he stopped to see Jacob Schweitzer, who had agreed to sell him a team of oxen. Howard paid for the oxen and stayed over at Schweitzer's for the night. By 6 o'clock the next morning he was on his way back to town to look for a better wagon. "Priced all the wagons I could hear or think of, but could not get a satisfactory price," he related. "At last I came across C. G. Paris. He had one. How much? $35. Make it $30 and I'll take it. He argued about ten minutes with me, saying he'd take 30 and never ask me for the other V. Told him I did not do business on that line; that I would not go into debt for even $5. Could apparently make no impression on him, so started for home without a wagon. I had not got out of town before he called me back, saying he'd take $30." At

Accompanied by a neighbor's child, a Kansas woman heads homeward with a barrow load of cow chips. Most pioneer stoves were fueled by the hardened droppings of cattle, dubbed the anthracite of the plains.

about 10 that night Howard was back home, oxen and wagon safely tied up in the yard.

Ownership of a team and a wagon gave a man a certain standing in a frontier community, and Howard Ruede was pleased a few days later to have an opportunity to display his new acquisitions. The occasion was a civic enterprise—a meeting about the projected building of a schoolhouse. Fifteen residents of the area assembled to discuss the question of its location. The whole thing could have been wrapped up in an hour and a half, Howard said, "if there had not been so much side talk, such as 'How much spring wheat did you sow?' and other questions of equally great importance." Finally someone offered to donate two acres of land—"a beautiful site," declared Howard—and nearly everybody present pledged to give six days of work to

building the schoolhouse, which would double as a church on Sunday.

During the 18 months that Howard Ruede kept a Kansas diary, his account of prairie life moved along in the same buoyant vein. He went to numerous ice-cream socials and frequently attended church services (Roman Catholics and "hard-shell Baptists" worshiped together, he noted approvingly). The rest of his family arrived from Pennsylvania in due course, and settled comfortably into the homestead. Howard Ruede suffered only one notable mishap: his prize sow died one day, from unknown causes. The sow had cost $5 and had consumed no-telling-how-much feed. Howard was made despondent by the episode, but "the fit soon wore off."

Not everyone took so sunny a view of life on a prairie homestead. To some people, particularly to women, it seemed a pretty dismal existence. Miriam Davis Colt — well educated, aged 36 — had a premonition of the rigors in store for herself and her family when, fresh from upstate New York, they reached the flats of eastern Kansas in 1856. Meeting her first frontier wife — "with bare feet, and a white sack twisted up and thrown over her shoulder, with a few quarts of corn meal in the end that hung down her back" — Miriam thought to herself: "Is that what I have got to come to?" Little by little she realized that it was. Eventually she summarized her disillusionment in a book entitled *Went to Kansas; Being a Thrilling Account of an Ill-fated Expedition to That Fairy Land, and Its Sad Results.*

Miriam's dismay might best be characterized as washday blues. Often short of homemade lye-and-ashes soap, she would scrub her clothes in creek water until, she said, they were "clean for brown but awful dirty for white." Moreover, she had lost her "indispensable flat-irons" somewhere, and "a rub through the hand" had to suffice as a simulacrum of starching and pressing.

Even so routine a task as cooking dinner could try the patience of a prairie housewife. Most settlers used a cast-iron Franklin stove for cooking as well as heating, with a sheet-iron pipe rigged through the roof to carry off the smoke. In a country so short of firewood, prairie stoves were designed so that they could burn hay, dried corncobs and sunflower stalks. The most common fuel, however, was cow chips, the domesticated version of the buffalo dung that had heated the meals of earlier pioneers as they rumbled across these same grasslands by covered wagon. Cooking with cow chips was not easy, especially for novices, who tended to be finicky. The chips burned so quickly that veteran cooks found it most expeditious to toss them into the stove by the handful. A Nebraska boy who watched his mother baking described the whole procedure as follows: "Stoke the stove, get out the flour sack, stoke the stove, wash your hands, mix the biscuit dough, stoke the stove, wash your hands, cut out the biscuits with the top of the baking-powder can, stoke the stove, wash your hands, put the pan of biscuits in the oven, keep on stoking the stove until the biscuits are done." The cook's final step, of course, was to wash her hands and serve dinner, even if she herself was too tuckered out to eat.

No method that onerous was likely to last. In 1877 the editor of a newspaper in Meade County, Kansas,

As a cloud of Rocky Mountain locusts darkens the countryside, cattle flee and farmers use smoke to rout the voracious invaders from their crops. These grasshoppers devastated the farms on the prairies and plains from 1874 to 1877, and then they abruptly and mysteriously disappeared.

A dust storm races toward a farming community, carrying a freight of particles from soil shriveled by drought. Such storms spread havoc on the plains, where, as a popular saying put it, "Between Amarillo and the North Pole, there is nothing to stop the wind but a barbed wire fence."

traced the decline of delicacy in the kitchen. "It was comical to see how gingerly our wives handled these chips at first," he wrote. "They commenced by picking them up between two sticks. . . . Soon they used a rag, and then a corner of their apron. Finally, growing hardened, a wash after handling them was sufficient. And now? Now it is out of the bread, into the chips and back again—and not even a dust of the hands."

If the housewife overcame her scruples about cow chips, she had another problem to contend with: the lack of flour to make biscuits or bread. Wheat did not grow easily in some parts of the plains, and sodbusters learned to make do with corn. One Nebraska newspaper ran an article listing 33 ways to fix the stuff. "I live entirely on food made of corn," Miriam Colt reported. "Hominy and milk and johnny-cake and milk

—and try to persuade the children to do the same, leaving the wheat bread for grand-ma and grand-pa. Today, at dinner, I told Willie momma had got some good johnny-cake, and asked him to have some in his milk. He said, 'Willie *rather have white bread;*' and the little fellow will relish it much better than children with pampered appetites do their round of goodies."

Schoolteacher Mollie Sanford, who was boarding with a family of transplanted Southerners, found the fare no less monotonous. "Their manner of living is so different from ours," wrote Mollie, "that it just about used me up. For breakfast we had corn bread, salt pork and black coffee. For dinner, greens, wild ones at that, boiled pork, and cold corn bread washed down with 'beverage.' The 'beverage' was put upon the table in a wooden pail and dished out in tin cups. When asked if

I would have some of the 'aforesaid,' I said 'yes,' thinking it perhaps was cider, but found out it was vinegar and brown sugar and warm creek water."

Besides cooking, washing and cleaning house, women on the prairies were expected to help the men with the plowing, to tote water and fuel, and perhaps grow a kitchen garden of herbs and vegetables. And in a land with few doctors, it was up to them to keep the family healthy. They devised all kinds of remedies from the materials — and the folk wisdom — at hand: coal oil for dandruff, warm manure for snakebite, warm urine poured into the ear for earache (also said to be good for freckles and sunburn), sassafras tea to cure spring fever, a roasted mouse (well done) ingested to cure measles, nine pellets from a shotgun shell swallowed for boils, buttercup tea for asthma, a bean thrown into a well

over the left shoulder for warts and a potato carried in the pocket for rheumatism.

Despite the dubious value of these curatives, prairie families managed to survive in reasonable health and security. But occasional catastrophes occurred for which no remedies existed, and which spelled the end to many a homesteader's dreams. Most disasters were brought on by the capricious prairie climate.

One instance was the horrendous drought that gripped Kansas and Nebraska just as the earliest wave of pioneers was beginning to settle in. For 18 months — from June 19, 1859 until November 1860 — not a single good rain fell. The earth broke into hideous cracks, the prairie grass withered to a walnut brown and no crops grew. Dry, scorching winds blew in periodically from the southwest, further desiccating the

Harvesting wheat on the northern plains, farm hands break for lunch around the mobile steam engine that powers their threshers. This machine, introduced in the 1870s, could perform the work of a dozen teamed horses, although it required an auxiliary wagon (left) to carry the water supply.

land. Thousands of sodbusters were left destitute, and Marcus J. Parrott, the Kansas representative in Washington, reported that "many people were then living on acorns and were clothed in bark."

Summer hailstorms could be almost as destructive, flattening crops and often battering the pioneers themselves. One such storm in the 1870s hit Zedekiah Blake as he rode to Fort Riley, Kansas, with a wooden tub full of vegetables. Bombarded by hailstones the size of eggs, Zedekiah saved his life by emptying his vegetable tub, turning it over and crouching beneath it.

One of the most terrifying hazards to a sodbuster's life and livelihood was the prairie fire. In the autumn, when the grass turned tinder-dry, it could be set ablaze by the merest spark from an ember of an untended campfire, by a stroke of lightning or by the discharge of a gun. The result was awesome. "The sky," one man testified, "is pierced with tall pyramids of flame or covered with writhing, leaping, lurid serpents, or transformed into a broad ocean lit up by a blazing sunset. Now a whole avalanche of fire slides off into the prairie, and then opening its great devouring jaws closes in upon the deadened grass."

Settlers would try to deal with small fires by smothering them with damp blankets and clothing, by lighting backfires or by adopting the cattleman's tactic of dragging the bloody carcasses of slaughtered livestock over the flaming grass. When all else failed they retreated to their dugouts and prayed. The heavy sod roofs usually saved them, but their fields went up in smoke.

On the prairies of southwestern Minnesota in the summer of 1871, hail and fire completely wiped out the crops. The winter that followed was unusually severe, and many settlers had no money to buy food and clothing. One desperate farmer wrote a letter to the governor's office: "I have been sick for months and my wife is not well from exposure and hunger and I thought that there was no other way than to ask you to help me — If you can let me have $25 and some close for my wife and daughter and myself as we have not close to cover our backs or heads."

The most terrible scourges of all were the plagues of locusts that swarmed through the prairies in the 1870s, devouring everything that grew and a lot that didn't. "They came in untold millions," wrote the editor of the Wichita City *Eagle* in 1874, "in clouds upon clouds, until their fluttering wings looked like a sweeping snowstorm in the heavens, until their dark bodies covered everything green upon the earth." The insects blanketed the ground in a writhing layer as much as six inches deep, and the combined weight of their bodies snapped the limbs off cottonwood trees.

Nothing escaped their appetite. They consumed crops, prairie grass, the leaves and bark of trees, leather boots and harness straps, even fence posts, door frames and the sweat-stained wooden handles of axes and plows. A Topeka editor reported that one year these invaders, having finished off the corn crop, "attacked innumerable piles of cord-wood and cut it up into very respectable chunks for the stove; this would have been a fair offset if the fiends had only taken the trouble to split it." No one seemed to know what caused the locusts to swarm, or what eventually prompted them to depart. But the wreckage that they left in their wake was all too painfully recognizable.

Winter, with its fierce blizzards and arctic temperatures, brought still another set of woes. Wind-driven snowflakes seeped through the cracks of the tightest sod house. In Lawrence, Kansas, in the winter of 1855-1856, the temperature sank to between 20° and 30° below zero; settlers sitting down to breakfast found the water frozen in their drinking glasses, and had to thaw their loaves of bread on the stove before slicing them. That same winter, in Fremont, Nebraska, one homesteader kept his wife and child from freezing only by sheltering them inside a tent of blankets he improvised around the stove.

Prairie blizzards could blow up, with startling rapidity, out of a clear blue sky. One of the most devastating, remembered as the "schoolchildren's blizzard" because it struck during school hours, howled across the entire breadth of the plains and prairies in January of 1888. Yet it took everyone by surprise. O. W. Coursey, a schoolboy in the Dakota Territory at the time, later described the storm's onset. That morning, he recalled, "was mild and warm. At recess, during the forenoon, we were all out playing in our shirt sleeves, without hats or mittens. Suddenly we looked up and saw something coming rolling toward us with great fury from the northwest, and making a loud noise. It looked like a long string of big bales of cotton, each one bound tightly with heavy cords of silver. These cotton bales

looked to be about twenty-five feet high; above them it was perfectly clear."

The children ran for the frame schoolhouse and barely reached it in time. The blizzard struck with such force that it almost lifted the building from its cobblestone foundations. The youngsters huddled inside all that night. By morning the storm had blown itself out, and they were able to set out safely for home, wading through snowdrifts.

Other settlers were not so lucky. Hundreds of people, caught out of doors by the full fury of the storm and blinded by the swirling snow, lost their way and froze to death. A couple in Buffalo County, Dakota, perished while looking for each other just outside their sod house. And another group of Dakota children, caught without fuel in their schoolhouse, started for a settler's home 140 yards away. They lost the path and

plunged into a little ravine. There, half-frozen and exhausted, they found a pile of straw and tunneled into it for the night. As it turned out, they had missed the settler's house by only six feet. All the children survived, though one girl's feet were so badly frostbitten they had to be amputated.

As fearsome as the blizzards and droughts and other unpredictable assaults of nature could be, there was a human threat that terrified sodbusters even more — the Indians. The hazard was more often imagined than real. The great majority of the prairie Indians had been packed off to reservations before pioneers arrived in numbers; even in the early days, most encounters between white man and Indian ended amicably enough. Occasionally a housewife would take fright when a strange Indian strode into her kitchen demanding food, but this was simply because she misunderstood the In-

dians' brusque and forthright way of approaching strangers and making friends.

Thus Matilda Peterson, busy frying doughnuts one day in her home in eastern Nebraska, was scared speechless when an Indian named No-Flesh ambled unannounced into her cabin with several companions and hunkered down near the stove. Trying to maintain her composure, Matilda kept turning out doughnuts, but she dropped one on the floor. It rolled in front of No-Flesh, and he thrust it into his mouth. From the way he smacked his lips and gestured for more, it was obvious he had never tasted anything so good. For more than an hour Matilda stood over the fire cooking more doughnuts for her apparently insatiable guests, until her husband, John, returned to the cabin and chased them away. A few days later No-Flesh, still hungry for Matilda's cooking, paid a formal call on John Peterson. He wanted to trade wives. Peterson jokingly agreed, only to discover that No-Flesh was serious. It took a bushel of doughnuts to smooth the Indian's ruffled pride.

Not all Indian scares proved to be baseless. Inevitably, some tribes began to feel a mounting shock of injustice and betrayal, and took to the warpath. Their grievances were many. More and more settlers were moving into their former hunting grounds, and even poaching on their reservation lands; white merchants were preying on them. For the Sioux of Minnesota in 1862, the final straw was the failure of the government's promised annual payment to arrive on time — after a winter of near famine. In the fall of that year, Sioux warriors burst out of their reservation and proceeded to burn and pillage every homestead within reach, usually murdering the inhabitants. "We do not go to bed without fear, and my rifle is always loaded," wrote a Norwegian farmer in Dodge County. The Sioux killed some 450 settlers before a hastily recruited local militia managed to subdue them and quell what became known as the Minnesota Massacre, one of the bloodiest Indian episodes in the history of the West. Two years later in Colorado the Cheyennes started raiding settlements, stealing cattle and killing people. The U.S. Cavalry galloped to the rescue, but sporadic Indian attacks continued throughout the decade.

As late as 1869 a war party of Cheyennes, having escaped from a skirmish with Lieutenant Colonel George A. Custer's Seventh Cavalry, roared into west-

ern Kansas. On May 30 at Spillman Creek they surprised a Danish settler named Eskild Lauritzen, his wife and a neighbor, and killed all three. Next they found a German couple, the Weichels, who had just finished planting their vegetable garden beside the creek. They gunned down Weichel and a companion, and took his wife prisoner.

Farther up the creek the Cheyenne warriors came upon Mrs. Timothy Kine, a young mother who had taken her new baby to visit neighbors, Susan Alderdice and her four children. The two women saw the Indians approaching across the prairie. Mrs. Kine plunged into the creek, at a point where she was hidden by some brush overhanging the bank, and held her baby high to keep it from drowning. But Mrs. Alderdice, paralyzed with fear, collapsed in a faint, surrounded by her four quaking children. The Cheyennes shot the three oldest boys, killing two of them. They then galloped off with Mrs. Alderdice and her youngest child. The baby cried so lustily that the Indians became enraged, choked it to death and left the body beside the trail. The gravely wounded mother later died, but the other woman captive, Mrs. Weichel, survived.

Eventually the Indian threat subsided: the U.S. Army established a *pax Americana* on the plains and prairies, and masses of settlers moved in. They flooded land offices with applications for homestead and pre-emption claims: 13,301 in Nebraska in 1885, and 11,874 in Kansas the same year. In the Dakotas, during the decade from 1880 to 1889, farmers claimed a total of 41,321,472 acres.

Windmills sprouted across the grasslands, and a lacework of irrigation ditches crisscrossed the arid plains of Colorado and Wyoming. A new kind of wheat, introduced in 1874 by Mennonite immigrants from Russia's Crimea, proved hardy enough to withstand severe extremes of climate, and began to replace the prairie grasses. Giant new machines — plows and reapers and combines pulled by lumbering steam tractors — allowed a sodbuster to cultivate in one afternoon the same amount of acreage that would have taken him weeks to work by hand. Barbed-wire fences enabled him to protect his holdings against intrusion. Like the earlier generation of pioneers who opened the Far West, the settlers on the grasslands were there to stay. They held on as stubbornly as the matted sod beneath their feet.

A bachelors' get-together features a watermelon feast, a friendly card game and a playful display of guns at hand.

A proud new world on the prairies

In the spring of 1886, a 30-year-old sodbuster who had worked briefly as a photographer back East hit upon the idea of producing an album of his fellow settlers. For the next 15 years, as the pioneer era drew to a close, Solomon D. Butcher crisscrossed Custer County, Nebraska, in a wagon that served as a studio. He announced his forays with notices in the local newspaper: "Farmers, have your farm photos taken for Butcher's Pioneer History."

The fact that Butcher was himself a farmer provided rapport with his subjects. But his genius as a photographer lay in allowing them to pose as they wished, against scenes of their own choosing. The portraits that resulted convey the dignity of pioneers in challenging circumstances, and they remain a classic record of a resolute breed.

A well-made sod house, sturdy youngsters and a new baby spell the good life for a pioneer couple.

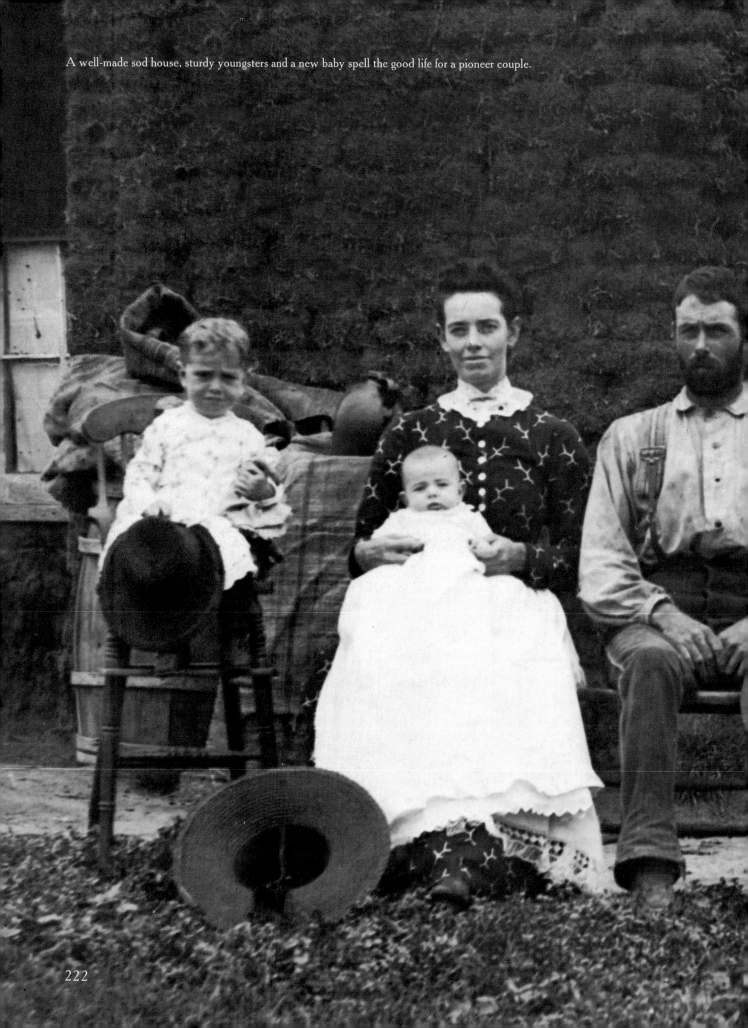

A prairie family's treasures include caged songbirds and a pile of antlers to be reduced to fertilizer.

Settlers cluster around a prized organ, hauled from the house to serve as their portrait's proud centerpiece.

A child's dolls are accorded the status of family members in this formal gathering of a pioneer clan.

Former slaves — "very highly respected citizens," the photographer noted — mark their new life as landowners.

Defying the chill of a prairie winter, hardy immigrants from Europe choose to be pictured in the snow.

TEXT CREDITS

For full reference on specific page credits see bibliography.

Chapter I: Particularly useful sources for information and quotes: *Far Western Frontier: 1830-1860*, Ray A. Billington, Harper & Row, 1956; *The Great Platte River Road*, M. J. Mattes, Nebraska State Historical Society, 1969; "Palmer's Journal of Travels . . . ," R. G. Thwaites, *Early Western Travels 1748-1846*, Vol. XXX, Arthur H. Clark Company, 1906; "Reminiscences of Experiences on the Oregon Trail in 1844," John Minto, *The Quarterly of the Oregon Historical Society*, Vol. II, March-Dec. 1901, pp. 119-167, 209-254; *The Sod House Frontier, 1854-1890*, Everett Dick, Johnsen Publishing Co., 1954; 24—Clyman quote excerpted from De Voto, pp. 55-56; 33—sea route description excerpted from Lewis, p. 49; 37—cold weather quote excerpted from Woodward, p. 59; Mollie Sanford quotes, Sanford, pp. 13, 112; deserted cabin and grasshopper quotes, Fite, pp. 200, 61. Chapter II: Particularly useful sources: *First White Women over the Rockies*, Vol. I, Clifford M. Drury, Arthur H. Clark Co., 1963; *Hall J. Kelley on Oregon*, Fred Wilbur Powell, Princeton Univ. Press, 1932; *Jason Lee, Prophet of the Oregon*, C. Brosnan, Macmillan, 1932; *John Marsh, Pioneer*, G. D. Lyman, Scribner's, 1930; *Marcus and Narcissa Whitman and the Opening of Old Oregon*, C. M. Drury, Vols. I & II, Arthur H. Clark Co., 1973; 43—Floyd and John Adams quotes, Ambler, p. 61; 64—Marsh letter excerpts, p. 315; 68—Williams quotes, Williams, pp. 25, 34; 69—Bidwell quotes, Bidwell, pp. 25, 34, quoted by permission of the Director, The Bancroft Library, University of Calif., Berkeley. Chapter III: Particularly useful sources: *The California Trail*, George R. Stewart, McGraw-Hill, 1962; *The Great Platte River Road*, M. J. Mattes, Nebraska State Historical Society, 1969; *Ordeal By Hunger*, George R. Stewart, Henry Holt, 1936; *Overland in '46*, Dale L. Morgan, Talisman Press, 1963; 85—soup mishap excerpted from Cummins, p. 19; 85, 86—Knight excerpts, Knight, pp. 38-53; 88—ox quote, Stewart, "Prairie Schooner," p. 99; 88, 89, 92—Delano excerpts, Delano, pp. 27-28, 85, 146; 90, 91—Applegate journey excerpted from Applegate, "Cow Column," pp. 3-22; 92—Parkman excerpts, Parkman, p. 8; 92, 93—buffalo excerpts, Minto, p. 132; 93—Alcove Springs excerpt, Bryant, p. 62; buffalo excerpts, Applegate, *Recollections*, p. 42; cooking skills excerpts, Paden, p. 45; 96—Long Texas paraphrased, Dick, *Tales*, pp. 260-262; 98—Ash Hollow excerpt, Wm. Kelly, p. 147; 99—Cummins excerpt, Cummins, pp. 35-36; 104—July 4th excerpt, Judson, p. 6; 107-110—Applegate story excerpts and paraphrases, Applegate, *Recollections*, pp. 25-122; 111—Young quote, Chas. Kelly, pp. 75-77. Chapter IV: Particularly useful sources: *Dictionary of Oregon History*, H. M. Corning, Binsford &

Mort, 1956; *Farthest Frontier*, S. Warren, Macmillan, 1949; *First White Women over the Rockies*, Vols. I & II, C. M. Drury, Arthur H. Clark Co., 1963; *Marcus and Narcissa Whitman and the Opening of Old Oregon*, Vols. I & II, C. M. Drury, Arthur H. Clark Co., 1973; *Mercer's Belles, The Journal of a Reporter*, R. Conant, Univ. of Washington Press, 1960; *The Oregon Trail*, Maude A. Rucker, Walter Neale, 1930; "Recollections and Opinions of an Old Pioneer," P. Burnett, *The Quarterly of the Oregon Historical Society*, Vol. V, No. 1, March 1904, pp. 64-99; "Palmer's Journal . . . ," R. G. Thwaites, *Early Western Travels 1748-1846*, Vol. XXX, Arthur H. Clark Co., 1906; 123—Hines quote excerpted from Hines, p. 151; Willamette valley excerpt, Davenport, p. 38; 127—Cartwright quote excerpted from Cartwright, pp. 56-57; 133—Cayuse excerpt, Ross, p. 86; 143-145—little girl excerpt, Bromberg, p. 307; 145—Howard quote and paraphrases from Bromberg, p. 308; women excerpt, Bagley, "Mercer Immigration," p. 7; 146—Mercer quote, Bagley, "Mercer Immigration," p. 16. Chapter V: Particularly useful sources: *Among the Mormons*, W. Mulder & A. R. Mortensen, Knopf, 1958; *Brigham Young*, M. R. Werner, Harcourt, Brace, 1925; *The Gathering of Zion*, Wallace Stegner, McGraw-Hill, 1964; *Great Basin Kingdom*, L. J. Arrington, Harvard Univ. Press, 1958; *History of Utah*, Hubert H. Bancroft, Bookcraft, 1964; *History of Utah 1847-1869*, Andrew L. Neff, Deseret News Press, 1940; *The Mountain Meadows Massacre*, Juanita Brooks, Univ. of Oklahoma Press, 1950; *The Story of the Mormons*, W. A. Linn, Russell & Russell, 1963; 160—Larson quote, Larson, p. 2; bathing frolic quote, Morgan, p. 200; Morgan quote, Morgan, p. 20; 167—Smith quote, Selby, p. 168; 173—morning frost quote, Morgan, p. 214; 174—beaver quote, Ricks, p. 64; 178—Brigham Young quote, West, p. 254; Tyler letter, Auchampaugh, pp. 180-181; 181—Lincoln quote, Hirshon, p. 263. Chapter VI: Particularly useful sources: *The Farmers' Frontier*, G. C. Fite, Holt, Rinehart & Winston, 1966; *The Great Plains*, W. P. Webb, Ginn, 1959; *Sod-House Days*, H. Ruede, Cooper Square, 1966; *The Sod House Frontier*, Everett Dick, Johnsen Publishing Co., 1954; 194-195—Gilpin quote, Emmons, pp. 10-11; 195—advice to Norwegians quote, Blegen, p. 433; Ebbutt's advice excerpted, Ebbutt, pp. 229-232; 202—skillet quote, Welsch, p. 339; 210—bare feet quote, Colt, p. 42; stove quote, O'Kieffe, p. 26; 210, 212—cow chips quote, Miller et al., p. 156; corn quote, Colt, p. 83; 212, 213—Sanford quote, Sanford, p. 87; 216—cord wood quote, Miller et al., p. 91; 216, 217—snow storm excerpt, O'Gara, p. 38; 217, 219—Indian assault excerpts, Bernhardt, pp. 25-32.

PICTURE CREDITS

The sources for the illustrations in this book are shown below. Credits from left to right are separated by semicolons and from top to bottom by dashes.

Cover—*Advice on the Prairie*, William Ranney, copied by Paulus Leeser, courtesy J. Maxwell Moran Collection. 2—Courtesy Utah State Historical Society. 6,7—*Covered Wagons Crossing Medicine Bow Creek*, Samuel Colman, copied by Paulus Leeser, courtesy Private Collection. 8,9—*The Emigrant Train Bedding Down for the Night*, Benjamin Franklin Reinhart, copied by Paulus Leeser, in the Collection of the Corcoran Gallery of Art, Gift of Mr. & Mrs. Lansdell K. Christie. 10,11—*The Prairie Fire*, William Ranney, copied by Paulus Leeser, courtesy J. Maxwell Moran Collection. 12,13—*The Attack on an Emigrant Train*, Charles Wimar, copied by Paulus Leeser, courtesy The University of Michigan Museum of Art, bequest of Henry C. Lewis. 14,15

—*The Pioneers*, William Ranney, collection of Claude J. Ranney, Malvern, Pa., courtesy American Heritage Publishing Co. 16—Courtesy The Bancroft Library. 18, 19—Courtesy of the New-York Historical Society. 21—Pierre Boulat, courtesy Bibliothèque Nationale, Paris. 22,23—Map by Rafael Palacios. 25—Courtesy Oregon Historical Society. 27—Courtesy Picture Collection, The Branch Libraries, The New York Public Library. 28,29—Missouri Historical Society, courtesy American Heritage Publishing Co. 31—Courtesy California Historical Society. 32, 33—Courtesy California State Library. 35—Courtesy Rare Book Division, The New York Public Library, Astor, Lenox and Tilden Foundations. 36—From The Medorem Crawford Papers, Special Collections, University of Oregon, Eugene. 37 — Courtesy Oregon Historical Society. 38, 39 — Courtesy of National Collection of Fine Arts, Smithsonian Institution. 40 — From *John Marsh, Pioneer,* George Lyman, courtesy General Research and Humanities Division, The New York Public Library, Astor, Lenox and Tilden Foundations; courtesy Oregon Historical Society. 41 — Courtesy Oregon Historical Society except top left, courtesy Washington State Historical Society, Tacoma. 42 — Courtesy James K. Polk Ancestral Home, Columbia, Tenn. 44, 45 — Courtesy Missouri Historical Society. 46 — Courtesy Culver Pictures. 47 — Courtesy American History Division, The New York Public Library, Astor, Lenox and Tilden Foundations. 50 — Courtesy National Archives. 51 — Courtesy Library of Congress. 53 — Courtesy Royal Ontario Museum, Toronto. 55 — Reproduced by permission of the Director, The Bancroft Library. 56, 57 — Courtesy Denver Public Library, Western History Department. 59 — Courtesy Whitman College, used by special permission of the copyright owners. 60 — J.R. Eyerman, courtesy Oregon Historical Society. 62, 63 — J.R. Eyerman, courtesy Carl Schaefer Dentzel Collection. 65 — Courtesy State Historical Society of Missouri. 66, 67 — Courtesy California Historical Society. 70, 71 — From *Wilderness Kingdom: The Journals and Paintings of Nicholas Point, S.J.* Copyright © 1967 by Loyola University Press, Chicago. Reproduced by permission of Holt, Rinehart and Winston, Inc. 72 — Courtesy Library of Congress — Courtesy Rare Book Division, The New York Public Library, Astor, Lenox and Tilden Foundations. 73 — From *Wilderness Kingdom: The Journals and Paintings of Nicholas Point, S.J.* Copyright © 1967 by Loyola University Press, Chicago. Reproduced by permission of Holt, Rinehart and Winston, Inc. — Courtesy Rare Book Division, The New York Public Library, Astor, Lenox and Tilden Foundations. 74, 75 — Herb Orth, Time-Life Picture Agency © 1972, Time Incorporated, from *Wilderness Kingdom: The Journals and Paintings of Nicholas Point, S.J.* Copyright © 1967 by Loyola University Press, Chicago. Reproduced by permission of Holt, Rinehart and Winston, Inc. 76, 77 — Courtesy Kansas State Historical Society, Topeka. 78, 79 — Courtesy Denver Public Library, Western History Department. 80, 81 — Courtesy Nebraska State Historical Society. 82, 83 — Courtesy Western History Research Center, University of Wyoming. 84 — Courtesy Denver Public Library, Western History Department. 86 — Courtesy California Historical Society. 87 — Clyde Arbuckle Collection, San Jose, California, courtesy American Heritage Publishing Co. 89 — Courtesy of the New-York Historical Society. 90, 91 — Courtesy The Bancroft Library. 94, 95 — Courtesy Denver Public Library, Western History Department. 96 — Courtesy Sy Seidman. 97 — Courtesy Denver Public Library, Western History Department. 100 — Harald Sund, courtesy Oregon Historical Society. 101 — Drawings by Nicholas Fasciano. 102, 103 — Harald Sund, courtesy Oregon Historical Society. 105 — Courtesy The Bancroft Library. 106 — Courtesy Culver Pictures. 108, 109 — Courtesy Denver Public Library, Western History Department. 110 — Courtesy Oregon Historical Society. 112 — Courtesy Sy Seidman. 114 — Courtesy California Department of Parks and Recreation. 115 — Courtesy California State Library. 116, 118, 119 — Courtesy The Bancroft Library. 120, 121 — Lithograph by Currier & Ives, courtesy Harry T. Peters Collection, Museum of the City of New York. 122 — Courtesy Picture Collection, The Branch Libraries, The New York Public Library. 124, 125 — Courtesy Idaho Historical Society. 126, 128 — Courtesy Picture Collection, The Branch Libraries, The New York Public Library. 130, 131 — Courtesy Oregon Historical Society. 132, 133 — Courtesy Sy Seidman. 134, 135 — Courtesy Oregon Historical Society. 136 — From *Marcus Whitman, M.D.,* Clifford Drury, published by Caxton Printers Ltd., Caldwell, Idaho. Used by special permission of the copyright owners. 137 — Courtesy Royal Ontario Museum, Toronto. 138, 139 — Lorenzo Lorain, courtesy Oregon Historical Society. 140, 141 — Courtesy Bettmann Archives. 142 — Courtesy General Research and Humanities Division, The New York Public Library, Astor, Lenox and Tilden Foundations. 143 — Courtesy Seattle Historical Society. 144, 145 — Courtesy Special Collections, University of Oregon Library, Eugene. 147 — Courtesy Oregon Historical Society. 148 through 157 — Courtesy The Church of Jesus Christ of Latter-day Saints. 158 — Courtesy Utah State Historical Society. 160 — Courtesy The Church of Jesus Christ of Latter-day Saints. 161 — Courtesy The Huntington Library, San Marino. 162 — Courtesy Denver Public Library, Western History Department. 164, 165 — Courtesy Nelson Wadsworth. 166 — Collection of Mr. & Mrs. C. Lincoln Avery, courtesy Utah State Historical Society. 167 — A.J. Russell, courtesy Union Pacific Railroad Museum Collection. 168, 169 — Courtesy Denver Public Library, Western History Department. 171 — Courtesy The Church of Jesus Christ of Latter-day Saints. 172 — Courtesy Utah State Historical Society. 174, 175 — Courtesy The Church of Jesus Christ of Latter-day Saints. 177 — Courtesy Denver Public Library, Western History Department. 179 — Courtesy Utah State Historical Society — Courtesy Denver Public Library, Western History Department. 180 — Courtesy General Research and Humanities Division, The New York Public Library, Astor, Lenox and Tilden Foundations. 182, 183 — A. J. Russell, courtesy The Oakland Museum. 184, 185 — Top left and inset courtesy Denver Public Library, Western History Department — Courtesy The Huntington Library, San Marino. 186, 187 — Courtesy Utah State Historical Society. 188, 189 — Courtesy A. A. Forbes Collection, Western History Collection, University of Oklahoma Library. 190 — Courtesy Baker Library, Harvard Business School. 192, 193 — Courtesy The Kansas State Historical Society, Topeka. 194 — Courtesy Nebraska State Historical Society. 195 — From *Beyond the Mississippi,* Albert D. Richardson. 196, 197 — Courtesy Solomon D. Butcher Collection, Nebraska State Historical Society. 198 — Courtesy Nebraska State Historical Society. 201 — Courtesy Prints Division, The New York Public Library, Astor, Lenox and Tilden Foundations. 203 through 207 — Courtesy Solomon D. Butcher Collection, Nebraska State Historical Society. 209 — Courtesy The Kansas State Historical Society, Topeka. 210, 211 — Courtesy General Research and Humanities Division, The New York Public Library, Astor, Lenox and Tilden Foundations. 212, 213 — Weather Bureau Photo No. 27-S-2, courtesy National Archives. 214, 215 — Courtesy Minnesota Historical Society. 217 — Courtesy Solomon D. Butcher Collection, Neb. State Hist. Soc. 218 — Courtesy the Kansas State Historical Society. 220 through 233 — Courtesy Solomon D. Butcher Collection, Neb. State Hist. Soc.

ACKNOWLEDGMENTS

The editors give special thanks to the following persons who read and commented on portions of the book: Dr. Clifford M. Drury, Pasadena; Nick Eggenhofer, Cody, Wyo.; Paul W. Gates, Ithaca, N.Y.; Dr. Rodman W. Paul, The Edward S. Harkness Professor of History, Calif. Institute of Technology, Pasadena.

The editors also acknowledge the assistance of Dale Archibald, Chief Curator, Oregon Historical Society Museum, Portland; Ray A. Billington, Western History Research Dir., Henry E. Huntington Library, San Marino, Calif.; Brenda Boswell, Information Section, State of Calif. Dept. of Parks and Recreation, Sacramento; Susan Burns, Assoc. Researcher, The Oakland Museum, Oakland, Calif.; Lee L. Burtis, Librarian, Photographs and Genealogy, Catherine Hoover, Asst. Curator, Maude K. Swingle, Ref. Librarian, Jay Williar, Ref. Librarian, Calif. Historical Society, San Francisco; Cynthia Carey, Librarian, Pasadena Public Library, Pasadena; William B. Carpenter, Church of Jesus Christ of Latter-day Saints, Graphics Dept., Salt Lake City; Maud Cole, Rare Book Room, The New York Public Library, New York City; James H. Davis, Picture Librarian, Western History Dept., Denver Public Library, Denver; Eugene Decker, Archivist, Kansas State Historical Society, Topeka; Carl S. Dentzel, Dir., Southwest Museum, Los Angeles; Lawrence L. Dodd, Curator of Manuscripts and Special Collections, Penrose Memorial Library, Whitman College, Walla Walla, Wash.; Richard H. Engeman, Photographs & Maps Librarian, Susan Sudduth, Oregon Historical Society, Portland; Pauline Fowler, Archivist, Jackson County Historical Society, Independence, Mo.; Kathleen Grasing, Dir., Library Services Div., Oregon State Library, Salem, Ore.; Frank Green, Librarian, Washington State Historical Society, Tacoma; Joan Hoffmann, Beinecke Rare Book and Manuscript Library, Yale Univ., New Haven; Opal Jacobsen, Photo Librarian, Nebraska State Historical Society, Lincoln; Jerry Kearns, Prints & Photographs Div., Library of Congress, Washington, D.C.; Margaret D. Lester, Curator of Photographic Collections, Utah Historical Society, Salt Lake City; Leona Morris, Research Asst., State Historical Society of Missouri, Columbia; Arthur Olivas, Photographic Archivist, Museum of New Mexico, Santa Fe; Kenneth I. Pettitt, Head Librarian, Wesley Catlin, Librarian, Calif. Section, Calif. State Library, Sacramento; Marsha Rodney, Photo Editor, Royal Ontario Museum, Toronto; Elizabeth Roth, Prints Div., The New York Public Library, New York City; Katharine Schwartz, Special Collections, Univ. of Oregon Library, Eugene; Bertha Stratford, Museum of History and Industry, Seattle; Dr. John Barr Thompkins, Curator of Pictorial Collections, Suzanne Gallup, Ref. Librarian, The Bancroft Library, Univ. of Calif., Berkeley; James Thorpe, Dir., Carey S. Bliss, Curator, Rare Book Dept., Mary Isabel Fry, Readers Service Librarian, Gary Kurutz, Rare Books, Jean F. Preston, Curator of Manuscripts, Henry E. Huntington Library, San Marino; Nelson Wadsworth, Provo, Utah; Dr. David Williams, Assoc. Prof. of History, Calif. State Univ., Long Beach.

BIBLIOGRAPHY

Ambler, C. H., *Life and Diary of John Floyd*. Richmond Press, 1918.

Applegate, Jesse, *A Day with the Cow Column in 1843*. Joseph Schafer, ed. Printed for the Caxton Club, Chicago, 1934.

Applegate, Jesse A., *Recollections of My Boyhood*. Joseph Schafer, ed. Printed for the Caxton Club, Chicago, 1934.

Arrington, L. J., *Great Basin Kingdom*. Harvard Univ. Press, 1958.

Auchampaugh, Philip Gerard, *Robert Tyler*. H. Stein, 1934.

Bagley, Clarence B.:
   The Acquisition and Pioneering of Old Oregon. Argus Print, 1924.
   "The Mercer Immigration: Two Cargoes of Maidens for the Sound Country." *The Quarterly of the Oregon Historical Society*. Vol. V, No. 1, March 1904, pp. 1-24.

Bancroft, Hubert H.:
   History of the Pacific States. Vols. 13-19. Bancroft & Co., 1885.
   History of Utah. Bookcraft Inc., 1964.

Bernhardt, Christian, *Indian Raids in Lincoln City, Kansas*. Lincoln Sentinel Print, 1910. Chicago, 1934.

Bidwell, John, *A Journey to California*. Friends of The Bancroft Library, 1964. Designed and printed by Lawton Kennedy.

Billington, Ray A., *Far Western Frontier: 1830-1860*. Harper & Row, 1956.

Black, P. M., "Nebraska Folk Cures." *Nebraska Univ. Studies in Language, Literature and Criticism*. Univ. of Nebraska Press, 1935.

Blegen, Theodore, *Land of Their Choice, The Immigrants Write Home*. Univ. of Minnesota Press, 1955.

Brodie, F. M., *No Man Knows My History*. Alfred A. Knopf, 1946.

Bromberg, Erik, "Frontier Humor: Plain and Fancy." *Oregon Historical Quarterly*. Vol. 61, No. 3, Sept. 1960, pp. 261-342.

Brooks, Juanita, *The Mountain Meadows Massacre*. Univ. of Oklahoma Press, 1950.

Brosnan, Cornelius, *Jason Lee, Prophet of the Oregon*. The Macmillan Company, 1932.

Bryant, Edwin, *What I Saw In California*. Ross & Haines, 1967.

Burnett, Peter H., "Recollections and Opinions of an Old Pioneer." *The Quarterly of the Oregon Historical Society*. Vol. V, No. 1, March 1904, pp. 64-99.

California Historical Society, "The Leese Scrapbook." *California Historical Quarterly*. Vol. 8, 1931, pp. 9-37.

Carley, Kenneth, *The Sioux Uprising of 1862*. Minnesota Historical Society, 1961.

Cartwright, Mrs. C. M., "Early Days in Oregon." *The Quarterly of the Oregon Historical Society*. Vol. IV, No. 1, March 1903, pp. 55-69.

Colt, Miriam Davis, *Went to Kansas*. Univ. Microfilms, Inc., 1966.

Conant, Roger, *Mercer's Belles: The Journal of a Reporter*. Univ. of Washington Press, 1960.

Corning, Howard McKinley, ed., *Dictionary of Oregon History*. Binfords & Mort, 1956.

Coy, Owen C., *The Great Trek*. Powell Publishing Co., 1931.

Cummins, Sarah J., *Autobiography and Reminiscence:...1845*. LeGrande Printing Co., 1914.

Davenport, T. W., "An Object Lesson in Paternalism." *The Quarterly of the Oregon Historical Society*. Vol. IV, No. 1, March 1903, pp. 33-54.

Davis, William Heath, *Seventy-five Years in California*. Harold A. Small, ed. John Howell-Books, 1967.

Dawson, Nicholas, *California in '41, Texas in '51*. The Pemberton Press, 1969.

Day, Mrs. F. H., "Sketches of the Early Settlers of California: Jacob P. Leese." *The Hesperian*. Vol. 2, No. 4, June 1859.

Delano, Alonzo, *Life on the Plains and Among the Diggings*. Miller, Orton & Mulligan, 1854.

De Voto, B., *The Year of Decision 1846*. Little, Brown & Co., 1943.

Dick, Everett:

The Sod House Frontier, 1854-1890. Johnsen Publishing Co., 1954.

Tales of the Frontier. Univ. of Nebraska Press, 1963.

"Water: A Frontier Problem." *Nebraska History*. Vol. 49. Nebraska State Historical Society, 1968.

Drury, Clifford M.:

The Diaries and Letters of Henry H. Spalding and Asa Bowen Smith. The Arthur H. Clark Co., 1958.

First White Women over the Rockies. Vols. I & II. The Arthur H. Clark Co., 1963.

Marcus and Narcissa Whitman and the Opening of the Oregon. Vols. I & II. The Arthur H. Clark Co., 1973.

Ebbutt, Percy, *Emigrant Life in Kansas*. Swan-Sonnerschein, 1882.

Eggenhofer, Nick, *Wagons, Mules and Men*. Hastings House Publishers, Inc., 1961.

Emmons, David M., *Garden in the Grasslands*. Univ. of Nebraska Press, 1971.

Fite, G. C., *The Farmers' Frontier*. Holt, Rinehart and Winston, 1966.

Florin, Cambert, *Western Wagon Wheels*. Superior Pub. Co., 1970.

Franzwa, Gregory M., *The Oregon Trail Revisited*. Patrice Press, Inc., 1972.

Gates, Paul, *History of Public Land Law Development*. Public Land Law Review Commission, 1968.

Gedney, Elizabeth, "Cross Section of Pioneer Life at Fourth Plain." *Oregon Historical Quarterly*. Vol. XLIII, March 1942, pp. 14-36.

Giffen, Helen S., *Trail-Blazing Pioneer: Col. Joseph Ballinger Chiles*. John Howell-Books, 1969.

Hilton, Lynn M., ed., *The Story of Salt Lake Stake*. Salt Lake Stake, 1972.

Hines, G., *Life on the Plains of the Pacific*. George H. Derby, 1851.

Hirshon, Stanley P., *The Lion of the Lord*. Alfred A. Knopf, 1969.

Judson, Phoebe Goodell, *A Pioneer's Search for an Ideal Home*. Union Printing, Binding & Stationery Co., 1925.

Kelly, Charles, *Salt Desert Trails*. Western Printing Co., 1930.

Kelly, Wm., *An Excursion to California*. Chapman & Hall, 1851.

Kennedy, G. W., *The Pioneer Campfire*. Clarke-Kundret, 1914.

Knight, Amelia, "Diary." *Transactions*. Ore. Pioneer Assoc., 1928.

Larson, Gustive O., *The "Americanization" of Utah for Statehood*. The Huntington Library, 1971.

"Letter of Dr. John Marsh to Hon. Lewis Cass." *California Historical Society Quarterly*. Vol. XXII, No. 4, Dec. 1943, pp. 315-322. (Letter is property of Calif. State Library, Sacramento.)

Lewis, O., *Sea Routes to the Gold Fields*. Alfred A. Knopf, 1949.

Linn, W. A., *The Story of the Mormons*. Russell & Russell, 1963.

Lockley, Fred. *History of the Columbia River Valley*. S. J. Clarke Publishing Co., 1928.

Lyman, G. D., *John Marsh, Pioneer*. Charles Scribner's Sons, 1930.

McGlashan, C. F., *History of the Donner Party*. Rev. ed. Stanford Univ. Press, 1954.

Mattes, Merrill J., *The Great Platte River Road*. Nebraska State Historical Society, 1969.

Miller, N., E. Langsdorf and R. Richmond, *Kansas—A Pictorial History*. Kansas State Historical Society, 1961.

Minto, John, "Reminiscences of Experiences on the Oregon Trail in 1844." *The Quarterly of the Oregon Historical Society*. Vol. II, March 1901-Dec. 1901, pp. 119-167, 209-254.

Morgan, Dale L.:

The Great Salt Lake. Bobbs-Merrill, 1947.

Overland in 1846: Diaries and Letters of the California-Oregon Trail. The Talisman Press, 1963.

Mulder, William and A. Russell Mortensen, *Among the Mormons*. Alfred A. Knopf, 1958.

Neff, Andrew L., *History of Utah 1847-69*. Deseret News Press, 1940.

O'Gara, Wm. H., *In All Its Fury: A History of the Blizzard of January 12, 1888*. Blizzard Club, 1947.

O'Kieffe, C., *Western Story*. Univ. of Nebraska Press, Lincoln, 1960.

Paden, Irene D., *The Wake of the Prairie Schooner*. The Macmillan Company, copyright 1943, renewed 1971 by Irene D. Paden.

Parkman, Francis, *The Oregon Trail*. Heritage Press, 1943.

Powell, Fred Wilbur, *Hall J. Kelley on Oregon*. Princeton Univ. Press, 1932.

Raynor, Wallace A., *The Everlasting Spires*. Deseret Book Co., 1965.

Ricks, Joel E. and Everett L. Cooley, eds., *The History of a Valley*. Deseret News Publishing Co., 1956.

Ross, Nancy Wilson, "Murder at the Place of Rye Grass." *American Heritage*. Vol. X, No. 5, August 1959, pp. 42-53, 85-91.

Rucker, Maude A., *The Oregon Trail*. Walter Neale, 1930.

Ruede, Howard, *Sod-House Days*. Cooper Square Pubs., 1966.

Sanford, Mollie D., *Mollie: Journal of Mollie Dorsey Sanford in Nebraska & Colorado Territories, 1857-1866*. Univ. of Nebraska Press, 1959.

Selby, Mary Jane Smith (Mrs. Paul), "Recollections." *Illinois State Historical Journal*. Vol. 16, p. 168.

Stegner, Wallace, *The Gathering of Zion*. McGraw-Hill Book Co., Inc., 1964.

Stewart, George R.:

The California Trail. McGraw-Hill Book Co., Inc., 1962.

Ordeal by Hunger. Henry Holt and Company, 1936.

"The Prairie Schooner Got Them There." *American Heritage*. Vol. XIII, No. 2, Feb. 1962, pp. 4-17, 98-102.

Talmage, James E., *The House of the Lord*. Deseret Book Co., 1971.

Throckmorton, Arthur L., *Oregon Argonauts*. Oregon Historical Society, 1961.

Thwaites, Reuben Gold, "Palmer's Journal of Travels over the Rocky Mountains, 1845-1846." *Early Western Travels 1748-1846*. Vol. XXX. The Arthur H. Clark Company, 1906.

Warren, Sidney, *Farthest Frontier*. The Macmillan Company, 1949.

Webb, Walter Prescott, *The Great Plains*. Ginn & Company, 1959.

Welsch, Roger L., "The Nebraska Soddy." *Nebraska History*. Vol. 48. Nebraska State Historical Society, 1967.

Werner, M. R., *Brigham Young*. Harcourt, Brace & Co., 1925.

West, Ray B., *Kingdom of the Saints*. Viking Press, 1957.

Williams, J., *Narrative of a Tour from the State of Indiana to the Oregon Territory*. Cadmus Book Shop, 1921.

Winther, O. O., *The Great Northwest*. Alfred A. Knopf, 1947.

Woodward, Mary Dodge, *The Checkered Years*. Mary Boynton Cowdrey, ed. The Caxton Printers, 1937.

Wyeth, John B., *Oregon*. Univ. Microfilms, Inc., 1966.